The Social Science Jargon Buster

The Social Science Jargon Buster

The Key Terms You Need to Know

Zina O'Leary

SAGE Publications
Los Angeles · London · New Delhi · Singapore

SAGE Publications Ltd
1 Oliver's Yard
55 City Road
London EC1Y 1SP

SAGE Publications Inc.
2455 Teller Road
Thousand Oaks, California 91320

SAGE Publications India Pvt Ltd
B-1/I 1 Mohan Cooperative Industrial Area
Mathura Road, Post Bag 7
New Delhi 110 044

SAGE Publications Asia-Pacific Pte Ltd
33 Pekin Street #02-01
Far East Square
Singapore 048763

Library of Congress Control Number 2007922040

British Library Cataloguing in Publication data

A catalogue record for this book is available from the British Library

ISBN 978-1-4129-2176-3
ISBN 978-1-4129-2177-0 (pbk)

Typeset by C&M Digitals (P) Ltd., Chennai, India
Printed in Great Britain by The Cromwell Press Ltd, Trowbridge, Wiltshire
Printed on paper from sustainable resources

Contents

Preface

Welcome to the world of the social sciences; a world where terms are often obscure, meanings can be dense, and professors tend to forget you're new to the lingo and unfamiliar with the 'jargon'. And there's an awful lot of 'jargon' to get your head around. Philosophers, sociologists, economists – in fact social theorists of all sorts – have adopted, adapted, modified, twisted, created, and re-created a bevy of terms that are not intended to confuse you, but can certainly do the job.

Now as tempting as it might be to skirt around such 'jargon' or simply apply everyday understandings to key social science terms, engaging 'jargon' is actually central to our understanding. Yes, I realize that, when you're standing on the outside, it might seem like social science terms are somewhat vague, abstract, pretentious or even meaningless. But such 'jargon' does have a function. It actually represents key constructs, fundamental concepts, critical theories, and influential schools of thought. So even if it seems like a huge barrier, there's a need to engage with as much of it as possible.

There are quite a few ways to come to grips with 'jargon'. For one, you can seek out your professors, lecturers and tutors – and this is an excellent idea. But they're not always available and some have a tendency to confuse you even more. Another option is to turn to one of the social science dictionaries on the market. But while they can be a great resource, they can also be dense, circular and presume a fair bit of knowledge. Of course there's always the web. And this is another terrific resource. There are any number of general and specialist dictionaries and encyclopaedias (*Wikipedia* being one of my favourites) as well as websites dedicated to various dimensions of the social sciences and all major social science theorists. So yes, the information is definitely out there and worth exploring, but you have to wade through an awful lot of stuff, some of it confusing, some of it conflicting, and a lot that is less than credible.

Hopefully this book will help streamline the task. It attempts to tackle and demystify 150 of the most confusing constructs in the social sciences. The idea is to help you grasp these in very grounded ways. If you can do this, you'll find that even the ideas you found most obscure begin to take focus. Constructs, even those articulated 200 years ago, begin to make sense. With some reflection, not only do you begin to understand what Marx, Durkheim or Weber were saying and why – but how and why it still might shed light on today's world.

The 150 key terms directly covered in this book (with many more referred to in the text and referencable in the index) were chosen for both their importance and their tendency to confuse, and are drawn from a number of disciplines, for example, sociology, cultural studies, media studies, cultural geography, political science, economics, psychology and even philosophy (this area underpins much social science thought and provides central concepts that can be notoriously difficult to understand). While this might seem quite broad, it's important to remember that our world is messy and chaotic, and not nearly as discrete as the academic disciplines we've created. Capturing the complexity of our world requires us to be able to cut across various disciplines and 'their' jargon.

In a bid to help you engage with key ideas, each of the 150 entries begins with a clear and concise *core definition*, great for a quick review or test preparation. This is followed by a *longer explanation* that attempts to make terms 'real' and understood at more than just the level of rote memorization. Since very few terms are without contention, *debates and controversies* are offered as a means to get you contrasting various perspectives. But where you really get to flex your thinking skills is in *practical applications*. These sections link each term with contemporary issues and the current social order. It's important to note, however, that the connections I highlight are not the only possibilities. Terms can be applied in any number of ways, in unlimited contexts, and your goal here should be to use this section as a thought-provoking entry into a much wider variety of real-world applications. Also covered are *key figures* that will introduce you to both classic and contemporary theorists and *recommended reading* chosen to take you down a path from straightforward introductions through to deeper theoretical engagement with classic works. Each entry also highlights a quote drawn from classic theorists through to media personalities; each chosen to provide greater depth, clarify your understandings, get you thinking, or simply amuse you with its insight. While Homer Simpson may not have Marx's credibility, his insights (often drawn from rich social science theory) still have the ability to get you thinking!

Each entry on its own should offer you a path for demystifying a particular bit of 'jargon'. But taken together, the entries actually give good coverage to some of the most fundamental questions asked in our social world. For example:

- ***Why are things the way the are?*** Entries such as chaos theory, conflict theory, functionalism, historicism, modernity, postmodernity, social constructionism, social Darwinism, structuralism/post-structuralism, systems theory, teleology, and theory/social theory all attempt to shed light on the nature of social order.

- ***What is 'real', what is important?*** Entries including aesthetics, essentialism, ethics, existentialism, idealism, instrumentalism, materialism, nominalism, ontology, pragmatism, rationalism, realism, relativism, social constructionism, subjectivism, and utilitarianism engage in this fundamental debate at various levels.

- **What constitutes knowledge and how can it be produced?** These are key questions across the social sciences and are addressed by terms such as action research, a priori/ a posteriori, causation, critical/radical, cultural studies, deconstruction, deductive/inductive reasoning, dichotomy, empiricism, epistemology, ethnography, ethnomethodology, genealogy, grounded theory, hegemony, hermeneutics, hypothesis/hypothetico deductive method, ideology, knowledge, methodology, methods, paradigm, phenomenology, positivism, post-positivism, qualitative/quantitative, rationalism, reductionism, reflexivity, research credibility (positivist and post-positivist), scientific method, semiotics, social science research, technology, and theory/social theory.

- **Who am I and how am I 'constructed'?** These are questions that connect the individual to the social world and are addressed in entries such as agency, behaviourism, body, class, cognitive dissonance, culture, determinism, deviant behaviour, game theory, hybridity, id/ego/superego, identity, ideology, labelling theory, marginalization, nationalism, norms, paradigm, personality, power, reflexivity, reification, role, self, sexuality, social Darwinism, social stratification, socialization, sociobiology, socioeconomic status, sociolinguistics, subject, and symbolic interactionism.

- **Who are 'we'?** Entries including class, collective, community, culture, ethics, ethnocentrism, human/social ecology, humanism, hybridity, individualism, justice, liberalism, multiculturalism, nationalism, norms, other, pluralism, predjudice/discrimination, reification, risk society, social movements, society, sociolinguistics, solidarity, and the state attempt to tackle the complexities of understanding individuals as part of larger social networks.

- **What are the processes that drive change?** Understanding change is one of the most fundamental tasks of the social sciences. Driving forces are covered in capitalism, colonization, communism, conflict theory, conservativism, dialectic, globalization, historical materialism, industrialization, Marxism, pedagogy/critical pedagogy, post-industrial, praxis, Protestant ethic, revolution, social change, social movements, socialism, and technology.

- **What is the price of change?** The implications of change are as important as drivers of the process. Entries on alienation, anomie, bureaucracy, class, commodification, developed/developing countries, globalization, industrialization, labour, marginalization, McDonaldization, modernism/postmodernism, revolution, risk society, secularization, social mobility, social stratification, socioeconomic status, and urbanization discuss the challenges that face a changing world order.

- **How is power exercised?** This is a huge question that can be explored at the level of the individual through to national and even global dimensions. Exploring entries on authority, capital, capitalism, class, colonization, communism, conflict theory, democracy, developed/developing countries, deviant behaviour, discourse, egalitarianism, fascism, feminism, fundamentalism, genealogy, governance, hegemony, ideology, imperialism, individualism, justice, knowledge, labelling theory, leadership, liberalism, marginalization, metanarrative, micro/macroeconomics, norms, other, paradigm, patriarchy, power, prejudice/discrimination, social control, social movements, social stratification, socialism, socioeconomic status, the state, technology, and totalitarianism will help you explore this central social science construct.

Of course these are not the only questions a social scientist can ask or the only ways the terms can be grouped. Questions posed by your professors, issues that crop up in your reading, and of course your own curiosity will hopefully take you down a number of paths and give you an unending array of road maps into social science exploration.

So good luck in your journey through the social sciences. For me, there's nothing more enjoyable than helping students unravel the mysteries of the social world and giving them the ability to grasp concepts they thought were beyond their reach. I hope I've succeeded, and that this book will offer you plenty of moments of clarity.

Zina

The Social Science
Jargon Buster

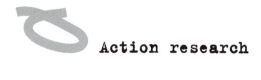
Action research

Core definition
Research strategies that tackle real-world problems in participatory, collaborative and cyclical ways in order to produce both **knowledge** and action.

Longer explanation

The goal here is to improve situations by engaging with others in multiple cycles of learning and doing. There are actually four key principals that make action research (AR) distinct: (1) it addresses real-world problems – AR generally begins by identifying and understanding practical problems within a particular setting in order to seek and implement solutions within that setting; (2) it pursues action and knowledge – AR does not premise knowledge over change. Whether developing skills, changing programmes and policies, or working towards more *radical* (see *critical/radical*) transformation, AR works towards change as knowledge is produced; (3) it is participatory – in a bid to empower stakeholders, AR minimizes the distinction between the researcher and the researched and calls for participation of, and collaboration between, researchers, practitioners, and any other interested parties; (4) it is cyclical – the goal is to learn, do, reflect, learn how to do better, do it better, learn from that, do it better still, so on, and so forth. The idea is to work through a number of cycles that converge towards better situation understanding and improved action.

Debates and controversies

On a theoretical level, AR literature can be pretty confusing and therefore difficult to get your head around. Perspectives across various disciplines have lead to any number of varieties, offshoots, and approaches, including action science, participative inquiry, cooperative inquiry, participatory rural appraisal, and participatory action research. On a practical level, goals of empowerment, participation and cyclical learning are certainly worthwhile. But it's precisely these goals that can make AR a thorny process. Facilitating rather than directing, keeping project scope manageable, assuring rigour in methods, getting stakeholders together with common purpose, keeping up momentum, managing people, protecting the welfare of participants, ensuring sustainability, and negotiating ownership of research outcomes are common challenges in the world of AR.

Practical application

The key principles of AR set it apart from traditional *positivist* research and is often called upon when the goal is to improve professional practice (think educators and healthcare workers); empowerment of the researched is paramount (as in development work); ownership of change is a high priority (e.g. changing the culture in a workplace); and producing knowledge and change are both priorities.

Key figures

While AR has certainly evolved since his day, Kurt Lewin, the social psychologist who coined the term, believed that social experiments in natural settings could and should enact social change. Other key figures include Chris Argyris, who developed action science, John Heron and Peter Reason, who coined the term cooperative inquiry, and Paulo Freire, who evolved participatory action research.

> *An ounce of action is worth a ton of theory.*
>
> *Friedrich Engels* (1820–1895) German political/social philosopher – in Groves, R. *The Strange Case of Victor Grayson* (1975)

Recommended reading

Action research books abound. The ones I've found most practical and accessible include *Doing Action Research in Your Own Organization* (Coghlan and Brannick 2004), *Action Research* (Stringer 1999), *Action Research: Principles and Practice* (McNiff and Whitehead 2002), and *Handbook of Action Research* (Reason and Bradbury 2001).

 **Aesthetics**

Core definition

The quality and nature of sensory perceptions and emotive feelings related to art, nature, and various cultural products.

Longer explanation

I'll start here by asking you to think about the antonym of aesthetic, 'anesthetic'. Now something with an anesthetic action dulls your senses, makes you groggy and basically puts you to sleep. So in contrast, something with an aesthetic action should make your senses feel alive. This pretty much sums up philosophical aesthetics. Rather than an appeal that relies on an object's material value or cultural worth, aesthetics is about the immediate sensory and emotive appeal that comes from reflecting on the direct experience of an object.

Debates and controversies

A major question here is whether aesthetic appeal is objective and simply exists in an entity independent of any outside factors (perhaps a sunset), or if it's *subjective* and always tied to cultural, historical (and personal) biases (a portrait of Elvis on black velvet). For those who believe it's objective, the challenge is identifying what it is that creates an appeal that transcends history and culture. For those who believe it's subjective, the challenge is understanding how power is associated with defining and owning what is aesthetically appealing. So are particular examples of say, abstract art, inherently beautiful? Or are they simply defined as such by a powerful art world that some might even call pretentious?

Practical application

Understanding what gives something aesthetic appeal, whether objective or subjective, is not just a philosophical pastime. It's actually the goal of anyone attempting to capture, create, sell, or capitalize on 'beauty' – and that describes a fair portion of the world. From high art, to *the body*, to advertising, aesthetics can be explored as big business tied to the all-important concepts of power and money. As George Steinbrenner once said, 'Don't talk to me about aesthetics … talk to me about what sells'.

Key figures

Those who've contemplated aesthetics reads like a who's who of philosophy. Key figures include ancient Greeks such as Socrates, who contemplated the value of beauty, Plato, who provided a systematic reflection of art, and Aristotle, who attempted to identify beauty's objective principles. Eighteenth-century philosophers include Baumgarten, who introduced the term, Kant, who questioned beauty's objectivity, and Schelling and Hegel, who offered philosophies of art and fine art respectively. More recent thinkers include Bollough and Wittgenstein, who offer reflections and critiques of aesthetics as a philosophical construct.

Nothing is beautiful, only man ... nothing
is ugly but degenerate man –
the domain of aesthetic judgment
is therewith defined.

Friedrich Nietzsche (1844–1900)
German philosopher – in 'Expeditions of
an Untimely Man', *Twilight of the Idols* (1889)

Recommended reading

Because the thoughts of so many theorists are relevant here, anthologies tend to be a good place to start. For coverage of Western philosophies and philosophers, I like *Aesthetics* (Feagin and Maynard 1998), *Aesthetics: A Reader in Philosophy of the Arts* (Goldblatt and Brown 2004), and *The Routledge Companion to Aesthetics* (Lopes and Gaut 2002). *A History of Modern Japanese Aesthetics* (Marra 2001) gives a different starting point for exploring the objective/subjective nature of the term.

Agency

Core definition

The ability of individuals to affect change, make autonomous and independent choices and act in self-determining ways.

Longer explanation

We like to think we're free agents who can act with independence and make a difference in the world. But is this the case? Do we have free will? And if so, can we use our free will to affect change? Or are our freedoms and choices constrained by the world around us? Well how much agency we believe we have is a core debate in both academic and everyday life. Think about the following phrases: 'It's in God's hands' – which implies there is no autonomy, God determines your future; 'Sometimes you just have to play the game' – which implies that the world operates by a set of rules that we can choose to play by or ignore; 'Each and every one of us can make a difference' – which implies that we can, indeed, influence the world; and finally, 'I can do whatever the hell I want' – which, on the surface, this implies full agency, but might point to an individual who's completely blind to constraints that dominant **ideologies** can place on free will.

Debates and controversies

There can be a tendency for philosophers and social scientists to **dichotomize** or divide into camps. In this case, those who believe we can exercise free will and affect change and those who believe the world around us limits our ability to act with independence. Of course, it's worth considering if there just might be an element of truth in both sentiments. Many theorists now recognize the complexity of agency and have begun to explore the interplay, tensions, and balances between free will of the individual and the constraints of the social world to which they belong.

Practical application

Agency should be of interest to anyone attempting to understand the construction and continuity of social structures, as well as those exploring the tendency for phenomena such as **social change**, **social movements**, political upheaval, and **revolutions**. At the level of social psychology, agency (and the lack of) can be an enlightening window for exploring concepts such as empowerment, disempowerment, **alienation**, and **anomie**.

Key figures

The concept of agency has been a key consideration of many **modern** thinkers. Durkheim believed that agency can be limited since social structures determine social actions. Althusser believed free will to be illusory since social structures and dominant ideologies create an individual's reality. Marx would have agreed but thought oppressed masses should and would exercise agency through revolution. Others, for example **ethnomethodologists** and **symbolic interactionists**, believe individuals have full agency since it is they who create the social world. More contemporary theorists, such as Peter Berger, Thomas Luckman and Anthony Giddens, focus on the tensions and balances that create and constrain agency.

> You must believe in free will; there
> is no choice.
>
> **Isaac Bashevis Singer** (1902-1991)
> Nobel Prize winning author - in
> 'Isaac Singer's Promised City',
> *City Journal* (1997)

Recommended reading

I'd start by looking at Berger and Luckmann's *The Social Construction of Reality* (1967), and Giddens' *The Constitution of Society* (1986). To explore how agency manifests across the social landscape try *Structure, Agency and the Internal Conversation* (Archer 2003), *Making History: Agency, Structure, and Change in Social Theory* (Callinicos 2004) and *Agency, Structure and International Politics* (Friedman 1997).

 Alienation

Core definition
When individuals feel estranged or cut off from and by *modern* (see *modernity*) society.

Longer explanation
What is the difference between a cobbler who crafts a pair of shoes and a worker in a shoe factory? Well cobblers have a craft, have pride in their shoes and are likely to have relationships with both customers and any one else they might work with. What does the factory worker have? According to theorists like Marx, not a lot. When you work in a factory, you become part of a *capitalist* machine that only cares about exploiting your labour. You work on a production line, are isolated from others and no longer have a craft or feel ownership and pride over your end product. You are stripped of your creativity and are left feeling alienated from your craft, your co-workers, and even your essential human nature. This is the traditional meaning of alienation. It's a negative emotional state as well as a description of the economic and social realities of capitalism.

Debates and controversies
While *Marxists* may attribute alienation to capitalism, it's worth considering whether capitalism is truly the root cause of alienation, or whether alienation can be attributed to other aspects of *industrialized* society, such as mass production and high division of labour (a reality that can also exist under *socialism*). It's also worth considering whether alienation is common among professionals and white-collar workers, and if it will continue to have relevance in *post-industrial* societies.

Practical application
While workers in the developed world may not face the same alienation issues they did at the height of the industrial revolution, *globalization*, in particular the practice of multinational corporations moving into *developing countries* to exploit cheap labour, makes the concept extremely current. It's also worth noting that alienation, as an emotive state, is now often explored without explicit reference to the realities of capitalism, and can be used to explore and explain

things like job satisfaction, the apathy of voters, lack of community **solidarity**, the discontented nature of youth and rising rates of depression.

Key figures

While Marx is certainly a key figure here, the evolution of alienation as a broader construct can be traced to American sociologists of the mid-1950s, such as Melvin Seeman and Robert Blauner. Seeman identified various dimensions of alienation, while Blauner attempted to link these dimensions to different types of factory work. This saw the focus of the construct move from a critique of capitalism to the wider understanding of emotive states.

> Capitalist production, therefore, develops ... only by sapping the original sources of all wealth – the soil and the labourer.
>
> **Karl Marx** (1818–1883) German political/social philosopher – in *Das Kapital* (1867)

Recommended reading

For a good contemporary take on alienation, I'd recommend *The Future of Alienation* (Schacht 1994) or *Alienation and Freedom* (Schmitt 2002). But I'd also turn to Marx – perhaps start with a third-person introduction, such as *Alienation: Marx's Conception of Man in a Capitalist Society* (Ollman 1977) and work your way up to Marx's *The Economic and Philosophic Manuscripts of 1844* (*1844* 1988). Also worth a look is Blauner's seminal work *Alienation and Freedom* (1964).

 **Anomie**

Longer explanation

It's difficult to play the game when you seem to be the only one playing by the rules, or when you don't know the rules, or when the rules suddenly change. How do you know what to do, how to feel, or where to turn? And what if the game is life itself? Well, as Durkheim will tell you, when you feel lost in the game of life, the stakes can be extraordinarily high. Durkheim believed that societal rules or **norms** help keep an individual's aspirations and desires in check. Without such norms, aspirations can extend beyond the means to achieve them and can leave individuals feeling helpless, lost, and in fact, suicidal. Durkheim attributed the loss of traditional rules and norms of the family and church, and its resultant anomie, to rapid **industrialization** and the move towards norms that value an individual's material-based ambitions and acquisitions. Like **alienation**, anomie is therefore both a structural characteristic of **capitalist** society and a psychological state.

Debates and controversies

Some social scientists believe the concept of anomie is losing currency. The destabilization caused by rapid industrialization no longer describes the reality of the developed world. Others feel that the concept has been stripped of its societal focus and is now little more than a soft set of personality traits less and less useful to social scientists.

Practical application

Despite the criticisms above, many would argue that as we move from an **industrial** to **post-industrial** society, a sense of normlessness continues to plague us. Perhaps a sense of destabilization has become a cultural reality, which can help to explain why so many search for meaning and **solidarity** through avenues such as Eastern spirituality, new age philosophies, cults, sects, and even gangs, who do offer both a sense of *community* and clear rules of the game.

Key figures

In addition to Durkheim, another key figure here is Robert Merton, who felt that a disparity between societal goals and means to achieve these goals caused anomie. In particular, he believed that the pervasive cultural goals of success and material wealth evident in the USA were not achievable for the masses, leaving them with a sense of anomie and no choice but to innovate (subvert the system), retreat (withdraw from *society*), rebel (fight the system), or ritualize (blindly follow the rules).

```
I used to be with it. Then they
changed what it was. Now what
I'm with isn't it, and what's it
seems weird and scary to me.
```
Abraham Simpson (*The Simpsons*)

Recommended reading

For wide-ranging readings that explore anomie in a contemporary world try *The Future of Anomie Theory* (Passas and Agnew 1997) and *The Legacy of Anomie Theory* (Adler and Laufer 1999). It's also worth exploring Durkheim's *The Division of Labor in Society* (*1893* 1997) and *Suicide* (*1897* 1997) as well as Merton's seminal work *Social Theory and Social Structure* (*1949* 1968).

A posteriori/a priori

Core definition

A posteriori – knowledge based on facts derived from personal and societal experience. A priori – knowledge that comes before the facts.

Longer explanation

These terms refer to the basis on which any proposition might be known. A posteriori propositions are pretty straightforward since we tend to be comfortable with knowledge based on memories, experiences and data derived from our senses. 'I had breakfast this morning', 'lemons are sour', and 'I have a cold', are all a posteriori statements based on factual experience. A priori arguments are a bit trickier since they come 'before the facts' and stand without experiential evidence. Truth-value here relies on reason, for example, 'triangles have three sides' and 'a straight line is the shortest distance between two points' (see *rationalism*). On a more colloquial level, a priori literally means beliefs that do come 'before the facts' and can refer to propositions based on things like hearsay and folklore, for example the urban myth that colonies of alligators prowl the New York sewer system.

Debates and controversies

Questions related to a posteriori propositions often centre on the nature of 'experience'. Most philosophers go beyond sensory experience and include memory and introspection. You also need to consider who's experience counts, how much experience warrants knowledge, and if there just might be an exception to an a posteriori argument that we have yet to come across. 'Dinosaurs are extinct' is only true until we manage to find or clone one.

One of the main critiques of a priori propositions is that justifications for knowing can be semantic – a play on words. Take for example, the 'logical' argument: 'Nobody's perfect. I am a nobody, therefore I am perfect.' The other difficulty with a priori arguments is being able to divorce experience from faith. For some, belief in God is based on pure faith, and therefore a priori. But for others, belief in God must rest on tangible evidence of his existence.

Practical application

There are a few good reasons to get your head around these terms. First, understanding knowledge creation underpins all the social sciences. Second, it's fascinating to consider the foundations for some of our most core beliefs. Is there experiential a posteriori evidence that supports mathematics, philosophy, God, even aliens? Or are these concepts built solely on a priori faith and/or reason? Third, professors love to use these terms, particularly a priori, but often without offering clear explanations. And finally, students consistently misuse them.

Key figures

Questioning the nature of knowledge is taken up by many historical and contemporary philosophers, for example Descartes ('I think, therefore I am') and Wittgenstein, who articulated the foundations of logic. But it's Kant, who argued that although knowledge is derived from experience, it's possible to have knowledge of objects prior to experience, that is most closely associated with these terms.

> Any necessary truth, whether a priori
> or a posteriori, could not
> have turned out otherwise.
>
> *Saul Kripke* (1940–) US philosopher –
> in *Naming and Necessity* (1980)

Recommended reading

For contemporary readings, try *In Defence of Pure Reason* (BonJour 1997) and *A Priori Justification* (Casullo 2003). But if you want to jump right into the philosophical heavyweights, try Descartes' *Discourse on Method and Meditations on First Philosophy* (*1641* 1993), Kant's *Prolegomena to Any Future Metaphysics* (*1783* 2004) and Wittgenstein's *On Certainty* (*1951* 1972).

 Authority

Core definition
Power that is seen as legitimate by those who posses it and those who are subjected to it.

Longer explanation
Why do we listen to the boss? Why do we accept the decisions of the president? Why do we turn to certain people in times of crisis? The answer lies in the notion of authority. Authority is the exercise of power accepted (although sometimes resisted) by those under it. Individuals can have authority over knowledge and be *an* authority on a subject (e.g. academics and doctors). But we generally talk about authority as power over conduct (e.g. a military sergeant). Three types of 'authority over conduct' were offered by Weber: legal rational – where rules, *roles*, and procedures are publicly and politically accepted (e.g. a US president); traditional – where traditions, customs and rituals legitimize power (e.g. the Queen Elizabeth II); and charismatic – where power comes directly from the characteristics of the leader (e.g. a cult leader like Charles Manson). In reality, authority figures generally have characteristics of more than one type.

Debates and controversies
What does it mean to have legitimate power? Is power legitimized by all ruled by it, or are some forced under its rule by default? Is authority a hidden form of coercive power or does authority offer social cohesion that can help protect individual liberty? And what happens if authority is questioned by the masses? Is power lost, or is power maintained through force? Well, the ability to question authority and have a voice in the selection of authority figures is central to our notion of *democracy*.

Practical application
Some might argue that in contemporary societies authority comes from a legal rational basis and that in modern politics, tradition and charisma have become less important. But I'd argue that Weber's trilogy of authority types is more relevant than you might realize. Look at the media – it's all about image and

spin-doctoring. Yes, authority figures are voted in a rational legal manner, but who gets to the polls is largely about charisma. You can also think of traditional authority in the same way. Our political systems are steeped in history and tradition. Think of how hard it is for someone outside one of the major political parties to get into office. In fact, I'd say that understanding the way authority is created and managed is crucial to understanding any political machine.

Key figures

While classical theorists such as Thomas Hobbes, David Hume, and John Locke all discuss the nature of authority, power, and leadership, the figure most closely associated with this construct is Max Weber. His trilogy of ideal types has defined the term for almost 100 years.

> I have as much authority as the Pope,
> I just don't have as many
> people who believe it.
>
> *George Carlin* (1937-) Stand-up
> comedian - attributed

Recommended reading

Weber's writings on authority are contained in *Economy and Society* (pt 1, ch 3) (*1921–22* 1978). Also worth a look are the BBC lectures by Bertrand Russell, *Authority and the Individual* (*1949* 1995). For more contemporary coverage try *Authority: Construction and Corrosion* (Lincoln 1995) or *Governing Globalization: Power, Authority and Global Governance* (Held and McGrew 2002).

 Behaviourism

Core definition
School of psychology that explains human behaviour by studying observable and measurable responses to environmental stimuli.

Longer explanation

In a nutshell, behaviourists believe that the best way to understand people is to study their behaviours. Behaviourists put little credibility in psycho-analytic approaches that focus on consciousness, mental states, and feelings. Understanding individuals through introspection or self-reflection is seen as too vague and subjective to be of use in the science of psychology. Behaviourists also believe that all behaviours can be learned or unlearned by changing stimuli, that is through the use of positive or negative reinforcements (operant conditioning). In *The Simpsons*, Lisa uses operant conditioning to determine which is smarter, Bart or a hamster. To do this she sees how long it takes for each to learn to avoid food that gives them an electric shock – not surprisingly, the hamster won.

Debates and controversies

Behaviourism became a key strand of psychology in the twentieth century, but is not without criticism. Many feel that the controlled and clinical nature of behaviourist studies limits its application in the real world. Unlike a maze navigated by a rat, the real world is not a controlled environment. The dismissal of anything not observable is also seen as problematic since this is at odds with mainstay psycho-analytic approaches. Finally, the ethicality of some behaviourist therapies is highly questionable. In the 1950s and 1960s it was not uncommon to try to 'cure' homosexuality. And aversion therapy, which involved administering nauseating drugs or electric shocks to gay men as they looked at pictures of naked men, was thought to be an effective cure.

Practical application

While we've gratefully moved past aversion therapy as a treatment for sexual 'deviance', behaviourist approaches, for example desensitizing individuals to their phobias, are often used to elicit behavioural change. But even more common is the belief in 'behaviourism' outside clinical psychology. The concept of modifying behaviours through reward and punishment is central to our processes of **socialization**, child-rearing, and rehabilitation, and can be found in virtually all institutions from the family, to the workplace, to the prison.

Key figures

You may have heard of Ivan Pavlov whose dogs were conditioned to salivate at the ringing of a bell. Pavlov rang a bell when his dogs sighted food, and eventually removed the food as a stimulus but kept the bell. The dogs salivated nonetheless, showing that reflexes could be learned. Other famous behaviourists include J. B. Watson, who was the first Western psychologist to fully articulate behaviourism, and his student B. F. Skinner, who believed that operant conditioning could cure both individual anxieties and social ills.

```
        Of course, Behaviorism 'works'...
            Just give me a no-nonsense,
        down-to-earth behaviorist, a few
                    drugs, and simple
                electrical appliances...

  W. H. Auden (1907-1973) Anglo-American
              poet - in 'Behaviorism',
            A Certain World (1970)
```

Recommended reading

Good choices in contemporary overviews include *Understanding Behaviorism: Behavior, Culture, and Evolution* (Baum 2004) and *The Philosophical Legacy of Behaviorism* (Thyer 2006). But if you want to get a sense of the behaviourism's foundations, try Watson's *Behaviourism* (*1930* 1998) and Skinner's *Beyond Dignity and Freedom* (*1971* 2002).

 (The) Body

Core definition
Physical or material structure of an individual, increasingly recognized as a social/cultural entity as well as biological one.

Longer explanation
Philosophers and sociologists have often separated the body from the mind, the body from the spirit, the body from consciousness, and the body from society. The body was left to anatomists, medical professionals, and even artists. But this is changing. Today, the body is recognized as central to understanding both the *self* and the social world. We now recognize that the world sees and reacts to our physical form, which can affect our self-esteem, our interpersonal interactions, and our position in the world. Perhaps even more interesting is that the body is no longer accepted as an immutable physical reality. We now have the ability to unmake and remake ourselves in order to change our opportunities. Our obsession with dieting, the proliferation of bodybuilding, and the increase in cosmetic surgery are examples of how we can change ourselves … and change how others see and react to us. For the wealthy, even getting old is becoming an option.

Debates and controversies
Most constructs have a defined history, but the body is a relatively new and broad 'social science' construct. So offering a precise definition is quite difficult. But perhaps understanding the body as an isolated social science construct is not the goal. Perhaps the goal is to understand how the self, with mind and body inextricably linked, is entwined in all our social and cultural interactions and is instrumental in understanding every aspect of humans as social beings.

Practical application
I think there are two key ways the body can have practical application in the social sciences. First, key understandings of the social world have not generally integrated the construct of the body into these understandings, so there's an opportunity to add complexity, richness and depth to virtually all realms of existing social knowledge. Second, there are a host of contemporary social

issues where the body has a starring role. Whether it be body image, eating disorders, dieting obsession, medical ethics (i.e. cloning or assisted suicide), the list of absolutely fascinating body-related social issues is unending.

Key figures

Recognition of the importance of the body to our social understandings has come from postmodern theorists like Michel Foucault, who saw the body as a site for surveillance, discipline and control, feminists such as Simone de Beauvoir, who saw women as prisoners of their bodies, and more mainstream sociologists like Bryan Turner, who believes the body should be the axis of sociological analysis.

> *I definitely believe in*
> *plastic surgery. I don't want to*
> *be an old hag.*
> *There's no fun in that.*
>
> **Scarlett Johansson** (1984–)
> American actor – attributed

Recommended reading

There are a number of interesting works that offer a good introduction to 'the body' as a social science construct: *The Body and Society* (Turner 1996), *The Body and Social Theory* (Shilling 2003) and *Real Bodies: A Sociological Introduction* (Evans and Lee 2002). But I'd also have a look at magazines such as *Vogue*, *WHO*, *Penthouse*, or any other magazine that shows the importance of the body in contemporary society.

 **Bureaucracy**

Core definition

A complex administration system designed to help an organization reach its goals efficiently.

Longer explanation

Bureaucracies are organizations characterized by specialized duties and professional salaried roles; hierarchical structures of *authority* with formal rules and regulations; thorough documentation; recruitment and promotion based on qualifications and merit; impersonal relationships; and authority vested in offices rather than individuals. And while all this is designed for efficiency, it doesn't always work. The word 'bureaucracy' can definitely have a negative connotation and this is because bureaucratic systems have a tendency to become so dense they can actually impede effective action. Now for us, bureaucratic red tape is a reality. We've grown up with bureaucratic governments, agencies, institutions, and corporations. So while we might complain bitterly when caught up in pedantic bureaucratic regulations, we realize this is how the world works. But when theorists like Max Weber first explored bureaucracies, this was not the case. At the turn of the twentieth century, the growth of bureaucracies represented a shift from traditional to more rational systems of administration. The impact this might have on both individuals and social institutions was a significant question of the day.

Debates and controversies

So is the modern bureaucracy good or bad, efficient or inefficient, equitable or unjust, organized or unresponsive? There's probably a bit of truth in all the above. Yes, specialization can lead to expertise, but it can also lead to compartmentalized thinking; hierarchical authority and formal rules should efficiently standardize work practices, but there's usually a way to skirt around rules and hide behind regulations at the expense of organizational goals; thorough documentation should lead to accountability, but it's amazing how common it is to pass the buck; impersonal relationships should lead to equity, but they can also lead to *alienation* and *anomie*. The system has it flaws and even its strengths can be exploited.

Practical application

There are two major questions social scientists can ask here: (1) given that bureaucracies are a reality of a *modern* and even *post-modernizing* world (see *modernity* and *postmodernity*) how can they best operate so that goals do not get lost to an administrative system? In other words, what do contemporary bureaucracies need to learn about *governance*?; (2) Do we have other choices? Are there alternative ways for our institutions to meet their goals without going down the bureaucratic highway?

Key figures

Weber is certainly a key figure here and offers a comprehensive portrait of the modern bureaucracy. But I also find Foucault, who saw the proliferation of databases, records, and documents as a means of bureaucratic surveillance and control over the individual, incredibly interesting.

> Join in the new game that's sweeping
> the country. It's called 'Bureaucracy'
> Everybody stands in a circle.
> The first person to do anything loses.
>
> **Anonymous**

Recommended reading

Contemporary works look at everything from the value of modern bureaucracies (see *In Praise of Bureaucracy* (du Gay 2000) and *The Case for Bureaucracy* (Goodsell 2003)) to our potential to move beyond them (see *The End of Bureaucracy* and *the Rise of the Intelligent Organization* (Pinchot and Pinchot 1994)). But I'd also turn to the classics, for example Weber's seminal work *Economy and Society* (pt 2, ch 9) (*1921–22* 1978) and Foucault's *Discipline and Punish* (pt 3) (*1977* 1995).

 **Capital**

Core definition

Any resource, for example, money, equipment, skills, or social networks that can be used for the production of wealth.

Longer explanation

To become wealthy you need what it takes to create wealth – what we call capital. But capital can take many forms. Classic theorists often focus on economic capital or assets (buildings, tools, machinery) and money – 'you need to have money to make money'. But there are other types of capital, such as human capital or an individual's skills, talents, and capabilities – '*knowledge* is *power*'; social capital, which is based on social networks – 'it's not what you know, but who you know'; cultural capital or higher social status indicated by manner of speech and appreciation of high-brow culture (think opera) – 'it helps to be born with a silver spoon in your mouth'. It's also worth thinking about 'body' capital since the young and beautiful generally get further in life than the fat and ugly!

Debates and controversies

The main issue here is one of equity. Yes, when the economy's good there might be opportunity for all to create wealth. But in periods of stagnation or depression, the race to build capital generally comes at someone's expense. Marx felt that the only way *capitalists* could build wealth was on the backs of workers who would never see the profits of their labour. Similarly, if there's capital value in things like middle-class culture, social networks, and knowledge and skills derived from education, then the starting line for success is certainly not fair. Those with limited opportunity to acquire various types of capital struggle to find a way to create wealth, perpetuating society's inequities.

Practical application

Understanding what it takes to create wealth – could there be anything more practical? The concept of capital can be a gateway to exploring issues such as who has the potential for wealth creation; what barriers, both personal and systemic, get in the way of having it; whether wealth creation is always at the expense of others (at both local and global scales); whether there are opportunities for the traditionally disadvantaged to build less mainstream forms of capital; how communities can better utilize their social capital.

Key figures

Since the dawn of the industrial revolution, theorists have explored the notion of economic capital, but Marx was passionate about the evils of an economic system based on capital. He said: 'capital is dead labour, which, vampire-like, lives only by sucking living labour' (1867 1999). Capital as a construct that extends beyond economics is best explored by Bourdieu, who introduced the concepts of cultural and social capital.

> Capital isn't scarce; vision is.
>
> **Sam Walton** (1918-1992) Founder of Wal-Mart, the largest retail chain in the USA — attributed

Recommended readings

Economic Growth Theory: Capital, Knowledge and Economic Structures (Zhang 2005) offers a good introduction to economic capital, while Bourdieu's *The Forms of Capital* (1986) is an excellent choice for anyone interested in the connection been social capital and material wealth. To get into Marx you can try *Das Kapital* (*1867* 1999) or an analysis of his work, such as *Understanding Capital: Marx's Economic Theory* (Foley 1986).

 **Capitalism**

Core definition
An economic system in which the means of production (factories and equipment) is privately owned and goods are sold through markets in order to build profit.

Longer explanation
In a barter system, you're basically trading for equal value … say 12 eggs for two loaves of bread. There's no profit, but you do trade some of your surplus stock for other things you need. In a capitalist system, you're trying to do more than break even – you're trying to get ahead. So you sell your eggs at the market for a bit more than what they cost you – and with the profit you buy another hen or build a chicken coop. The idea is to produce more eggs, so you can build more profit and eventually grow a thriving business. With a bit of business savvy you may end up with your own factory, as well as a Porsche for yourself – after all you can't live on eggs alone.

Debates and controversies
So is this virtuous or evil? Well many think capitalism respects the freedom of entrepreneurs and encourages creativity, thereby encouraging economic, **technological** and social progress. So not only does your factory employ many in the **community**, it's also responsible for technological advances that see it producing the largest chicken eggs ever seen. But what about the downside? Critics fear that only the privileged benefit from capitalism. Most are not in a position to build **capital** and are left to rely on their own labour power – which is tough when factory owners want to maximize profits, and the more work they can squeeze out of labourers (for less), the better. So yes, the drive for profit may see the development of new technologies, but it may also lead to worker exploitation. In fact, **Marxists** believe that capitalism works best if you strip workers of traditional sources of **solidarity**, leaving them at the mercy of industry. As the great Simpson's capitalist, C. Montgomery Burns of the Springfield Nuclear Power Plant once said: 'Family. Religion. Friendship. These are the three demons you must slay if you wish to succeed in business.'

Practical application

It is definitely worth exploring capitalism as a far-reaching economic system, but this system is also central to how much of the world operates at the level of government, laws, morals, ethics, values, social standards, in fact virtually all aspects of 'Western' culture. But forces of **globalization** have meant that such capitalist values are no longer confined to the West.

Key figures

Understanding the impacts of capitalism is foundational to the social sciences. Marx believed that capitalism, and its exploitative ways, was doomed to failure; Weber was interested in how capitalism was linked to a world becoming more and more rational and bureaucratic; while Durkheim explored how capitalism was changing the face of community and its means of creating social bonds.

> Sell a man a fish, he eats
> for a day, teach a man
> how to fish, you ruin a wonderful
> business opportunity.
>
> **Karl Marx** (1818–1883) German
> political/social
> philosopher – attributed

Recommended readings

Capitalism: A Very Short Introduction (Fulcher 2004) is a good starting point, while *Knowing Capitalism* (Thrift 2005) offers more depth. If you'd prefer to get into the classics, try working through Marx's *Das Kapital* (*1867* 1999), Durkheim's *The Division of Labor in Society* (*1893* 1997) and Weber's *Economy and Society* (*1921–22* 1978).

 **Causation**

Core definition
When one thing brings about something else.

Longer explanation
In philosophy, in the physical sciences, in the social sciences, and even in our day-to-day knowing, we search for cause. We want to know the reasons why – we want to know what makes us happy, what causes cancer, what's responsible for racist attitudes, and what it'll take to get parents off our backs. We want to know because to want to be able to precipitate the good things and avoid the bad. We believe that if we understand cause and effect, we can manipulate environments to make things better. In the social sciences, understanding causation is absolutely central, particularly in research where we often try to figure out how one variable or factor affects another.

Debates and controversies
Sounds simple, but finding causality is rarely straightforward. I remember hearing on the radio that researchers had found that 'eating fish increases IQ'; children who eat fish at least once a week have higher IQs than non-fish eaters. But is this really cause and effect or simply a correlation? Can we be sure that eating fish makes you smart or could it be that smart people eat more fish? And of course an intervening variable might also come into play. Maybe it's not the fish that makes children smart; maybe smart parents feed their children fish, and IQ is determined by genetics. There are multiple possibilities because when you're dealing with people and social phenomenon, there is one thing you can count on, and that's complexity. Not only can 'effects' be hard to measure, they can be even harder to attribute to a particular cause.

Practical application
The main application for social science students is in the conduct of research. In fact, the *hypotheses* or conjectures that tend to drive research are often

cause-and-effect statements. Whether in the lab, in the field, through experiments, interviews or surveys, researchers are on a never-ending quest to find causality.

Key figures

While the concept of causality may be widely accepted, and is used to drive social science research, as a philosophical construct it has long been a topic of exploration, debate and controversy. Two key figures here are Aristotle, who identified various classes of causes, and David Hume, who saw cause as regular associations but questioned whether laws of cause and effect could ever be proven.

Shallow men believe in luck,
believe in circumstances ...
Strong men believe in
cause and effect.

Ralph Waldo Emerson (1803–1882)
US essayist, poet, philosopher –
in *The Conduct of Life* (1860)

Recommended readings

A good generalist introduction to causation is *Making Things Happen: A Theory of Causal Explanation* (Woodward 2005). But if you want to delve into debates and controversies that sit on the philosophical side of causation, try *Causality and Explanation* (Salmon 1997). To explore the mathematical end of the spectrum, I'd turn to *Causality: Models, Reasoning, and Inference* (Pearl 2000).

 Chaos theory

Longer explanation

If you drop a coin from eye level on to a plate, you're likely to hit the target. Even if the target is moved, you can make appropriate adjustments and still be confident you can hit the mark. But try it with paper money and it gets more difficult. Even if the target stays still, it's hard to predict the trajectory and landing spot of that note. Yes, it may fall within a particular boundary, but it will tend to move in a chaotic fashion that resists prediction. But what if you were to do it over and over? Could you mathematically model, and therefore predict, the fall of the note? This is the idea behind chaos theory, which is now commonly used to predict chaotic systems such as the weather and the stock market. Okay, but what's the connection with the social sciences? Well there's nothing more complex and chaotic than the social world, so social phenomena, with their inherent mix of structure and people, can be described as chaotic. In fact, some social scientists are fully embracing chaos theory and are attempting to mathematically model social phenomena. Others, however, apply chaos theory metaphorically in an attempt to acknowledge and capture the social's chaos and complexity.

Debates and controversies

For those who want to mathematically model social complexity, the question is whether social phenomena can be predicted in the same way as physical systems (i.e. the weather). For those using chaos theory as a metaphor, the question is whether the theory, stripped of its mathematical roots, can add to our understanding of complex social systems.

Practical application

Even though its roots lie in fractal geometry, chaos theory involves key social science concepts such as prediction, *causation* and the importance of subtle or less significant variables. Social scientists who adopt chaos theory attempt to understand the interaction of complex systems, and try to avoid easy answers.

Key figures

A key figure here is Edward Lorenz, whose work on weather prediction in the 1960s showed that small changes in the initial conditions of chaotic systems could produce large changes in long-term outcomes. This has become known as the 'butterfly effect' – that a butterfly flapping its wings in Paris could eventually cause a tornado in Sydney. Researchers applying chaos theory to the social world include Mary Lee, Brian Berry, Euel Elliott, Frederick Turner, and David Harvey.

> *Chaos theory is a new theory invented by scientists panicked by the thought that the public were beginning to understand the old ones!*
>
> ***Anonymous***

Recommended readings

Chaos Theory Tamed (Williams 1997) provides a clear introduction, while *Nonlinearity, Chaos, and Complexity* (Bertuglia and Vaio 2005) provides a bit more depth. For an introduction to the application of chaos theory to the social world, try *Chaos, Complexity, and Sociology* (Eve and Horsfall 1997) and *Chaos Theory in the Social Sciences* (Keil and Elliott 1997).

 **Class**

Core definition

A way of categorizing the population according to the nature of their employment, wealth and/or social status.

Longer explanation

We live in a world that categorizes. We stratify, classify, compartmentalize, and subdivide. And when it comes to individuals, one of the most common means for doing this is on the basis of employment (which then indicates things like wealth and social status). There are actually a number of overlapping class typologies that arose as theorists attempted to understand the impacts of **industrialization** on social systems and social relationships. These typologies can be roughly broken up as follows (each list starts with the term originally used by Marx): *bourgeoisie, upper class, ruling class* – individuals who own and control the means of production (i.e. industrialists, financiers, media moguls); *petite bourgeoisie, middle class, white collar* – professionals, small business owners, and other individuals who work behind a desk (i.e. managers, administrators, technicians, lawyers, politicians and a variety of middlemen); *proletariat, working class, blue collar* – those who sell their labour power (i.e. skilled and unskilled manual workers); and *lumpenproletariat, underclass* – those who do not make a contribution to the economy (i.e. the elderly, those on welfare, the unemployed, petty criminals, and the homeless).

Debates and controversies

There are a couple of issues here. First things like domestic labour, or running a home and raising a family, are not included as occupations. Class has its roots as a **patriarchal** concept that describes the realities of men. Women simply assumed the class of their fathers and husbands. Second is the issue of **social mobility**. In some societies, class is fixed from birth, while in others, the opportunity to improve class standing is core in national **ideology**. Third is that the meaningfulness of traditional class delineations needs to be questioned in a **post-industrial** world where the masses tend to be distributed among the middle rather than working class.

Practical application

Marx and Engels once said that 'the history of all hitherto existing society is the history of class struggles' (*1848* 2004). Even if this is only half true, 'class' would be central to understanding concepts such as conflict, revolution, change, and governance. Understanding class is also fundamental for anyone trying to 'sell' anything, whether it be ideas, services, and/or products. Political parties, companies, and the media all need to know the demographic profile of their market. We're constantly manipulated on the basis of our class categorization.

Key figures

Marx is definitely a key figure here. But so, too, is Weber, who offered three categories of class: (1) economic relationships (similar to Marx); (2) status (prestige and standing) and; (3) political party affiliations. Our current notion of class often embeds all of these conceptions.

> The classes that wash most are
> those that work least.
>
> **G. K. Chesterton** (1874–1936)
> British author – attributed

Recommended readings

To explore class in the twenty-first century, try *Social Stratification and Inequality* (Kerbo 2002) or *Social Stratification: Class, Race, and Gender in Sociological Perspective* (Grusky 2000). If you are up to the challenge, turn to Marx and Engels' *The Communist Manifesto* (*1848* 2004) and Gerth and Mills' *From Max Weber: Essays in Sociology* (1958). These will give you a living history of 'modern' class divisions.

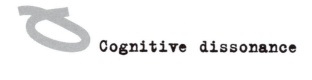

Cognitive dissonance

Longer explanation

Imagine you grew up believing that abortion was wrong. There's no two ways about it, abortion is murder. Or at least that was how you felt until you turned 17 and found yourself pregnant and very, very scared. So scared, in fact, that a large part of you desperately wanted to end the nightmare … and thoughts of abortion crept into your mind. Under this scenario, you're likely to find yourself with a very bad case of cognitive dissonance. The lack of consistency between your beliefs and what you want to do is really hard to deal with. Well, cognitive dissonance theory suggests that individuals do have a hard time living with inconsistency and attempt to resolve dissonance by aligning their beliefs, values, and actions. So in the scenario above, you might choose to keep the baby, which is likely to reinforce your anti-abortion stance, or you may choose to go ahead with the termination, in which case you just might adopt new values and beliefs that are more compatible with your actions (i.e. a women's right to choose).

Debates and controversies

Are we always able to align the head, heart, and body? While finding anecdotal evidence of cognitive dissonance theory at work is not difficult (just think of the irrational justifications that smokers often use), I'd suggest that the ability to resolve dissonance might be becoming increasingly difficult in a *postmodern* (see *postmodernity*) information age where (1) we have access to more evidentiary knowledge than ever before, and (2) we are encouraged to reflect on every aspect of ourselves.

Practical application

Have you ever wondered why people often adopt beliefs or engage in actions that seem to defy reason? Cognitive dissonance theory can help you make sense of their choices. Cognitive dissonance can also explain why people who live with inconsistencies often suffer from stress related to angst, guilt, and regret. Perhaps this is the cost of self-reflection in an information age.

Key figures

The main figure here is Leon Festinger, a social-psychologist who was interested in how cults deal with the dissonance caused by failed prophecy (i.e. when the flying saucers don't show up to carry their members away as predicted). He first articulated cognitive dissonance theory in 1957. Contemporary researchers working in this area include Eddie Harmon-Jones and Jack Brehm.

> *Our ideas must agree with realities,*
> *be such realities concrete or*
> *abstract, be they facts or be they*
> *principles, under penalty of endless*
> *inconsistency and frustration.*
>
> **William James** (1842–1910)
> US philosopher, psychologist –
> in 'Pragmatism's Conception
> of Truth', *Pragmatism* (1907)

Recommended readings

For a contemporary take on cognitive dissonance, try *A Radical Dissonance Theory* (Joule 1996) or the collection of papers presented at a 1997 cognitive dissonance conference, *Cognitive Dissonance: Progress on a Pivotal Theory in Social Psychology* (Harmon-Jones and Mills 1999). Still worth a look is Festinger's seminal work, *Theory of Cognitive Dissonance* (1957).

 Collective

Core definition
A number of people who act together as a single group.

Longer explanation
Have you ever done anything outrageous, daring, brave, illegal or just plain stupid when you were in a group, something you'd never do if you were on your own? If the answer is yes, you're not alone. There is power in the collective – a power that transcends the individual and even transcends an array of individuals. Now there are a number of important social science terms that are premised on the notion of the collective. A few include: *collective action* – social action undertaken by a group for the purpose of advancing common interest (i.e. a community group lobbying to save a park); *collective bargaining* – the negotiation of wages and employment conditions by employees who are represented by a union or other authorized party; *collective behaviour* – how people behave in groups or crowds, which includes everything from organized social movements (i.e. Sydney's gay and lesbian Mardi Gras) to more spontaneous behaviours (i.e. soccer riots); *collective conscious* – sets of beliefs and sentiments that are common to 'typical' members of a society; and *collective unconscious* – the ancient and shared experience of the human race that arguably (1) resides in all individuals; (2) sits independent of personal psychology; and (3) acts to direct social and personal beliefs and behaviours.

Debates and controversies
There's not a lot of debate on whether there's power in collectivity – it's generally accepted that there is. Debates more often centre on how collectivity affects the intellectual, emotional and physical responses of individuals. For example, an issue often explored revolves around personal responsibility and how crowd mentality can overcome an individual's personal psychology, causing them to act to ways outside their normal character.

Practical application
We often look at how individuals negotiate the social world and how they interact within groups. But we sometimes forget that the whole can be more than

the sum of the parts, and that there's power in a collectivity that transcends individuals or even the sum of individuals. In a world where group mentality, advocacy and action are all central to conflict and change, the collective is an extremely important social science construct.

Key figures

Several theorists have contributed to our understanding of collective attitudes and behaviours, including Emile Durkheim, who argued that a collective conscience offers *solidarity* to the *community* and guidance to the individual, and Carl Jung, who argues that a collective unconscious underpins all of humanity.

> In not my, but our collective,
> hands is held the promise of change.
>
> **Mark Sanford** *(1960–)* Governor of
> South Carolina, Inaugural Address,
> 15 January 2003

Recommended readings

Various notions of collective are covered in *Introduction to Collective Behavior and Collective Action* (Miller 2000), *An Introduction to Collective Bargaining and Industrial Relations* (Katz and Kochan 2003) and *The Wisdom of Crowds* (Surowiecki 2004). To read more on the collective conscious you can try Durkheim's *The Division of Labor in Society* (*1893* 1997) and *Sociology and Philosophy* (*1906* 1974). To explore the collective unconscious turn to *Blake, Jung, and the Collective Unconscious* (Singer 2000) or attempt Jung's *The Archetypes and the Collective Unconscious* (*1934* 1991).

Colonization

Core definition

The practice of dominant nations establishing economic and political infra-structure in foreign territories through settlement. Often follows armed conflict and results in a fundamental (and often legal) distinction between settlers and indigenous populations.

Longer explanation

Rich, fertile, faraway lands bursting with natural resources. Occupied? Not really … except for the 'savages', but no real civilization to speak of. Quick, let's get over there, set up a colony, and claim that land as part of our empire. While this practice has occurred throughout history (see **imperialism**), the 'modern' period of colonization began with the discovery of 'new worlds'. Spain and Portugal created colonies in South America, and Great Britain had colonies in Canada, Australia, and New Zealand, not to mention their North American colonies, which quickly fought for and gained independence and became a colonial power in its own right. In the early twentieth century, the process of colonization involved the European quest for Africa and parts of Asia. This modern period of colonization ended after the Second World War. Since that time there's been a trend towards 'decolonization', in which many nations have fought for and won independence. The question is whether this allows autonomy and freedom or whether these new 'independent' countries remain economically and culturally subservient to their colonizing nation (a situation referred to as neo-colonialism).

Debates and controversies

So what's the fate of indigenous populations facing colonial futures? Well, Ian Smith, prime minister of the former African colony, Rhodesia, once said: 'Colonialism is a wonderful thing. It spread civilization to Africa. Before it they had no written language, no wheel as we know it, no schools, no hospitals, not even normal clothing.' And while this may be true, before colonization the natives of many lands also had no experience of genocide, slavery, life in a reservation, patronizing attempts to be 'civilized', and treatment as second-class citizens.

Practical application

Colonization, as well as the process of decolonization, are massive exercises in power that involve issues such as race, *class*, the 'primitive', civilization, warfare, invasion, genocide, trade, *globalization*, development, *revolution*, nation building (see *nationalism*) and humanitarian rights. Understanding processes of colonization provides an exceptional window for exploring key social science constructs in the context of dynamic local and global change.

Key figures

Colonization is a global practice that has been explored, often critically, by both theorists and activists. Examples here are Andre Gunder Frank, the founder of dependency theory (that the wealth of many nations relies on poorer states), and Frantz Fanon, who believed that revolution is the only means of ending colonial repression.

> We must find new lands from which
> we can easily obtain raw materials
> and at the same time exploit the
> cheap slave labour that is available
> from the natives.
>
> **Cecil Rhodes** (1853-1902) Founder
> of Rhodesia as well as founder of
> De Beers Diamond Corporation,
> which at one time controlled 90% of
> the world's diamonds - attributed

Recommended readings

Colonialism: A Theoretical Overview (Osterhammel 2005) offers a good, short introduction, while *Colonialism: An International Social Cultural and Political Encyclopedia* (Page and Sonnenburg 2003) provides much more depth. *Colonialism in Question: Theory, Knowledge, History* (Cooper 2005) offers a rich historical overview, while *The Decolonization Reader* (Le Sueur 2003) explores nations after colonial rule.

Commodification

Core definition

The conversion of use-value (the value of a chicken in feeding one's hunger) to monetary or exchange-value at a market (on sale for $7.95).

Longer explanation

What value does an object have? Is it the value that an object brings to our lives – or is it $$? Is the value of a sweater warmth or $29.95? Is the value of bread sustenance or $2.50? And what about sex? Is the value the ecstasy it brings, or is it about $100 per hour? In a commodified society everything has a monetary value, even people. According to *Forbes Magazine*, Oprah Winfrey is 'worth' $1.3 billion. Even Maggie Simpson has a barcode. At the supermarket she rings up at $847.63 (the US mean annual cost of raising a baby in *The Simpsons'* first season).

Debates and controversies

So what implications are there for societies that are highly commodified? Well, Marxists believe that commodification is dehumanizing because it reduces all human interactions to economic transactions. Similarly, what was once thought of as priceless, suddenly becomes a marketable object sold for profit. Money becomes the sole language of worth. Another issue here is equity. We accept that the poor may not be able to afford nice 'things', but in a society where services and even relationships become commodified, the poor may not be able to afford education, basic healthcare, sex, the path to true love, a new hip, a womb, or the sperm/egg necessary for a child. The more a *society* is commodified, the more potential there is for economic inequity.

Practical application

As the basis of an ever-growing global economic system, the commodification of 'goods' is a central concept in understanding *globalization* and the growth of *capitalism* in *developing countries*. Closer to home, we know that 'things' have monetary value, but as commodification reaches beyond goods into services, relationships, and even the self (how much did your nose cost you?), it will be fascinating to explore the implications for societal relationships and personal psychology.

Key figures

Marx was highly critical of an economic system based on the production and sale of commodities, that is **capitalism**. He believed that if worth is reduced to a price tag, commodities can actually become more important than the people and social relationships that create them. The commodity (i.e a car, house, or shiny new appliance) becomes an object of worship that has power over even those that produce it. Marx referred to this as commodity fetishism.

> Marge, there's an empty spot
> I've always had inside me.
> I tried to fill it with family,
> religion, community service,
> but those were dead ends.
> I think this chair is the answer.
>
> **Homer Simpson** (The Simpsons)

Recommended readings

For a contemporary overview of Western commodification, try *Commodifying Everything: Relationships of the Market* (Strasser 2003) or *Rethinking Commodification: Cases and Readings in Law and Culture* (Ertman and Williams 2005). Marx's discussion of commodification is in his classic work, *Das Kapital* (pt 1) (*1867* 1999).

 Communism

Core definition

A form of society in which the means of production and sustenance, that is land, resources, and financial *capital*, belong to the *community*.

Longer explanation

Communism can be described as a community-based economic system of cooperative ownership and control. But is communism a utopian path or a flawed economic system? For Marx and Engels, communism was certainly a utopian vision of a humane society. They believed workers would unite against the exploitation of *capitalism* and fight for a more equitable form of society. Communism would be the realization of this struggle since under this economic/political system there would be no need for exploitation. Now while communist revolutions did occur (i.e. Russia in 1917 and China in 1949), the utopias Marx and Engel's predicted did not evolve. Communist regimes took power, but were characterized by party rule and dictatorial centralization. By the 1980s it was clear that communist societies were not moving towards equity and freedom, and were struggling to compete economically with capitalist societies. By the early 1990s most of the World's communist states, including the Soviet Union, had collapsed and those that remained, for example China, were attempting to compete in global capitalist markets.

Debates and controversies

The question here is what went wrong? It's hard to malign the *Marxist* goals of communism, but easy to critique the eventuating political regimes. A number of explanations have been put forward to explain this 'gap': the poor economic status of countries in which communist revolutions occurred; the economic and political pressure of capitalist countries like the USA; internal corruption and greed that undermined the notion of classlessness; and a growing belief in the 'survival of the fittest' (see *social Darwinism*). In fact, many now question whether a genuine communist vision can ever be realized on the ground.

Practical application

Should communism be relegated to the history books, or is there still practical application in the social sciences? Well, it's important to understand the birth of communism as a critique of the inequities inherent in capitalism. In fact, Marx wrote more about capitalism than he did about communism. So while communist societies have struggled, we still search for an economic system that allows both equity and prosperity. Much of the world still strives to reach utopian goals not dissimilar to those of Marx and Engels.

Key figures

Revolutionaries and leaders of communist regimes include Lenin, who came to power in Russia in 1917 as leader of the Bolsheviks (which became the Communist party in 1918), Stalin, who after Lenin's death attempted to make Russia an industrial power within a communist framework, and Mao Zedong, who in 1949 established the People's Republic of China. Communism's visionaries, however, are clearly Marx and Engels.

> Let's not talk about Communism.
> Communism was just an idea,
> just pie in the sky.
>
> **Boris Yeltsin** (1931–2007) Former
> Russian President – in
> *The Independent*, London,
> 13 September 1989

Recommended readings

Good starting points here are *The Complete Idiot's Guide to Communism* (Carlisle and Lide 2002) or *Communism: A History* (Pipes 2003). The classics are Marx's *The Economic and Philosophic Manuscripts of 1844* (*1844* 1988) and Marx and Engel's *Communist Manifesto* (*1848* 2004).

 Community

Core definition
A group of people who share a sense of belonging based on commonalities such as residential area, *culture*, race, religion, profession or interests.

Longer explanation
While communities can be based on any number of commonalities, one of the most widespread conceptions of community is the feeling of belonging that comes from where you live, your neighbourhood. Nostalgically, we tend to think of community as a place where neighbours meet up at the corner coffee shop and interact regularly with the local doctor, teacher, and minister. Everybody knows and cares about everybody else. But is that the way the real world works? Do we take the time to know our neighbours? Do we even have a local coffee shop (or are we stuck with Starbucks at the mega mall)? Are we surrounded by communities that provide a sense of place and fulfil our social needs? Or have societies gone through cultural and economic transformations that have left us without deeper community connections?

Debates and controversies
'Community' tends to be a warm and fuzzy word, and you often hear people mourning its loss. Old folks talk of times when community was like an extended family and there was a definite sense of *solidarity*. But 'community' is a loaded term, and we often forget that some communities can actually be dysfunctional (think of street gangs), stifling, and/or highly *alienating* to those left on the outside. For example, in rural areas today, where a sense of community is considered strong, there are plenty of teenagers who can't wait to escape its confines.

Practical application
Yes, *urbanization*, rationalization, *secularization* and more hours at work may be dampening a traditional spirit of local community, but does this mean community is dead? Or does it still exist, but in other forms? Workplaces, for one, can be an important source of community. After all, outside family, work mates can be the only people we spend time with. I think we seek community

where we can, and that might mean at work, at social clubs based on common attributes or interests, or at an ever-increasing rate, in virtual internet communities. And this makes community a shifting construct that's worth exploring.

Key figures

In the late nineteenth century Ferdinand Tönnies distinguished between communities and societies, arguing that communities are cohesive social entities within larger **societies**. Emile Durkheim, Tönnies' contemporary, feared that traditional sources of community solidarity might be threatened by **industrialization**. Twentieth-century theorists who engaged with the concept of community include Talcott Parsons, Robert E. Park, Louis Wirth and Robert Redfield.

> *A community needs a soul if it is to become a true home for human beings. You, the people must give it this soul.*
>
> **Pope John Paul II** (1920–2005)
> Polish ecclesiastic – attributed

Recommended readings

For a contemporary take on community, try *Psychological Sense of Community* (Fisher et al. 2002), *Native to Nowhere: Sustaining Home and Community in a Global Age* (Beatley 2004), or *The Virtual Community: Homesteading on the Electronic Frontier* (Rheingold 2000). The classic readings are Tönnies' *Community and Civil Society* (*1887* 2001) and Durkheim's *The Division of Labor in Society* (bk 1, ch 2) (*1893* 1997).

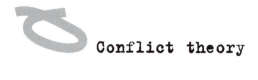

Conflict theory

Core definition

Theoretical perspective that focuses on how both change and order arise from struggles (coercion, physical force, competition) between individuals and social groups who wish to maximize their wealth and *power*.

Longer explanation

So what makes societies tick? Do individuals and groups strive to make functional contributions in cooperative ways? Do we seek consensus and harmony? Or is the reality that we're much more self-centred and ready to enter into conflict to get what we want? Conflict theory argues that from personal to global scales, conflict is inevitable. The desire for wealth and power has always led to tensions. The powerful coerce, exploit, and control the weak, while the weak do what they can to resist. At times, the end result is protection of the status quo. Other times, it's change. Conflict theorists argue that this is how the world operates and that as long as there is competition for scarce resources, conflict will be our driving force.

Debates and controversies

So does this mean we're driven by conflict rather than consensus, dysfunction rather than function? Well, conflict does seem inevitable and does lead to social change, but this doesn't necessarily negate theories that focus on cohesion, norms, and function (see *functionalism*). The social world is infinitely complex, and theories are simply an attempt to get our heads around what might be happening out there. Rather than a reflection of reality, theories are better seen as tools that help us gather insights into complexity. So while conflict theory is central to understanding society, it provides only partial understanding and should be explored in conjunction with other key sociological theories, such as functionalism and *symbolic interactionism*.

Practical application

So much of our world revolves around conflict. Tradition and transformation are often at war, and it's not uncommon for families, communities and nations to come to blows. The ways in which such conflict leads to social change, which can be slow and evolutionary, dramatic and revolutionary, or anything in between, is something that conflict theory can certainly help illuminate.

Key figures

While the study of conflict as a major source of social order and change can be traced back to the likes of Karl Marx, Max Weber, Georg Simmel and others, conflict theory as a label is most closely associated with theorists of the 1950s and 1960s who opposed more functional perspectives on society. Key figures here include John Rex in the UK, Lewis A. Coser and Randall Collins in the USA, and Ralf Dahrendorf in Germany.

> *Only in the frictionless vacuum of*
> *a nonexistent abstract world can*
> *movement or change occur without*
> *that abrasive friction of conflict.*
>
> **Saul Alinsky** (1909–1972) US radical
> activist – in 'The Purpose',
> *Rules for Radicals* (1971)

Recommended readings

Using Conflict Theory (Bartos and Wehr 2002), *Class and Class Conflict in Industrial Society* (Dahrendorf 1959) and *Functions of Social Conflict* (Coser (*1956* 1999) should give you a feel for the development of twentieth-century conflict theory. But if you want to go right back to the founding fathers, turn to Marx's *Das Kapital* (pt 3) (*1867* 1999), Weber's *Economy and Society* (pt 2, ch 10) (*1921–22* 1978) and Simmel's *Conflict and the Web of Group Affiliations* (*1908 1964*).

 Conservatism

Core definition

A tendency to oppose change and preserve what exists. While conservatism can be described as an attitude, it's also associated with political principals that stress the value of existing systems and structures.

Longer explanation

Some people want to change the world. Others think we should leave well enough alone. It's this second sentiment that is the basis of conservatism. Whether it's preserving the existing government, the current economic system, religious institutions and values, or traditional notions of family, conservatism stresses the need to rely on what is. Of course 'what is' depends on your time and place in history. So rather than any defined personal or political platforms, conservatism is more a belief in notions like the value of the tried and true (whatever that may be) over the new and innovative, order over chaos, and what exists over what might be possible. In fact, conservatives believe that people can be overly passionate, yet somewhat short-sighted. Stability and tradition can therefore save society from the unanticipated and unwanted political, economic, and social consequences of *radical* (see *critical/radical*) change and 'utopian' visions.

Debates and controversies

I think the question here is 'Does tradition and stability protect us from our own recklessness, as conservatives would have us believe, or is there also a risk in stagnancy?' Is change always the biggest threat? It's also interesting to note that what conservatives want so badly to preserve is often the result of previous battles for change. As Leo Rosten once said: 'A conservative is one who admires radicals centuries after they're dead.'

Practical application

Conservatism can be a window for exploring the tension between stability and change and how disagreements, debates, arguments, political platforms, and revolutionary actions can (1) lead back to stability and the status quo; (2) lead to change that is slow and incremental; and (3) open the door to more quick, dramatic and even radical change that temporarily destabilizes conservative sensibilities.

Key figures

Key figures here include the eighteenth-century philospoher David Hume, who was suspicious of attempts to reform society in ways that departed from tradition, and Edmund Burke, an eighteenth-century political scholar who believed that a desire for change, even when argued with logic and reason, is still likely to be tied to vested interests or misguided and unrealistic visions. He argued that the wisdom of individuals and radical fringe groups cannot equal the collective wisdom of a society with its embedded customs, practices, institutions, and legal systems. Conservatism therefore protects us from our own fallibility.

> What is conservatism?
> Is it not adherence to the old and
> tried, against the new and untried.
>
> **Abraham Lincoln** (1809-1865)
> US president - speech,
> 27 February 1860, in Basler,
> R. P. Collected Works of
> Abraham Lincoln (1953)

Further readings

The Meaning of Conservatism (Scruton 2002) and *Conservatism* (Muller 1997) will introduce you to the concept's major tenets and key thinkers. I also like *The Inevitability of Conservatism* (Perkinson 2005), which argues the unavoidable nature of conservative thought and action in Western political and social systems.

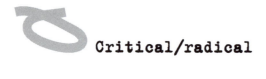

Critical/radical

Core definition

<u>Critical</u> – to challenge taken-for-granted ways of knowing; to ask not only what is, but why it is, who benefits, and what are the alternatives. <u>Radical</u> – belief in the necessity of fundamental or revolutionary changes in practices, conditions, institutions, or ideologies.

Longer explanation

First question – do these words belong together in the same entry? Since they're not really antonyms or synonyms you might wonder why I've combined them. Well I have two reasons. First, these adjectives refer to ways of thinking or doing that question the status quo. Second, they both have social science definitions that are distinct from their everyday meanings, which makes them often misunderstood and misused by students. For example, when students are asked to think critically, they tend to think they're being asked to be negative or engage in criticism. What professors really want, however, is intellectual engagement that involves going below the surface, looking at the how and why, and challenging what is often taken for granted. More than simple fault-finding, the goal is to uncover and unmask hidden assumptions.

The word 'radical' creates a similar situation – the mind thinks 'extremes' or 'living at the edge'. But the trick here is to go back to the Latin root, which just happens to be 'root'. So to be radical is to pull something up by its roots. Radicals believe that tweaking an ideology or system is not enough – to make a difference you need to grab something by its roots, turn it upside down and inside out, and acknowledge the need for fundamental change.

I'll give you an example. Take the statement: 'Divorce is one of the biggest problems facing Western society.' To look at this *factually* might involve turning to statistics, that is the number or divorces and recent trends. But to look at this *critically* you would not only explore divorce as a social problem, you might also explore it as an answer to the social problem of bad marriages. Apply some *radical* thinking and you might argue that the real problem here is the concept of marriage itself. Marriage might have worked when women were dependent on men for financial support, and men were dependent on women for domestic duties, but in a world where two autonomous individuals don't need to be dependent on each other for care or money, the institution of marriage, as we know it, may need to be turned on its head.

Practical application

I was one of the many students who went through an undergraduate degree inappropriately using my everyday understandings of these words within the social sciences – no wonder I was confused. Not only will getting your head around these terms open up new understandings, it will also help you distinguish the difference between concepts such as **ethnography** and critical ethnography, **feminism** and radical feminism, so on and so forth.

Think off-center.

George Carlin (1937-) Stand-up
comedian - attributed

Recommended readings

Critical Thinking (Moore and Parker 2005) or *Critical Thinking* (Fisher 2001) both offer good introductions to criticality, while *Thought Dreams: Radical Theory for the 21st Century* (Albert 2004) will introduce you to the power of radical thought. If you're more interested in exploring a range of contemporary critical and radical theorists, have a look at *Fifty Key Contemporary Thinkers* (Lechte 2006).

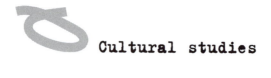

Cultural studies

Core definition

A field of scholarly inquiry that explores the production and circulation of meaning and covers all forms of cultural practice. Objects of inquiry are broad and include literary texts, products of mass media, objects of industrial production, consumer culture, marginality, and other aspects of everyday life.

Longer explanation

Cultural studies emerged during the second half of the twentieth century in response to the *marginalization* of topics thought to be somewhat trivial in the humanities and social sciences (i.e. popular literature, popular culture, various subcultures, and fashion). It was thought that traditional objects of study, such as classic literature, key religions, social institutions, and economic forces, should not be considered the only things that shed light on the human condition. The products of popular *culture* and everyday life, whether they be TV shows, films, clothing, hairstyles, advertisements, graffiti, gadgets, magazines, or novels should also be considered rich 'texts' worthy of study. After all, these are genuine cultural artifacts that can tell us a lot about ourselves, our culture, and how it all nests within larger socioeconomic/political contexts.

Debates and controversies

Cultural studies is a highly diverse area of inquiry that includes a wide array of approaches, methods, and perspectives. Proponents argue that this is a strength, and that the breadth of cultural studies comes from the need to open up traditional (and quite narrowly focused) disciplines. But others argue that cultural studies lacks a distinct and coherent disciplinary core, and have even accused it of being an academic fad that fails to address fundamental questions of social life.

Practical application

I once interviewed a cross-section of girls at a middle-class high school about their everyday interactions. I remember being quite impressed and thinking, 'what a nice, polite group of kids'. Then I innocently went to the bathroom... So much for my 'nice kids' hypothesis. I spent at least 25 minutes reading the absolutely compelling words of wisdom, vulgar vilification and crucial data (i.e. who's a slag, who's well hung, etc.) scrawled on the toilet walls. I, for one, would strongly argue that there are times when the products of everyday culture can be extremely informative.

Key figures

There are a huge array of cultural theorists that include the likes of Richard Hoggart, Stuart Hall, Theodor Adorno, Roland Barthes, Homi K. Bhabha, Pierre Bourdieu, John Guillory, Michel Foucault, Donna Haraway, Raymond Williams, bell hooks, Max Horkheimer, and Jean-François Lyotard. The readers below will introduce you to these as well as a host of other contributors to cultural studies.

> It's generally my belief and those
> of others in this field of
> cultural studies that popular culture
> has a big effect on the people
> who consume it.
>
> *Michael Asimow* (1939–) UCLA Law
> professor – quoted in *Canadian Press*,
> 16 February 2006

Recommended readings

I'd start with either *Introducing Cultural Studies* (Sardar 2005) or *The Uses of Cultural Studies* (McRobbie 2005). To delve deeper into the work of an array of cultural theorists, I'd turn to readers such as *Introducing Cultural Studies* (Longhurst et al. 2000), *What is Cultural Studies?* (Storey 1996) and *The Cultural Studies Reader* (During 2007).

 **Culture**

> ## Core definition
> The knowledge, values, beliefs, traditions, spirituality, emotive features, material products, lifestyles, and notions of **community** that exist in a **society**.

Longer explanation

They say 'culture' is notoriously hard to define. I think this is because culture not only surrounds us, but actually creates us. Yes, culture is socially constructed (see **social constructionism**). Social groups construct culture in any variety of ways (which leads to cultural diversity across the globe and even within neighbourhoods). But culture also constructs people. Think about it … infants don't know much when they're born (other than maybe suck and poop), but even before they set foot in school they're not only familiar with the food, values, spirituality, language, and family structures that define their culture, it's actually this social heritage that defines them as individuals. Perhaps this is why culture is so hard for us to see, so hard to for us define, yet is so staunchly defended when under threat. Not only is it embedded in individuals as true and natural, it also creates an individual's knowing about themselves, others, and the world that surrounds them.

Debates and controversies

Basically, culture is everything that is socially (rather than biologically) learned and shared. It's what gives us meaning and power, and offers us a way to relate to our world. But this can cause us to become quite **ethnocentric** where we see our own culture as inherently superior to all others. In fact, a tremendous amount of global bloodshed, war, genocide, and terrorism has at its root, a need to define, defend, spread, devalue, and destroy 'cultures'.

Practical application

Not that long ago, exploring other cultures (which allowed us to 'see' our own culture) meant travelling far and wide. But we now live in an ever-shrinking world full of multicultural communities in which cultures are increasingly visible, and often represent issues to be managed. The importance of culture to a community, the challenges of managing cultural diversity, and the role of culture in global conflict makes this an extremely important social science construct.

Key figures

Key figures here include Edward Burnett Tylor, an anthropologist who provided an early definition in 1871 and argued that all cultures move along a single evolutionary path, and Franz Boas, who in the early 1900s argued that diverse historical circumstances lead to diverse cultures and that cultural plurality (see **pluralism**) is an inevitable feature of humankind. More contemporary theorists can be found under the **cultural studies** entry.

> *Culture is roughly anything we do and the monkeys don't.*
>
> **Lord Raglan** (1885–1964)
> British soldier, farmer and
> scholar – attributed

Recommended readings

Arguably more interesting than understanding culture as a broad social science construct is exploring the implication of 'culture' on our world. Some interesting works here are *Culture and Everyday Life* (Bennett 2005) and *Cultures and Societies in a Changing World* (Griswold 2003). I also like *Introducing Cultural Studies* (Sardar 2005) and *Cultural Studies* (During 2005), which explore culture as it relates to globalization, the media, identity and sexuality.

 Deconstruction

Core definition

To reveal a 'text's' inherent contradictions and underlying assumptions in order to unpack its cultural, linguistic and historical layers of meaning.

Longer explanation

Deconstruction helps us understand that our 'texts', which go beyond formal writing and include social products such as TV, movies, magazines and gadgets are not universal, timeless, or apolitical. They're actually 'constructions' built on the back of historical, linguistic and cultural forces. So they shouldn't be taken at face value; what we accept as truth is but one possibility. Take graffiti as an example. According to *Wordnet,* graffiti is 'rude decoration inscribed on rocks or walls'. Now while definitions are generally thought of as neutral, they're actually imbued with value judgements. In this case, the word 'rude' may be a give away, but conisder the choice of 'decoration' rather than 'art', or 'rocks and walls' instead of 'natural canvas'. There's no mention of 'self-expression' or 'political statement' either. Deconstructionists would argue that graffiti is a construct that rests on a particular ideology with defined views on art, youth, and deviance. An NYPD 'reward' poster says it best: 'Reward up to $500.00 for the arrest and conviction of anyone who commits Graffiti Vandalism… Remember graffiti vandalism is a crime.' Deconstruction reminds us that there are other ways to understand constructs like graffiti. An alternative reading is offered by Simon and Garfunkel in *Sounds of Silence*: 'The words of the prophets were written on the subway walls and tenement halls.'

Debates and controversies

A major criticism of deconstruction is that you can discredit something simply by looking at contradictions within it – there's no need to refute its actual arguments. Critics suggest that this takes all power out of our constructs and leaves them quite useless. Deconstruction is also notoriously difficult to understand – a criticism for which I have a lot of sympathy. Deconstruction is based on dense and complicated jargon that can confuse almost anyone.

Practical application

While the roots of deconstruction lie in literary criticism, deconstruction can be immensely useful to social scientists who consider society a 'text'. Deconstruction can help uncover cultural biases, power struggles and hidden ideological beliefs. It opens up new possibilities for understanding taken-for-granted constructs.

Key figures

The main key figure here is Jacques Derrida, a French literary critic and philosopher who argued that Western thought is based on **dichotmoties** or oppositions (i.e. male/female, good/bad, black/white). He believed that while such oppositions are offered as descriptive and therefore neutral, they're not. One of the oppositional elements is, in fact, privileged, thereby biasing our understandings without us even knowing it. Derrida believed that deconstruction was needed to reveal such biases.

> This is deconstruction – to peel away like an onion the layers of constructed meaning.
>
> **Richard Appignanesi** (1940–) Novelist, editor and philosopher – in *Introducing Postmodernism* (1995)

Recommended readings

They say that attempting to define deconstruction is to miss the point. I don't necessarily agree with that, but I do recognize that it takes more than 500 words to capture deconstruction's complexities and subtleties. To read more, try *Deconstruction for Beginners* (Powell 2005) or *Deconstructions: A User's Guide* (Royle 2000). If you're game enough to tackle Derrida, try *Of Grammatology* (*1976* 1998).

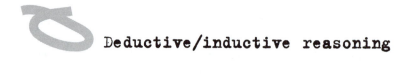

Deductive/inductive reasoning

Core definition

Types of reasoning often used to ground various approaches to social science research. <u>Deductive reasoning</u> moves from general *theory* down to particular examples, while <u>inductive reasoning</u> moves from particular examples up to general theory.

Longer explanation

In social science research, methods that rely on deductive reasoning start with a theory, which is narrowed to a testable *hypothesis*. Data is then collected and analysed to see if the hypothesis can be confirmed and the theory, substantiated. For example, say you hypothesize that one cause of divorce is women feeling unfulfilled by an identity of wife and mother. Deduction would involve collecting data, say from a survey that asks women about attitudes towards marriage with specific reference to issues of identity. Results are then analysed to see if they support your hypothesis/theory.

Inductive reasoning works the other way around and starts with a question, followed by data collection. Data is then explored for regularities, patterns and themes that lead to generalizations and eventually theory. So say your question is 'why are so many women leaving marriages?' Data collection might involve in-depth interviews with a sample of relevant women. But rather than looking to confirm a preordained hypothesis, you remain open to various possibilities (often called *grounded theory* generation). In the end, the goal is to put forth findings and even theories that help explain what's really going on.

Debates and controversies

Which approach is better or more effective? There are actually three ways to answer this question. The first is to take a side in a longstanding *paradigm* debate. *Quantitative* researchers tend to see hypothesis testing (deductive reasoning) as the core of proper scientific method. But those who do *qualitative* research tend to believe that only inductive methods let the data tell the story in an unbiased way. The second approach is to recognize how context-sensitive research is. Researchers often explore their questions, objectives, settings, and skills before determining the best way to proceed. The third way forward is to acknowledge that most research involves cycles of inductive and deductive reasoning – even if not formally articulated as such. For example, we move from theory down to data, but when we anaylse our data we might recognize a need to modify theory. Similarly, if we move from data to theory, we will eventually seek to confirm that theory with further data observation.

Practical application

Reasoning and logic are central in philosophy, and deductive and inductive approaches offer two alternatives in the production of knowledge. Most students of the social sciences, however, will engage with these two types of reasoning when conducting research.

> It is difficult to distinguish deduction from what in other circumstances is called problem-solving. And concept learning, inference, and reasoning by analogy are all instances of inductive reasoning.
>
> **Frank Smith** (1928–) Canadian educator – in *To Think* (1990)

Recommended readings

Logic, Inductive and Deductive: An Introduction to Scientific Method (Jones *1909* 2004) is an important seminal work, while *Scientific Method in Practice* (Gauch 2002) is a contemporary alternative. Another choice here is Glaser and Strauss's *The Discovery of Grounded Theory* (1967), which represents a shift towards more **post-positivist** approaches to inductive research methods.

 Democracy

Core definition

A system of government in which citizens have an equal right to participate in political decision-making. In larger political systems this generally involves indirect decision-making via the election of government representatives.

Longer explanation

The Western world prides itself on being democratic. In a democracy, there are no dictators or aristocracy. **Power** rests with common people. Each has an equal voice in all realms of political, economic and social life. Citizens are guaranteed a vote in free elections and are assured basic human rights. As the American Constitution states: 'We hold these truths to be self-evident: that all men are created equal'. But then again, when they said 'men' they actually meant men, and free white ones at that. Slaves were not allowed to vote until emancipation in 1863 (although voting criteria such as poll taxes and literacy tests discriminated against black voters for many more years). Women were not granted a right to vote until 1920.

Debates and controversies

Three general criticisms are common here. The first is that the concept of democracy itself is flawed. It's perilous to trust the running of a nation to commoners who might be (a) politically ignorant; (b) easily duped by political rhetoric; or (c) quite apathetic. Winston Churchill sums this up well: 'The best argument against democracy is a five-minute conversation with the average voter.' The second line of criticism accepts the *theory* of democracy but suggests that its goals are not realized in practice. For one, and as indicted above, the concept of 'all' does not necessarily mean everybody. Recent 'democratic' elections in Kuwait excluded women. Second, equal voice should mean an equal share in political power, yet there's a known correlation between economic power and political power, and wealth is far from equally distributed. As George Orwell says in *Animal Farm*: 'All animals are created equal, but some are more equal than others.' Finally, while we may be allocated a vote, we need to look critically at the choices we're offered. Is there real diversity among political parties or are they all tarred with the same brush?

Practical application

The principles of democracy, its practice, diffusion, and implications give social scientists plenty to explore. Not only are we governed by some form of democracy, our longing to protect and foster democracy across the globe has been a justification for war for centuries.

Key figures

Since the time of Plato and Aristotle, numerous theorists have explored and critiqued notions of democracy. In the USA, eighteenth and nineteenth-century democratic theorists included Thomas Paine, Thomas Jefferson, and James Madison. British contemporaries included John Stuart Mill and Jeremy Bentham. A more recent democratic theorist is Robert Dahl, who questions whether modern democracy gives power to the people or simply shifts power from one group of power elites to another.

> Democracy is the government of
> the people, by the people,
> for the people.
>
> **Abraham Lincoln** (1809–1865)
> US President Address to Congress,
> 4 July 1861

Recommended readings

Some good introductory choices here are *Understanding Democratic Politics* (Axtmann 2003) and *Models of Democracy* (Held 1997). Also worth a look are *The State of Democratic Theory* (Shapiro 2003), *Democracy: A History* (Dunn 2006) or for a more **critical** view, Dahl's *On Democracy* (2000).

 **Determinism**

Longer explanation

Are our lives predetermined, or is it up to us to chart our own course? Do we get to write our destiny, or has the script already been penned? Determinists believe that our future is dictated by particular circumstances, so our ability to control our destiny, or our free will, is constrained. In other words, it's not by chance, luck, or even, to an extent, conscious decision-making that finds you studying at univeristy. Given your genes, *socialization*, time and place in history, and psychological profile, there's nothing else you could be doing – a somewhat scary thought. Types of determinism include: *genetic/biological* – your destiny is determined by your genetic make-up, including IQ, race, and gender; *environmental (anthropological)* – that a society's path is determined by external environments (i.e. fishing communities will develop on island nations, while hunters and gatherers will be found in desert climates); *environmental (psycho-sociological)* – that socialization determines your path; *theological* – what happens is God's will; and *economic* – that social structures, forms of *community*, avenues for *solidarity*, and life opportunities are determined by a society's economic system (a view championed by *Marxists*).

Debates and controversies

The extent to which our future is predetermined is a huge philosophical question. We like to think we're in control of our destiny, and that it's our decisions that direct our life course. But what if our paths are predetermined? We might as well go through life without even trying. After all, if your life is screwed up, you're not responsible. Determinism says there is no free will and is therefore often critiqued for it's disempowering tendencies.

Practical application

The concept of determinism is central to anyone trying to understand cause and effect, whether it be at the level of philosophy, psychology, anthropology, sociology, economic theory, and even quantum physics. Entries on **agency**, **chaos theory, causation,** and **essentialism** will give you additional perspectives on this central and hotly contested construct.

Key figures

A number of classic theorists, including Thomas Hobbes, David Hume, J. S. Mill and Immanuel Kant, have tackled the question of determinism and whether a belief in cause and effect allows for any level of free will. More recent theorists to tackle this issue include John Searle and Ted Honderich.

> The hand you are dealt is determinism;
> the way you play it is free will.
>
> *Jawaharlal Nehru* (1889–1964) First
> prime minister of India – attributed

Recommended readings

If you're after a good introductory text, try *How Free Are You?: The Determinism Problem* (Honderich 2002). To go further into cross-diciplinary debates and philosophical theory, try *The Illusion of Conscious Will* (Wegner 2003), *Freedom and Determinism* (Campbell et al. 2004), or *Between Chance and Choice: Interdisciplinary Perspectives on Determinism* (Atmanspacher and Bishop 2002).

Developed/developing countries

Core definition

A *dichotomy* used to describe a nation's economic status. <u>Developed countries</u> (sometimes referred to as first world) have a relatively high standard of living and a strong economy, while <u>developing countries</u> (third world) have a poor infrastructure and low average income.

Longer explanation

So what countries are considered developed, who is developing, and how is this decided? Well, the United Nations uses a statistic called the human development index (HDI) to measure development status. The index includes life expectancy, adult literacy rates, school enrolments at various levels, and gross domestic product. A score of .8 or more indicates high development, .5 to .8 indicates moderate development and under .5 is considered low development (a list of countries by HDI can be found on the free web encyclopedia, Wikipedia). It's interesting to note, however, that even with the introduction of the United Nation's HDI in the early 1990s, there's still no established convention for designation – countries can self-select. This leads to a number of anomalies. South Korea and Singapore, for example, for political and economic reasons, do not wish to be considered developed, even though both have HDIs over .9.

Debates and controversies

While the use of the adjectives 'developed' and 'developing' may seem fairly straightforward, it's important to recognize that these terms are not value-neutral. 'Developed', for example, implies that a pinnacle has been reached; there's no need to seek improvements at economic, social or humanitarian levels. 'Developing', on the other hand, implies (1) that a nation wants to develop an *industrialized*, Western, *capitalist* economic system; (2) that the wealth of developed countries is not dependent on countries that are less developed (there is room for all to develop); and (3) that economic growth is, indeed, occurring. 'Developing' implies that all nations should, can, and are becoming developed. An alternative here is the term 'underdeveloped', which still has a negative connotation, but better reflects the reality of the poorest countries whose economies are not moving forward along 'accepted' development criteria.

Practical application

The social sciences have always allowed for exploration along a continuum that ranges from individual to global perspectives. As our world gets ever smaller, however, global perspectives have increased in importance. International trade/tourism, *globalization*, a world economy, and even the spread of diseases such as AIDS, Bird Flu and SARS, has made us ever more conscious of the importance of a nation's economic status – not only as it effects those within that nation but as it affects the larger global picture.

> In an underdeveloped country don't drink the water. In a developed country don't breathe the air.
>
> **Jonathan Raban** (1942-) British travel writer and novelist – attributed

Recommended readings

To delve into the challenges facing developing countries, try *Politics and Culture in the Developing World* (Payne and Nassar 2002) or *The Challenge of Third World Development* (Handelman 2002). When it comes to developed nations, one of the biggest challenges is equity. *Egalitarian Capitalism: Jobs, Incomes, and Growth in Affluent Countries* (Kenworthy 2004) is an interesting work that compares growth and equity across 16 industrialized nations.

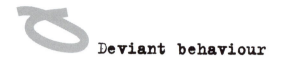 Deviant behaviour

Core definition

Behaviours that do not conform to societal expectations.

Longer explanation

Deviant behaviours are behaviours that 'deviate' from something. The question is what that something is and who gets to define it. Now deviant behaviours are often thought of as inherent to an individual, but they're actually socially (and often legally) defined. Take adultery as an example – is it a deviant act? Well it all depends on who is setting the standards of acceptability. When the Taliban sets the standard, adultery is so deviant it's punishable by stoning. Even in the USA, the original (and often still existing) penal codes of most states find adultery both deviant and illegal (punishable by imprisonment and even treatment of insanity). Today, however, adultery has actually become the **norm** (think Hollywood). So while the religious right might still see adultery as deviant (and sinful), in many places it's actually become common, expected, and even accepted. Remember – deviant behaviours are labelled by a society's norms. So just as these norms are broad-ranging, constructed, and ever-shifting, so too are the behaviours we consider deviant (i.e. what's eccentric, immoral, and illegal).

Debates and controversies

The world would be a better place if we could stop deviant behaviour. Well, maybe not. Many social theorists believe that deviance is functional (see **functionalism**) for a society. When we see others as weird, eccentric or immoral, it allows us to see ourselves as mainstream, normal, and perhaps even righteous. Deviance also bonds societies together. We tend to strengthen our bonds when we percieve a common threat. Finally, deviant behaviours can open a path for societal evolution. In the USA 50 years ago, sitting at the front of a bus or trying to get served at a lunch counter were considered deviant if you were black. But the persistence of, and frustration over, these forms of deviance was a catalyst for much needed **social change**.

Practical application

As long as we have people, places and power we will have norms… and there-fore deviance. And this is as true in the playground as it is in global politics. Deviance is thus a fascinating window for exploring our past values, our current values, what we may value in the future, as well as the values of others.

Key figures

While deviance has been explored by any number of sociologists, criminolo-gists and social psychologists (see Recommended readings), a classic figure here is Durkheim. Through his study of norms and normlessness, Durkheim was one of the first to articulate deviance, in this case **anomie**, as a product of societal forces. Durkheim also explored deviance as a normal and, in fact, func-tional part of society that allows the majority to bond through shared legal, eth-ical, moral, and social norms.

> *You have to be deviant if you're going to do anything new.*
>
> **David Lee** TV Producer, co-creator of *Frasier*

Recommended readings

For contemporary introduction, I like *Deviant Behavior* (Humphrey 2005). For a broader array of readings, try *Social Deviance: Readings in Theory and Research* (Pontell 2004) or *Deviant Behavior: A Text-Reader in the Sociology of Deviance* (Kelly and Clarke 2003). If you're interested in Durkheim, you can delve into *Suicide* (*1897* 1997), which discusses deviance from social **norms**, or *The Rules of Sociological Method* (ch 3) (*1895* 1982), which discusses the functions of 'pathology'.

 **Dialectic**

> ## Core definition
> A process of change that arises from the tension between a particular way of doing or thinking and its contradictory positioning.

Longer explanation

In our *society* we might hold a particular belief to be true (a thesis). But some simply don't agree, in fact they believe just the opposite (an antithesis). So what happens? Do the sides stay poles apart, or is there another option? Well, dialectic means working through the contradictions and tensions in order to create a position (a synthesis) that represents an evolution in thinking. For example, say your parents don't believe today's bands hold a candle to those of the 1970s and 1980s. You, on the other hand, can't believe that they still listen to that old school drivel and can't appreciate the musicality of bands like Good Charlotte or Simple Plan. But rather than walk away rolling your eyes, you both decide to listen with open minds and attempt to appreciate what the other values. In the end, you might just reach a position of synthesis, such as believing that contemporary bands reflect the values, beliefs and fears of its generation and in doing so is likely to be best appreciated by that generation.

Debates and controversies

If only opposition, contradiction and difference consistently lead to synthesis and positive change. But we tend to spend an awful lot of energy defending our own position rather than listening openly to alternate views. And this keeps us from using opposition to push our thinking to new levels. Ours is a power-hungry world where the need to be 'right' often comes at the expense of synthesis and forward thought.

Practical application

I think the importance of understanding dialectics is in its power to allow contradiction and opposition to do more than build resentment and antagonism; opposition and contradiction can be seen as central in processes of *social change*. Whether attempting to understand historical processes of transformation, attempting to reconcile contradictory data or opposing theory, or attempting to facilitate conflict resolution, dialectics can be an extremely powerful social science tool.

Key figures

While many thinkers have engaged with dialectics, there are definitely two key figures worth exploring. The first is Hegel, who believed that truth can only emerge when one-sided thinking finds, lives, and reconciles with its opposition. In Chinese culture this might be expressed as every concept needing both its yin and its yang. Marx applied this thinking to economic systems and saw dialectics as the logic that predicted the demise of *capitalism*. If belief in capitalism was a thesis, then the contradictions that Marx saw in capitalism were an antithesis. Out of the tension of these contradictions would come a new synthesis. For Marx, this was a *socialist* state before and ultimate state of *communism* (a process referred to as dialectic materialism).

> Wisdom lies neither in fixity nor
> in change, but in the dialectic
> between the two.
>
> *Octavio Paz* (1914-) Mexican poet -
> in *The Times*, London, 8 June 1989.

Recommended readings

While *Notes on Dialectics: Hegel, Marx, Lenin* (James 2005) will help you work through key theorists, *Dance of the Dialectic: Steps in Marx's Method* (Ollman 2003) finds an even more specific focus. For a contemporary read that looks at dialectics as a force for social change, try *Organizing for Social Change: A Dialectic Journey of Theory and Praxis* (Papa et al. 2005).

 Dichotomy

Longer explanation

We like things black and white. It makes it easy for us. It provides clarity and helps us get our head around various concepts. In fact, this book is full of examples where philosophers and social theorists have offered conceptions of the world as 'either/or'. So we compare things like masculine and feminine, *subject* and object, *qualitative* and *quantitative*, Eastern and Western, *agency* and *structure*, *democracy* and *totalitarianism*, *capitalism* and *communism*, *liberal* and *conservative*, *deductive* and *inductive*, *determinism* and free will, *developed* and *developing*, mind and *body*, sacred and *secular*, public and private, and so on. And we tend to look at these divisions as though they are made up of mutually exclusive opposites with no shades of grey.

Debates and controversies

Can the world be so readily divided into sets of two? After all, when was the last time you saw a person who was actually black or white in colour? In addition to leading us to gross generalizations, our tendency to dichotomize has also affected the way we understand the social world. Philosophers and social theorists spend an awful lot of time defending their positions and denigrating anything that stands in opposition. And of course this causes us to lose sight of the subtleties, complexities, and interconnections that are rife in the social world (see *systems theory*). An interesting alternative here is the Chinese conception of opposites, yin and yang. Here concepts are still divided into two, but the parts are seen as complementary opposites rather than absolute opposites. Yin and yang contain the seed of each other and are understood as highly interdependent. In fact, they have a dynamic relationship.

Practical application

In exploring the social world, it's certainly tempting to impose dichotomies on complex phenomenon – it can be highly clarifying and there's a long history of this practice. But it's important to remember that dichotomies are man-made. They're not actually real out there in the world. We create them as part of our need to understand and explain. So while they can be explanatory, you need to guard against having them obscure your ability to see and appreciate the chaos, complexity, context and dynamism of an ever-shifting world.

Key figures

While any number of social theorists have relied on dichotomies to understand the social, theorists are now questioning our tendency to be overly **reductionist** (see Recommended readings below). Jean-François Lyotard, for example, clearly warns against explanations that don't acknowledge difference, diversity, complexity, chaos, and possibility.

> We are drawn to easy labels. ...
> It's a human characteristic to
> dichotomize things into black and
> white because it makes things
> seem so clear.
>
> **Elayne Rapping** Contemporary media
> critic and professor of
> women's studies — attributed

Recommended readings

Several Western dichotomies have been captured in text, for example *Dismantling the East–West Dichotomy* (Hendry and Wong 2006), *The Two Cultures* (Snow *1959* 1993), which tackles the dichotomy between the arts and sciences, *The Science Wars* (Parson 2003), which explores debates within science, and *The Argument Culture* (Tannen 1999), which explores how dichotomization negatively affects the way we communicate. On a different note, if you're interested in exploring the ancient Chinese theory of opposites, try *Yin and Yang* (Palmer 1998).

 **Discourse**

Core definition

Communicative practices that provide us with meaning and set often invisible boundaries for what is said and left unsaid (and therefore what is thought and not thought) about a particular topic.

Longer explanation

In linguistics, discourse refers to utterances greater than a sentence, but in the social sciences (as influenced by Michel Foucault) it refers to 'language' that defines and constructs a topic at a particular historical moment. For Foucault, communicative practices do not reflect objective truth as much as they reflect the success of a particular way of thinking. These ways of thinking may not be visible, but because they are wrapped up in our language they become real. Discourses are therefore extraordinarily powerful because they create truth and give power to those who benefit from that truth. Meanwhile, those who might benefit from an alternative truth are *marginalized*. Now, because we are immersed in discourses they can be hard to see, but they do shift, evolve and clash and it is at these points they become visible. Take, for example, these opposing abortion discourses retrieved from pro-choice and pro-life websites respectively:

> A fetus does not have a right to be in the womb of any woman, but is there by her permission. This permission may be revoked by the woman at any time … there is no right to enslave … a woman is not a breeding pig owned by the state (or church).

> Abortion is murder. Go ahead and suck that baby out of the womb and spatter its red blood all over your grubby paws. The government says you can do that. But that doesn't change the fact that it is murder.

Debates and controversies

It's quite easy to accept that there are discourses in operation. The question is whether all we know, all we understand, and all we communicate is the product of various discourses. Is there objective truth? Can we ever capture and communicate it? Or is everything wrapped up in politically laden discourse?

Practical application

Our social world runs on **power**, so understanding the creation and mainte-nance of power through language affords us great insights into knowledge creation, dominance, and oppression. In fact, **semiotics**, **sociolinguistics**, **deconstruction,** and discourse analysis are some of the tools social scientists use to accomplish this task. But discourses can also help us work towards social transformation. In the quote offered below, Guy M. Condon advocates the creation of new discourses to help win social/cultural battles.

Key figures

Foucault was fascinated by the discourses that gave definition and meaning to things like **sexuality** and madness. He saw discourses as highly influential and oppressive constructions of reality since they offer little room for alternative thinking or being.

> The words we use, the way we talk,
> the stories we tell will ultimately
> determine what we believe and
> what we do. ... Our goal should be
> to shape public discourse.
>
> *Guy M. Condon* (1954–2000) Past
> president of *Care Net,*
> a pro-life network of
> pregnancy care centres – *attributed*

Recommended readings

For contemporary works, try *Discourse: A Critical Introduction* (Blommaert 2005), *Cultural Studies and Discourse Analysis* (Barker and Galasinski 2001), or *Constituting Cultural Difference through Discourse* (Collier 2000). Foucault's *Archeology of Knowledge* (*1969* 2002) is tough-going, but an important seminal text.

 **Egalitarianism**

Core definition
Philosophical/political positioning that all members of a society should be treated with equality.

Longer explanation
While egalitarianism may sound straightforward, there are actually various types of equality that underpin highly divergent political systems. For example, the *discourse* of the USA is that 'all men are created equal' in a 'land of opportunity'. These beliefs underpin a legal system that is supposedly blind to an individual's *socioeconomic status*, race, or gender; a *democratic* government in which all citizens have an equal right to participate in political decision-making; and a *social stratification* system with enough *social mobility* to allow everyone an opportunity to become what they wish – there are no legislated barriers to success. There is, however, no promise of material equality. As a *capitalist* society, wealth is not shared equally and is, in fact, intended to be earned entrepreneurially. Contrast this to the discourse of *communism*, in which resources are to be shared according to the need of each individual.

Debates and controversies
So do various economic systems live up to their promises of egalitarianism? Well, the collapse of the Soviet Bloc at the end of the twentieth century and the inequities that existed and continue to exist in communist societies suggests that while equality of conditions may have ideological merit, it's extremely difficult to achieve in practice. And many would argue that the same is true in democratic societies underpinned by legal, political, and opportunity equality. For any variety of reasons, members of minority groups often face inequity (i.e. longer periods of incarceration than peers from dominant sectors of society). Minorities are also less likely to be involved in political processes, and are highly underrepresented in the highest echelons of society.

Practical application
Egalitarianism is actually one of the most powerful ideas in modern history since it lays the foundation for any number of diverse political, religious and

social movements. Yet, it's notoriously difficult to achieve. While the desire to be treated with equality is central to ongoing battles for social *justice*, so too is the desire for *power*. And this tension makes egalitarianism, and its use as political rhetoric by those in power (who generally wish to remain in power), a fascinating construct to explore.

Key figures

Thomas Hobbes, John Locke and Jean-Jacques Rousseau were key figures in the seventeenth-century Enlightenment who strongly believed that individuals should be equal before a society's political and civil institutions. When it comes to political theory related to equality of material conditions, key figures would be Karl Marx and Fredrich Engels.

> Why would God punish a kid?
> I mean ... an American kid?
>
> **Bart Simpson** (The Simpsons)

Recommended readings

For a contemporary overview, try *The New Egalitarianism* (Giddens and Diamond 2005) or *Egalitarian Capitalism* (Kenworthy 2004). If you're interested in debates that surround the equitable redistribution of wealth, see *Recasting Egalitarianism* (Bowles and Gintis 1999) and *Globalization and Egalitarian Redistribution* (Bardhan et al. 2006). For a scathing attack on egalitarian philosophy, try *The Illusions of Egalitarianism* (Kekes 2003).

 **Empiricism**

Core definition

Philosophical positioning that *knowledge* is limited to what can be observed and tested through sensory input and observation.

Longer explanation

The scientific revolution of the seventeenth-century 'enlightened' us. It allowed us to understand the world in a concrete way. No longer did we need to rely on faith, intuition, pure reason, or abstract *theory* for our knowing. The key to knowledge was empirical methods of sensory data collection. We could now rely on science and *scientific method*, that is replicable, standardized, and objective methods based on tangible facts.

Debates and controversies

Empiricism, however, is not without debate. It's actually based on a number of assumptions (particularly when applied in the social sciences) that are each a source of controversy. Empiricism assumes:

- *if something exists, it can be measured* – but many, including *Marxists*, believe this finds us capturing superficial surfaces, rather than underlying conditions;
- *we can be objective* – but we all have our biases; *feminists* and *postmodern* theorists have argued that we all carry *ideological* and *discursive* baggage;
- *the social world is controlled by the same laws as the natural world* – *social constructionists*, however, believe that society cannot be taken as a given, it's actually created or invented by human actors;
- *our senses can gather all the data we need for understanding the world* – does sound exist in an isolated community of deaf individuals? Of course it does, but the knowledge produced within this community would be incomplete because it's based on only four senses. Well, what if we live in a world that has more sensory inputs than we can take on board? Wouldn't our empirical knowledge also fall short of completeness?

Practical application

To produce social science knowledge you need to be conversant with empiricism. The social sciences followed on from the natural sciences so there was a strong belief that the rules of scientific method, if applied with rigour, would allow the complexities of the social world to be uncovered in tangible ways. And while there is an ever-growing pool of *post-positivist* and *postmodern* (see *postmodernity*) forms of discovery, the empirical legacy continues with many approaches to *social science research* dependent on hypothesis testing and fact gathering through various forms of observation.

Key figures

In the late 1600s, John Locke was one of the principal advocates of the scientific revolution and is considered one of the founding fathers of empiricism. In the mid-1700s, David Hume attempted to apply empiricism to the study of the human mind.

> No man's knowledge here can go
> beyond his experience.
>
> *John Locke* (1632–1704) English
> philosopher – in Nidditch, P.
> *An Essay Concerning*
> *Human Understanding* (1975)

Recommended readings

For a solid introduction here, try *Introducing Empiricism* (Robinson 2004) or *The Structure of Empirical Knowledge* (BonJour 2005). If you're after a bit more theoretical depth, try *The Empirical Stance* (van Fraassen 2004). For the lowdown on empircal scientific method, see *Scientific Method in Practice* (Gauch 2002) or *A Beginner's Guide to Scientific Method* (Carey 2003).

Epistemology

Core definition

How it is that we come to have legitimate *knowledge* of the world; rules for knowing.

Longer explanation

It's in our nature to try to understand the world. We want to know, discover, uncover, and understand the mysteries of the *self*, the social world, the natural world, and even the supernatural. Well, it's our epistemology that tells us how we go about this and what rules there might be for the production of knowledge. Since the Enlightenment, the reigning epistemology has been *empiricism* – that all knowledge is limited to what can be observed through the senses – and this is still the cornerstone of *positivist* belief in the defined rules of *scientific method*. But there are competing epistemologies. For example: theistic or religious epistemologies – that truth is what is revealed by God in scriptures; indigenous epistemologies – where knowledge might come from myths, stories, and legends; *rationalism* or *a priorism* – that knowledge comes from reason alone; *realism* – that knowledge requires abstract *theory* since a real material world exists beyond what humans can know; and various offshoots of *postmodern* (see *postmodernity*) thought that question whether the construction of knowledge is more about *power* than 'truth'.

Debates and controversies

Epistemologies are more than philosophical – they are highly political. Those who define the rules of legitimate knowing and actually create knowledge are in a very powerful position. After all, 'knowledge is power'. The church was once all-knowing and all-powerful, and actively fought against an Enlightenment that would threaten its power base. Even within current *social science research* there's a huge, highly defensive, emotive, and often unproductive divide between empiricists and *post-positivist* researchers. Each believes they hold the key to legitimate knowing, which unfortunately lessens the potential for them to work together down a path of holistic knowing.

Practical application

We take a lot for granted, and I'd certainly include the rules for knowing in that list. Empiricism may rule, but until we realize there are, always have been, and always will be alternative ways of knowing that vary across **cultures**, **ideologies**, and **discourses**, social scientists will be limited in their ability to both appreciate and produce knowledge that confronts the biases of their own cultural and ideological positioning.

Key figures

Any number of theorists have contributed to knowledge across various epistemological frameworks. Entries for **empiricism**, **idealism**, **nominalism**, **positivism**, **post-positivism**, **rationalism**, **realism**, **and social construc-tionism** will introduce you to a range of key thinkers.

> All religions, arts and sciences are branches of the same tree ... directed towards ennobling man's life, lifting it from the sphere of mere physical existence and leading the individual towards freedom.
>
> **Albert Einstein** (1879-1955)
> German-born US theoretical
> physicist - in Moral Decay (1937)

Recommended readings

For a solid introduction to this area, try *Problems of Knowledge: A Critical Introduction to Epistemology* (Williams 2001). For a range of key readings, turn to *Epistemology: Contemporary Readings* (Huemer 2002) or *Contemporary Debates in Epistemology* (Steup and Sosa 2005). To delve into readings on specific epistemological frameworks, have a look under the entries that are highlighted under Key figures above.

 **Essentialism**

Longer explanation

Strip away what's constructed by time and place, culture and history and what's left? Many would say not much – we're the product of the world around us. But others believe there's always an essential core or an essence that provides a point of definition that can't be denied. For example, is the essential difference between men and women limited to anatomy – penis vs. vagina – or are women innately more nurturing and men more rational? And what about murder? Are circumstances and cultural beliefs relevant, or is killing another person universally wrong, no matter what? Well, essentialists would argue that there are indeed essences that define who we are and that there are universals that stand in spite of cultural (or any other) influences.

Debates and controversies

Essentialism, in relation to social groups, tends to be viewed quite negatively since essentialist positions often underpin various *prejudices,* such as racism and sexism. And in spite of growing recognition of the power of cultural influences, when it comes to things like gender, essentialist views are an entrenched part of Western *discourse.* For example, if you watch a couple of young boys running around like idiots and you're likely to hear someone say 'boys will be boys'. *Feminists* have long argued the danger of essentialist positions that see women as inferior. But ironically, some feminists actually make use of essentialism when arguing the superiority of women based on their innate biological ability to bear children.

Practical application

One of the biggest social science debates out there is 'nature versus nurture'; what is learnt and what is inherent. And essentialism helps us understand the 'nature' side of the argument. But it's also worth exploring essentialism as a rationale for prejudice and discrimination. At one extreme this can manifest as a 'good natured' battle of the sexes (consider John Gray's *Men are from Mars and Women are from Venus, 2004*). But on the other end of the spectrum, you have individuals like Hitler whose essentialist position on racial superiority and inferiority was the philosophical justification for genocide.

Key figures

An interesting social science essentialist is John Locke. Writing in the seventeenth century, Locke argued that objects of inquiry not only have core essences, but that the discovery of these essences (that may not be directly observable, yet do determine what can be observed) is the ultimate goal of scientific observation.

> *You're always a little disappointing in person because you can't be the edited essence of yourself.*
>
> **Mel Brooks** (1926–) US filmmaker, actor – attributed

Recommended readings

For a contemporary introduction to key issues, try *The Philosophy of Nature: A Guide to the New Essentialism* (Ellis 2002). To delve into arguments on each end of the essentialism debate, look at *Real Essentialism* (Oderberg 2006) and *Against Essentialism* (Fuchs 2005). I also found the psychologically based arguments in *The Essential Child: Origins Of Essentialism in Everyday Thought* (Gelman 2005) quite interesting.

 **Ethics**

Core definition
A branch of philosophy that investigates what guides us in deciding what is right and what is wrong.

Longer explanation

Ethics is basically the study of what we ought to do. The question is how we know what we ought to be doing? What are the principles that guide us in deciding right from wrong? There are actually quite a few schools of thought here – some which see ethics as *fundamental* and others that see ethics as dependent on social and cultural realities. For example, should we always do what brings the greatest good for the greatest number (*utilitarianism*), or what brings us, personally, the greatest pleasure (hedonism)? Maybe we should act in accordance with the word of God – in the Bible, the Qu'ran, commandments (divine command theory). Or maybe what's right is what will get us into heaven (salvation theory). Do we have 'duties', such as to tell the truth and act justly (deontology), or should we act in ways that protect a citizen's inalienable rights, that is life and liberty (contract theory). But then again maybe it's all about survival of the fittest (*social Darwinism*) or maybe there really is no such thing as morality, or maybe ethics is just a political power game (nihilism).

Debates and controversies

What's interesting about this list of ethical groundings is not just their diversity, but the contradictions, in both beliefs and behaviours, that can arise from this diversity. Not only do we have a world where people act in accordance with highly diverse ethical principles, these varied principles can lead to fundamental conflicts (i.e. certain religious tenets vs. basic human rights). No wonder we've never been a world at peace.

Practical application

As a contemplative species, ethics grounds just about everything we do, so as a philosophical theory it's a fascinating area of study. But I think applied ethics, particularly in a time of massive *technological*, economic and environmental change, should be of interest to all social scientists. Hot ethical issues include abortion, euthanasia, criminal justice, **globalization**, development, genetic engineering (both crops and people), the environment, terrorism, animal rights, war, reality TV, surveillance societies as well as issues of equity related to gender, race, **class** and **sexuality**.

Key figures

Key figures here include Kant, who believed that ethics should be based on categorical imperatives or rules of behaviour that would work as universal laws, Jeremy Bentham and John Stuart Mill, who were foundational in the articulation of utilitarianism, and John Locke, Thomas Hobbes, and more recently John Rawls, who explored the protection of rights in relation to contract theory.

> *Ethics are nothing but reverence for life. That is what gives me the fundamental principle of morality, namely, that good consists in maintaining, promoting, and enhancing life, and that destroying, injuring, and limiting life are evil.*
>
> **Albert Schweitzer** (1875–1965)
> French missionary –
> in *Kulturphilosophie* (1923)

Recommended readings

Two good introductory works here are *Philosophical Ethics: An Introduction to Moral Philosophy* (Beauchamp 2001) and *The Moral of the Story: An Introduction to Ethics* (Rosenstand 2002). Another way into this area is through broad readers. I'd recommend *Ethics: Theory and Contemporary Issues* (MacKinnon 2003) and *Great Traditions in Ethics* (Denise et al. 2004). For those who want to delve into the work of classic theorists, try *The Moral Philosophers: An Introduction to Ethics* (Norman 1998).

 Ethnocentrism

Longer explanation

Did you know that in Australia, they drive on the wrong side of the road, and that in China, as disgusting as it seems, they'll slurp down their soup at amazing decibels. And you want to talk about gross, in Palau, they chew this thing called a betel nut and hock their spit just about anywhere. Thank God we live in a civilized country! The above is a taste of ethnocentrism – an inherent belief that the way it's done at home is how it should be done. It's right, ethical, logical... basically superior. If others do things differently, it's got to be wrong, immoral, unjust, stupid, gross... in other words, inferior. When you're being ethnocentric, you act as if the culture of your own ethnic group is at the centre of the universe and make no attempt to understand the perspective of others.

Debates and controversies

In some ways it's not surprising that we tend towards ethnocentrism. After all, aren't we socialized to accept, internalize, and even revere the *norms*, values and practices of our culture? It's therefore only natural that we find other perspectives a bit weird. But what we tend to forget, or don't even consider, is that 'others' are also socialized, but in alternate, yet equally valid ways. And when we forget this, we run the risk of begin narrow-minded, racist, and classist, as well as a very ugly tourist!

Practical application

The causes and implications of ethnocentrism, particularly in a *globalizing* world, are certainly worthwhile topics of social science investigation. But I thought I'd focus here on the importance of avoiding ethnocentrism in social science research, since it's so easy for us to impose our values on to others. For example, if you're from a straight-laced, middle-class, Christian family and you plan on interviewing inner-city kids about day-to-day school life, you need to accept that their reality, which might include sex, drugs, and 'colorful' language, might be totally distinct from your own. You need to reserve judgement and remember that the only way to understand high school life is from the perspective of the kids within it.

Key figures

William Sumner, an American professor of political and social science coined this term in 1906 to describe the superiority felt by 'us' towards 'them'. Anthropologists such as Franz Boas, Bronislaw Malinowski, and Clifford Geertz (who attempted to understand, describe, and interpret a way of life from the point of view of its participants) argued that ethnocentrism was a key hurdle in authentic understandings.

> When science finally locates the
> center of the universe, some
> people will be surprised
> to learn they're not it.
>
> **Anonymous**

Recommended readings

Worth a look is *The Social Construction of Difference and Inequality* (Ore 2005) and *Identity: Community, Culture and Difference* (Rutherford 2003). *Us and Them: Understanding Your Tribal Mind* (Berreby 2005) explores ethnocentrism at the level of personal psychology, while *Ethnocentrism and the English Dictionary* (Benson 2001) explores English as a product of ethnocentric attitudes and beliefs. Finally, Geertz' seminal work, *The Interpretation of Cultures* (1973), argues the need to avoid ethnocentrism when studying the other.

 Ethnography

Longer explanation

If you were to come to my house for dinner and you were to reflect on that experience, you'd probably do so in relation to what happens in your own home, that is 'we do that', 'that's different', 'how bizarre'. You'd judge my family in relation to your own family or your own frame of reference. Well, when it comes to studying cultural groups this is precisely what ethnography tries to avoid. Ethnography explores a way of life from the point of view of its participants and tries to avoid assessing a *culture* using pre-existing frames of reference or from a particular worldview. The goal is to 'see' things the way group members do, and grasp the meanings they use to understand and make sense of the world. In other words, ethnographers attempt to suspend judgement and understand the symbolic world in which people live in order to interpret meaning from within a culture. To build this type of rich understanding, ethnographers tend to immerse themselves within a culture for a significant period of time. They participate, then reflect on their lived conversations and observations.

Debates and controversies

I guess the major question here is whether an outsider (particularly one from a very divergent culture) can ever truly know, describe, and interpret the reality of insiders. Even if you believe this is possible, it's still not easy to pull off a good ethnographic study. Because ethnographers try to immerse themselves in a culture, they need to gain access, build trust, deal with the potential to be emotionally involved, and avoid having an effect on the researched.

Practical application

While conventional research *methods* generally rely on surveys or interviews to understand the attitudes, beliefs, opinions, and/or behaviours of cultural groups, ethnography (which has it roots in cultural anthropology) attempts to go beyond this and explores how group members make sense of their experiences.

Morgan Spurlock, who made the *Supersize Me* documentary on McDonald's, recently launched a new reality TV series called *30 Days,* which has an ethnographic feel. For 30 days, Spurlock attempts to 'live' an experience in order to really know and appreciate what it feels like from within.

Key figures

Key figures include anthropologists Franz Boas, Bronislaw Malinowski, and most significantly Clifford Geertz, who attempted to explore, understand, discover, describe, and interpret cultures by building 'thick descriptions' (multiple layers of meaning). He argued that only through such descriptions could we uncover the underlying frameworks that produce both behaviour and meaning.

> A good interpretation of anything –
> a poem, a person, a history, a ritual,
> an institution, a society – takes
> us into the heart of that ...
> interpretation.
>
> *Clifford Geertz* (1926–2006) US
> anthropologist – in *The Interpretation
> of Cultures* (1973)

Recommended readings

A few good works here include the *Handbook of Ethnography* (Atkinson et al. 2001), *Ethnographic Research: A Reader* (Taylor 2002); and *Methodological Issues and Practices in Ethnography* (Troman et al. 2005) which covers relevant debates and controversies. Also worth a look is Geertz' classic, *The Interpretation of Cultures* (1973).

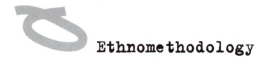

Ethnomethodology

Longer explanation

Ethnomethodology explores the interpretative processes individuals use to negotiate their way through the everyday. Throughout our day we interact – with our parents, friends, the check-out person at the grocery store. And we make judgements, sometimes conscious but mainly subconscious, about how we should act and what we should say. And we generally do this without too much stress because we're socialized with appropriate 'methods' (i.e. rules, **norms**, and patterns that help us wade through such interactions). For example, say someone comes up to you and says, 'I couldn't help but notice you'. To make sense of this you'd look for cues, find a 'pattern', and formulate an appropriate response. So if you were in a nightclub and the person speaking to you was of the opposite sex, the pattern might be 'the pick-up'. And you might reply with a disgusted, 'get lost, you loser' or a seductive, 'yeah… I noticed you too'. The other party then has to recognize the pattern that's building, in this case 'rejection' or 'flirtation', and form the appropriate response. You then use that response to generate your next response, and so on and so forth until the interaction ends.

Debate and controversies

It's argued that because ethnomethodology doesn't explore the 'meaning' of utterances or actions, it doesn't help us understand important constructs such as race, class or gender. Some even say that the 'rules' ethnomethodology draws out are obvious and not very interesting. Others, however, argue that ethnomethodology's interpretative work can help us understand how individuals produce, for example, racism or sexism.

Practical application

As a research **methodology**, ethnomethodology is often called upon because it: recognizes that individuals are not passive in making meaning and establishing social order; recognizes that traditional investigations of 'what's' said and 'why' it's said can be complemented by studies exploring 'how' conversation itself occurs; explores how group members make meaning and engage in interpretative work; and investigates how particular types of interaction are performed. For example, how juries deliberate or how doctors can deliver bad news in ways that minimize negative reactions.

Key figures

The founding father here is Harold Garfinkel, who was interested in how individuals construct their social world. Harvey Sacks is another important figure for his contribution to the analysis of conversation. I'll also mention Jerry Seinfeld, who, as a comedian, makes his living by exploring and deconstructing the minutiae of everyday life. Watch a couple of *Seinfeld* episodes … the 'show about nothing' is actually a show about what we take for granted as we manage the interactions that make up the everyday.

> *I know that you believe you understand*
> *what you think I said, but I'm not*
> *sure you realize that what you heard*
> *is not what I meant!*
>
> **Anonymous** (sometimes attributed
> to Richard Nixon)

Further readings

For a contemporary introduction (in addition to watching *Seinfeld* reruns) try *Ethnomethodology* (Coulon 1995), *An Invitation to Ethnomethodology* (Francis and Hester 2004) and *Understanding Qualitative Research and Ethnomethodology* (ten Have 2004). I'd also recommend Garfinkel's seminal work, *Studies in Ethnomethodology* (1967).

 **Existentialism**

Core definition

Philosophical doctrine that emphasizes the ultimate responsibility and freedom humans have in deciding how to journey through an absurd and meaningless world.

Longer explanation

Last night I went to bed knowing my life had meaning. I had goals, I had a purpose, and even if I didn't always know why something was happening, I knew it was God's will and that my life was unfolding the way it should. I had faith. But when I woke up *everything* was different. I suddenly realized my whole life was a sham. God was just a convenient excuse for my inability to take control. There was no God, only me. No one else to rely on or take responsibility for my life – a life where the only certainty is impending death. It's just me trying to live my life in an absurd, indifferent and meaningless world.

Sounds scary. And many would agree. To be fully responsible for your life in an absurd, indifferent and meaningless world is more than many can bear. But it also represents immense freedom. When there's no higher meaning, you're fully empowered to decide your course with no constraints. You can intentionally and authentically make your way through life, even if the only end point is death. It's up to you to invent yourself.

Debates and controversies

First question … is there a higher power? Is there a true, real, and fundamental basis for faith. If your answer is yes, then the premise of existentialism simply won't wash. Second question … even if you believe humans are fully responsible for their lives and that radical freedom is ours for the taking, does it have to be so damned bleak? Must existence necessarily cause **anomie** and anxiety or could those emotive states simply be the product of an oppressive world?

Practical application

So how does this heavy philosophical theory relate to the more 'mundane' social sciences? Well, there seem to be a lot of lost souls out there in the **postmodern** (see **postmodernity**) world. God's no longer omnipotent, **ideologies** no longer go unseen, and we're recognizing that we simply play a ***role*** in a constructed world. The question that many now ask is: Do I like 'my role' and can I make decisions that will lead to a more authentic life? Whether it be the housewife of 30 years or the executive who works 60 hours a week, the existential questions being asked are: 'Is that all there is?' and 'what power do I have to change it?'

Key figures

Sartre popularized existentialism in the mid-1900s, but much of his work was influenced by Kierkegaard, who believed human existence is completely unique, Nietzsche, who claimed modern science led to the death of God, and Heidegger, who saw man as a self-aware being whose only certainty is death.

> Man is the only animal for whom his
> own existence is a problem which he
> has to solve.
>
> **Erich Fromm** (1900–1980)
> US psychologist – in
> Man for Himself (1947)

Recommended readings

For a quick introduction to the key concepts, try *Teach Yourself 101 Key Ideas: Existentialism* (Myerson 2001). For a range of more in-depth readings, see *Existentialism* (Solomon 2004) or *Basic Writings of Existentialism* (Marino 2004). It's also worth having a look at Sartre. I'd recommend starting with *Essays in Existentialism* (1993).

 Fascism

Core definition

Specifically, the political regime in Italy from 1922 to 1945 under Benito Mussolini. Generically, highly nationalistic and authoritarian political doctrine that seeks to revitalize a nation's economy, *culture* and identity.

Longer explanation

The First World War left many European nations in a shambles. Economies were falling apart, there was intense fear of *communist revolution*, and belief in those that ruled was extraordinarily low. Many felt a need for strong and powerful leadership that could rebuild 'great nations'. There was a desire for revitalized national identity and economy. Mussolini's Italy, with its strong ties to the military and campaign of national propaganda was the first state to be identified as fascist. But between the World Wars many other European nations, for example, the Iron Guard's Romania, Hitler's Germany and Franco's Spain adopted similar 'fascist' doctrine. Now fascism is highly nationalistic, so actual doctrines are culturally specific. There are, however, certain common characteristics, including a hatred of communism and *Marxism*; a belief in *capitalism* (which is organized and managed through the *state*); cynicism over *democratic* principles; a belief in a need for charismatic leadership with authoritarian and even dictatorial powers; the complete immersion of education, the military, media, and the legal system into the political regime; *totalitarian* power and lack of *pluralism* in government; the right and ability to violently fend off any who dare question the regime; but yet a strong desire for public support (often built by both propaganda and terrorism). And while violent, terroristic, and dictatorial, many citizens (particularly those in the middle class) believed in a need for an all-powerful state that would protect them from communism, economic crisis, and the old ruling class.

Debates and controversies

There's really nothing here but controversy. We're talking about a notorious time in history where propaganda and terrorism combined to see the genocide of millions, and the oppression of many many more.

Practical application

I think modern fascism is a fascinating window for exploring boundaries of human morality, fear, and desperation. Exactly what atrocities are we capable of doing/supporting? But there's another big question here… could it happen again? Yes, small fascist movements have continuously occurred since the Second World War, but could social, economic, and *ideological* forces ever again align in ways that once gave a number of dominant states awesome repressive powers?

Key figures

Two theorists here include Giovanni Gentile, who wrote the *A Doctrine of Fascism* for Mussolini in 1932, and Antonio Gramsci, an Italian Marxist imprisoned by the Italian Fascist Party who, while incarcerated, explored the economic, political and ideological factors that lead to the Fascist state. Key political figures include some of the most notorious men in history, such as Mussolini and Hitler.

> The keystone of the Fascist doctrine
> is its conception of the State,
> of its essence, its functions, and
> its aims ... the State is absolute,
> individuals and groups relative.
>
> **Benito Mussolini** (1883–1945)
> Italian dictator – in *A Doctrine
> of Fascism* (actually authored
> by Giovanni Gentile (1932)

Recommended readings

Fascism: A Very Short Introduction (Passmore 2002) offers a good starting point, while *The Anatomy of Fascism* (Paxton 2005) and *Fascism, Totalitarianism, and Political Religion* (Griffin 2005) provide more depth. Also worth exploring are *Fascism Reader* (Kallis 2002) and *Fascism* (Griffin 1995), which offer readings from social theorists, fascist thinkers, as well as anti-fascist critics.

 Feminism

Longer explanation

There really isn't a universally accepted definition of feminism, but there are key themes: equal political and legal rights; equal opportunity; sexual autonomy; and a right to self-determination. And while these rights might seem self-evident, they didn't come about without a struggle – a struggle that continues in many parts of the world. Now there have actually been three waves of feminism. The first emerged from eighteenth-century Enlightenment thinking that advocated equality, reason, and freedom. And while Mary Wollstonecraft's treatise, *A Vindication of the Rights of Women,* was published in 1792, it wasn't until the 1920s that women in the UK and USA gained the right to vote. In the 1960s, a 'second wave' of feminism sprung from recognition and frustration over the marginalization of women. This wave was quite *radical* (see *critical/radical*) and challenged society's gender roles. It took the private (i.e. marriage, sex, birth control, abortion, and domesticity) and made it part of the public debate. This second wave, which at times denigrated traditional women's roles and premised Western, middle-class perspectives, was not without criticism. This opened the door for a 'third wave' that recognized the *plurality* of women both around the neighbourhood and around the globe, and the diverse challenges they face (i.e. everything from female circumcision in the Sudan to glass ceilings in London).

Debates and controversies

Where do I start...? Given biological differences, will men and women ever be 'equal'? Are there inherent personality differences that limit equality? Should men and women be treated the same, or are we after respect given difference? Should women strive to do everything men do? Would they want to? Or should we try to restructure a world without *patriarchy*? Maybe we'd be better off without men altogether? Are feminists ruining the family? Does feminism imply I should be embarrassed to be a wife and mother – or proud? Is feminism sexist? Is 'gender equality' a less sexist term? Debates such as these will rage on.

Practical application

In every corner of the globe, across every sector of society, the battle for equity given difference is, and will continue to be, an ongoing struggle. How we can best manage this struggle, particularly as it relates to gender, is one of the most fundamental questions any social scientist can ask.

Key figures

It's impossible to be comprehensive here, so here's a list of but a few feminists that are particularly important, interesting or inspirational: Mary Wollstonecraft, Simone de Beauvoir, Kate Millet, Juliet Mitchell, Betty Freidan, Germaine Greer, Gloria Steinem, Alice Rossi, Ann Oakley and bell hooks. For a more comprehensive list see readings below, particularly Schneir's anthology.

> My idea of feminism is
> self-determination, and it's
> very open-ended: every woman
> has the right to become herself,
> and do whatever she needs to do.
>
> **Ani Difranco** (1970–) Singer,
> guitarist, and songwriter – attributed

Recommended readings

For an introduction to feminist theory/history, try *Feminist Theory: A Reader* (Kolmar and Bartowski 2003) and *No Turning Back: The History of Feminism and the Future of Women* (Freedman 2003). It's also worth exploring works of key feminists, such as Greer's *The Female Eunuch* (*1970* 2002), de Beauvoir's *The Second Sex* (*1949* 1989) and Freidan's *The Feminine Mystique* (*1963* 2001). Another option is an anthology, such as *Feminism: The Essential Historical Writings* (Schneir 1994).

 Functionalism

Core definition

A sociological perspective that focuses on the contributions any particular social unit makes towards the larger social system. Each part of *society* is seen to perform a function necessary for the continuity of the whole.

Longer explanation

The question here is whether society, which consists of things like family, religion, and *community*, is analogous to an organic body dependent on its heart, lungs, limbs, brain, etc. For functionalists, the answer is yes. Functionalists attempt to understand society by focusing on the contribution (both intended and unintended) that each part makes to the survival or maintenance of the whole. So rather than explore causes, the focus is on function (i.e. what does religion or deviance contribute to society's continuity). Take our societal obsession with body image as a more specific example. Yes, historical causes can be examined, but functionalists would look at the contribution this obsession makes to our society. For example, analysis might focus on the profits reaped by the diet, cosmetic, and exercise industry, thereby serving a function in *capitalist* society. While many believe that functionalism implies positive contributions, as in the example above, contributions can be real, even if their value is debated.

Debates and controversies

Functionalism rests on a number of assumptions that are not without debate. First, it premises consequences and gives little weight to causes or intentions. Second, it assumes social units are necessary for the whole and cannot be purposeless. Third, it assumes that dysfunction serves a positive function (i.e. *deviant behaviour* sets normative boundaries). Functionalism is also critiqued as being *ideologically* conservative since its focus on continuity limits its ability to explain *social change* and conflict.

Practical application

Functionalism is central to understanding the workings and stability of social systems, but it's important to remember that it's only one of three main sociological perspectives, the others being **conflict theory** and **symbolic interactionism**. While functionalism can and should be applied to the study of any social unit or institution, I'd argue that any attempt to understand our complex social world would be enhanced by valuing the contribution each perspective offers.

Key figures

Durkheim was fascinated by the societal contribution offered by things like religion and deviance. As such, he's considered an early functionalist. Functionalism was also important in anthropology and was taken up in the early 1900s by the likes of Bronislaw Malinowski and Alfred Radcliffe-Brown. In the mid-1900s, functionalism was formalized by Talcott Parsons and became a central focus in sociological analysis.

> Cats are intended to teach us that not everything in nature has a function!
>
> **Garrison Keillor** (1942–) US author, humorist – attributed

Recommended readings

Causation and Functionalism in Sociology (Isajiw *1968* 2003) offers a solid introduction to classic functionalism, while *Dynamic Functionalism* (Faja 2006) gives the perspective a more dynamic and contemporary twist. If you'd like to go back to the classics, try Durkheim's *The Rules of Sociological Method* (*1895* 1982), Parsons's *The Social System* (*1951* 1991) and Malinowski's *Scientific Theory of Culture and Other Essays* (*1944* 2001).

 Fundamentalism

Core definition

Belief in the need to return to pure or fundamental religious faith as revealed literally in scripture (i.e. the Bible, the Qur'an or the Torah).

Longer explanation

Fundamentalists believe that man was blessed when he was given the word of God. And it's simple… the word, as revealed in sacred texts, must be followed to the letter. But fundamentalists believe mainstream religion has lost its way. People 'choose' their beliefs, 'interpret' texts, and still call themselves Protestants or Jews. Mary wasn't 'really' a virgin, – the world wasn't 'actually' created in six days, – it doesn't matter if you skip Mass. Even homosexuality is accepted. Enough! Fundamentalists want to turn away from liberal, relativistic, and modern notions of religion and return to traditional and orthodox beliefs as they were directly revealed to man in scripture. Now the term 'fundamentalism' comes from a set of Protestant tracts called *The Fundamentals* (1909). Not only was the goal to deride other Christian religions (i.e. Catholicism), but to critique liberal interpretations of Protestantism. The term, however, is now applied to conservative movements in both Christian and non-Christian religions (i.e. conservative Judaism, Islam, or even the Opus Dei movement in Catholicism). Fundamentalism is also often linked to politics, for example, the moral majority in the USA. 'Fundamental' Islam is another example of politicization, since certain Islamic groups seek strict political rule (i.e. the Taliban in Afghanistan).

Debates and controversies

There are two main controversies here. The first is based on the literal interpretation of God's written word that (a) contains contradictions; (b) relies on interpretations that must be read from within particular cultural frameworks; and (c) was written by 'fallible' men. The second controversy is in the application of the term 'fundamental'. While Protestant sects self-select the term, it's often applied to other religious movements in highly negative ways, particularly when talking about Islam. Yes, Muslims are 'fundamental' in the sense that they believe the perfect word of God was finally embodied in the Qur'an. But when

Westerners apply the term, they are often referring to political extremism, militancy and fanaticism.

Practical application

The concept of fundamentalism is interesting at two levels. First, in supposedly *secular*, *pluralistic*, enlightened societies, it's conservative and fundamental religious movements that are the fastest growing. In a world of choice and freedom, there seems to be a need for unambiguous rules and guidance. Second is the Western world's battle with Islamic extremism. The Western *discourse* that justifies war includes the protection of *democracy*, freedom and Christian values from Islamic fundamentalism. Understanding how these arguments are used to leverage public support is both fascinating and timely.

Key figures

W. E. Blackstone, J. H. Brookes, W. Moorehead, A. C. Dixon, and J. Hudson Taylor are some of the scholars considered founding fathers of Protestant fundamentalism. Labelling Islamic faith as 'fundamental', however, is more a media phenomenon than a social science one, so is without 'founding fathers'.

> *Fundamentalism isn't about religion,*
> *it's about power.*
>
> *Salman Rushdie* (1948–) Indian-born
> British author – attributed

Recommended readings

To explore how fundamentalism occurs across various 'tribes' have a look at *Fundamentalism and American Culture* (Marsden 2006), *The Clash of Fundamentalisms: Crusades, Jihads and Modernity* (Ali 2003) and *Fundamentalism: The Search for Meaning* (Ruthven 2004), which is a comparison of Christian, Islamic and 'political' fundamentalism.

Game theory

Core definition

The study of strategic situations, or 'games', where players with conflicting interests attempt to maximize their returns.

Longer explanation

Game theory is used to help understand and explain social action and inter-action in any situation where at least two people are competing at some level. Games can be 'zero sum', where benefits are fixed and one person's gain is another's loss, as in chess where for every winner there is a loser. But games can also be non-zero sum, where benefits can increase with cooperation. A classic example here is the prisoner's dilemma. In this 'game', two individuals suspected of burglary are separately interrogated. If they both stay quiet, they'll be charged with the lesser offence of trespassing and only get a year each. If they both confess, they'll be convicted and get five years a piece. But if only one confesses and rats out the other, the confessor gets off scot-free and the other gets ten years. This is quite an interesting dilemma because it explores the relationship between concepts such as self-interest, trust, cooperation, fear and rational decision-making. So just how much do you trust your co-conspirator? And how trustworthy are you? How much enticement does it take to get you to talk? For both zero and non-zero sum games any strategy a player adopts should take into account their competitor's strategies as well as their competitor's reaction to strategies they intend to use.

Debates and controversies

Game theory actually has its roots in mathematics and attempts to model human behaviour based on assumptions of rationality. But as any observer of the social knows, humans are far from rational, and this makes modelling predicative behaviour fraught with difficulty. As such, many social scientists side-step game theory's mathematical modelling and concentrate on broader psycho-social dimensions.

Practical application

The original application of game theory was in the study of economic behaviour, but it's now increasingly used in sociology to explore action, reaction, and interaction (including communication, competition, conflict, and cooperation) at various scales, including families, organizations, political parties, and countries. In philosophy, game theory is used to explore ethical behaviours, and can help illuminate concepts of trust, altruism, self-interest, and reciprocity.

Key figures

John von Neumann and Oskar Morgenstern published *The Theory of Games and Economic Behavior* in 1944, which gave game theory a credible presence in mathematics. Another key figure is John Nash (the subject of movie *A Beautiful Mind* staring Russell Crowe), who explored optimum game strategies known as Nash equilibrium.

> Life is a game. Money is how
> we keep score.
>
> *Ted Turner* (1938–) US broadcasting
> and sports executive – attributed

Recommended readings

A good place to start is with *An Introduction to Game Theory* (Osborne 2003) or *Game Theory: A Nontechnical Introduction* (Davis 1997). To delve into game theory modelling, try *Models in Cooperative Game Theory* (Branzei et al. 2005). You might also want to have a look at the von Neumann and Morgenstern reading mentioned under key figures, as well as *Classics in Game Theory* (Kuhn 1997), an edited volume of key essays.

 Genealogy

Core definition

Traditionally concerned with family lineage. In a **postmodern** framework (see **postmodernity**), however, it refers to the study of the ways in which particular notions of history become 'truth', and what alternatives might exist.

Longer explanation

Is history what happened in the past? Well, that's what we've been taught to believe. But in reality, history is simply what someone decided to *record* about the past. For postmodern genealogists, the real question is not so much what was recorded, but who did the recording and why. In addition to what was written, genealogists are interested in what *could* have been written. In other words, genealogists explore how our history, or rather our historical myths, come into being and what other truths these myths might obscure. As Winston Churchill reminds us, 'History is written by the victors'. What would our history books look like if they were written by indigenous populations, migrants, women, the poor, the oppressed? How would a different take on the past affect who we are now?

Debates and controversies

This postmodern form of genealogy is itself a critique. In fact it's a scathing critique of how we seek and accept clean, clear, linear stories with defined beginnings and endings. Genealogy rejects our reluctance to seek and accept complexity and **plurality**. But there are many traditional social scientists who believe postmodern theorists, genealogists included, are attempting to drain the truth from everything – nothing is sacred, nothing is real, not even the past. For these theorists, genealogy is all about pulling things apart, rather than making any significant contribution. These traditionalists believe in history and would scoff and the notion of, for example, 'herstory'.

Practical application

If you accept, at any level, that history is constructed, then exploring that construction, *deconstructing* that construction, and looking at alternatives can open up whole new understandings of both ourselves and our world. Questioning our historical myths is quite crucial since it is precisely these myths that have shaped, and continue to shape, individuals and *societies*.

Key figures

Friedrich Nietzsche was the first to co-opt the term 'genealogy' and used it when exploring how moral truths, rather than being universal or God-given, are actually created through power struggles. Foucault drew on this conception and developed a genealogical method for exploring marginalized knowledge that could shed light on alternative realities not immortalized as truth. In this way, he explored alternative possibilities related to, for example, madness and sexuality.

> What is history but a fable
> agreed upon?
>
> **Napoleon Bonaparte** (1808–1873)
> French emperor – attributed

Recommended readings

The heavyweight readings here are Nietzsche's, *The Genealogy of Morals* (*1887* 2003) or Foucault's works on the topic, which can be found in *The Foucault Reader* (Foucault 1984). For a more contemporary but still theoretical exploration, try *Political Genealogy after Foucault: Savage Identities* (Clifford 2001). On a somewhat different note, *The Politically Incorrect Guide to American History* (Woods 2004) clearly highlights the 'construction' of history.

 Globalization

Longer explanation

Not long ago, exploring far away lands was left to adventurers and anthropologists who travelled for months on end to discover natives who ate bizarre foods, traded with stones, and were ruled by tribal chiefs. It's a bit different now. Just about anyone can go on such an adventure… you just buy an 'authentic' cultural experience on the 'net', complain because getting half way round the world takes the better part of a day, and be grateful you didn't lose your Visa card. But at least you can head for the local McDonalds for exotic native foods like the 'Mc Oz' in Australia, the 'McLobster' in Canada, the 'Maharaja Mac' in India or the 'McKroket' in the Netherlands. How's that for cultural diversity? Globalization is transforming a once culturally diverse and geographically dispersed world. On an economic level, we're talking about world financial markets, capitalist economy, international free trade, multinational corporations, electronic communication, and global labour markets. On a cultural level, there's the impact that things such as the internet, mass media, travel, tourism, and international sport are having on cultural diversity and indigenous **cultures**. In politics, agencies now operate across national boundaries (i.e. the World Bank and World Trade Organization) as well as multinational corporations that are creating a powerful transnational capitalist class. Globalization is also environmental and recognizes that many 'local' challenges can only be met if we take a global perspective (i.e. air pollution, global warming, SARS, and Bird Flu).

Debates and controversies

So is globalization positive? There's plenty of debate here, but little agreement. As Jimmy Carter once said:

> Globalization, as defined by rich people like us, is a very nice thing … you are talking about the Internet … cell phones … computers. This doesn't affect two-thirds

of the people of the world. ... If you're totally illiterate and living on one dollar a day, the benefits of globalization never come to you.

But others argue that global trends towards **democracy**, longer life expectancy, higher global literacy, and **technological** advances that improve quality of life are benefits of globalization.

Practical application
Globalization is a major change phenomenon that can be studied across various dimensions, such as economics, politics, culture, ecology, health, and across various scales, from the family to the globe. While the local may not disappear, it's now recognized as part of a global system (sometimes referred to as glocalization). And this leaves virtually every aspect of the world open for new levels of exploration.

Key figures
The term 'globalization' has only appeared in the literature over the past 20 years or so, but since that time several key thinkers, including David Harvey and Anthony Giddens, have engaged in debates related to its major characteristics.

> It has been said that arguing against globalization is like arguing against the laws of gravity.
>
> **Kofi Annan** (1938–) Seventh secretary-general of the United Nations – attributed

Recommended readings
To explore the economic side of globalization, try *Globalization and Its Discontents* (Stiglitz 2003). For the political dimension, see *The Globalization of World Politics* (Baylis et al. 2004). Cultural issues are well addressed in *Globalization and Culture* (Pieterse 2003), while *Worlds Apart: Globalization and the Environment* (Speth 2003) tackles growing environmental pressures.

Governance

Core definition

The systems and processes used by *states* and organizations to manage their affairs.

Longer explanation

If government is who and what, then governance is who, what and *how*. Governance is more than just the political regime of a state or the hierarchal structure of an organization. Governance is the ways, means and attitudes adopted by those in power. It's the way *authority* is exercised and resources are managed for social and/or economic development. Emphasis is on the exercise of *power* and whether this leads to effective, equitable, empowering and just *leadership*. Good governance varies depending on what's being governed, but common elements include clear vision, strategic goals, participation, mediation of varied interests, accountability, transparency, responsiveness, effectiveness, efficiency, equity, and inclusiveness. It is also recognized that governance won't be fully effective if potential contributions and needs of relevant stakeholders are not thoughtfully considered, managed and coordinated in ways that optimize strengths and promote effective interaction. Within political regimes, stakeholders include the state, private enterprise, and the general populace. Within corporations it includes management, clients, consumers and employees, as well as *community* and government.

Debates and controversies

Is it enough that your employer pays you? As long as they do their job, do you care if your staff are 'happy'? Should we worry about the child labour used by multinational corporations? Are infuriating bureaucratic structures (see *bureaucracy*) unavoidable? I don't believe we're as accepting of inefficient and inequitable leadership as we once were. Public scandals, increased media coverage, growing recognition of the cost of unhappy staff, constituents and clients have put effective governance at the top of the agenda for corporations and governments alike.

Practical application

Governance has become a buzz word in diverse areas of political/organizational leadership including: *global governance* – how interdependent relationships are managed/coordinated when there's no overarching political authority; *local governance* – how local authorities work with community; *corporate governance* – how company objectives are set and met; *environmental governance* – how the environment (which knows no geographic/political boundaries) is managed; and *IT governance* – how IT is used within enterprises to achieve strategic goals. Exploring best practice across these areas is increasingly important in applied social sciences.

Key figures

Various forms of governance have been examined by key theorists such as Weber, who explored the development of the modern bureaucracy, Marx, who argued that national governance was dependent on modes of production, Althusser, who explored the means by which governing **ideology** is disseminated and adopted, and Durkheim, who was interested in the role of governance in creating social order.

A well-balanced, inclusive approach,
according to certain standards
and ideals, is essential
for proper governance.

Laisenia Qarase (1941–) Deposed
prime minister of Fiji –
Prime Minister's Corporate
Governance Summit, 12 March 2005

Recommended readings

The notion of effective governance has been addressed across various institutions. Have a look at *Comparing Local Governance* (Rose and Denters 2005), *The Politics of Global Governance* (Diehl 2005), *Corporate Governance* (Monks and Minow 2003), *Environmental Governance Reconsidered* (Durant et al. 2004), and finally *IT Governance* (Weill and Ross 2004).

Grounded theory

Longer explanation

How is theory generated in the social sciences? Traditionally, we have a 'theoretical' idea, perhaps sparked by personal experience, past research, or something we've read, and we develop a **hypothesis** accordingly. We then design and conduct a study in order to test that hypothesis. If we find what we're looking for, we've just added weight to our theory. The key is that we had the theory first and collected and explored data in order to provide evidence for that theory. In other words, we use a **deductive** process. Well, as a method, grounded theory, which focuses on the analysis of **qualitative** data, turns this on its head. There's no predetermined theory, no predestined categories of exploration. Theory evolves through the process of data analysis, which demands rich and ongoing engagement with data. The data holds the answers and it is up to the researcher to analyse that data in ways that allow findings and theory to emerge.

Debates and controversies

According to *Wikipedia*, grounded theory is referred to in **qualitative** data analysis more than any other method. I'm not surprised. Grounded theory is extremely well articulated (see Recommended readings) and is referred to as the cornerstone of qualitative data analysis in most social science methods texts. It's important to realize, however, that while grounded theory is certainly an important option in qualitative analysis, it's not the case that all theory in qualitative analysis must arise from data. The need to generate theory **inductively** (see **deductive/inductive reasoning**) (from the ground up) will not be appropriate for all researchers, particularly those whose aim is to test theory or mine data for predetermined themes.

Practical application

At some stage you may have to undertake a research project that involves working with qualitative data. If so, it's important to understand grounded theory as a methodology you may wish to adopt. But even if the inductive methods of grounded theory don't suit your investigation, being familiar with the clear step-by-step articulation of this approach can go a long way in helping you develop or adapt an approach more appropriate for meeting your own research goals.

Key figures

In the early 1960s, Barney Glaser and Anselm Strauss conducted a study on the awareness of dying in which they developed a constant comparative method of analysis later termed 'grounded theory'. While the two took the method in somewhat different directions in the 1970s, most researchers engaging in grounded theory return to their original 1967 work, *The Discovery of Grounded Theory.*

> The temptation to form premature theories upon insufficient data is the bane of our profession.
>
> **Sherlock Holmes** (Sir Arthur Conan Doyle, 1859-1930)

Recommended readings

I think the classics still hold up here. I'd have a look at Glaser and Strauss's *The Discovery of Grounded Theory* (1967) and Strauss and Corbin's *Basics of Qualitative Research: Techniques and Procedures for Developing Grounded Theory* (1998). Also worth a look are *Constructing Grounded Theory: A Practical Guide through Qualitative Analysis* (Charmaz 2006) or *Situational Analysis: Grounded Theory after the Postmodern Turn* (Clarke 2005).

Hegemony

Core definition

How the political, economic, cultural and ideological systems of those in *power* come to be accepted, legitimated and even celebrated by the masses at the expense of alternative ways of thinking and doing.

Longer explanation

Where do our values come from? Why do we tend to embrace the political, economic and cultural perspectives of our *society*? Even when inequities seem obvious, why do we accept and support them? For example, why do so many Americans, even those living in poverty, believe in *capitalism*? Why do so many Islamic women defend what Westerners see as blatant sexism? Why do we accept and even embrace a government position that sends youth to war? The answer, at least in part, is hegemony. Hegemony is when the values of a dominant group are transmitted and shared in ways, both overt and subtle, that make them seem like an inevitable part of the natural order. In fact, they become embedded in consciousness and can come to mask inequities such as racism, sexism, *class* conflict, and religious bigotry.

Debates and controversies

How important is hegemony to a society? On the upside, it unites, helps to develop patriotism, gives governments stability, and provides a common *culture*. On the downside, it works against *pluralism*, can give us blind allegiance to ineffective, inefficient and unjust governments, can mask inequities, and helps to silence those at the margins. Hegemony may be crucial to the stability of the status quo. The question is whether or not this is something we want.

Practical application

There are a number of fascinating applications here, for example, the study of citizenship (i.e. how we come to be socialized as citizens), in the exploration of culture/*multiculturalism*/cultural transmission, or in media studies since the media is key to the transmission of hegemonic (as well as alternative) ways of knowing. *Globalization* is also interesting since Western ways of thinking are finding new territories. Finally, hegemony is central in understanding war and its justification, particularly in the Middle East where Western/American values are being offered as a means of salvation.

Key figures

Karl Marx once said: 'The ideas of the ruling class are, in every epoch, the ruling ideas.' Those with power create intellectual and cultural realities. The question is how this occurs. The Italian Marxist, Antonio Gramsci, suggested that it's a complex process that involves more than just coercion or force. There needs to be 'consent', consent that becomes part of our consciousness as the beliefs of the ruling class become embedded in political propaganda and social institutions such as the legal system, the church, art, literature, and schools.

> Resistance is ... an obligation, I believe,
> for those who fear the consequences
> and detest the reality of the attempt to
> impose American hegemony.
>
> Noam Chomsky (1928–) US linguist, political
> analyst – in American Power and
> the New Mandarins (1969)

Recommended readings

Works on hegemony can take you down several interesting paths. Have a look at *Language and Hegemony in Gramsci* (Ives 2004), *Modernity and the Hegemony of Vision* (Levin 1993), *Hegemony: The New Shape of Global Power* (Agnew 2005) or the quite controversial work, *Hegemony or Survival: America's Quest for Global Dominance* (Chomsky 2003).

 **Hermeneutics**

Core definition

A *theory* and *methodology* for interpreting texts. Texts originally referred to biblical scriptures, but it is now used more broadly to include other literary forms, including books, artwork, theatre, and music.

Longer explanation

Summer has come and passed. The innocent can never last. Wake me up when September ends. – Billie Joe Armstrong (Green Day)

What are these lyrics about? What do they mean to me, to you, to Billie Joe Armstrong? Will we assign the same meaning to these lyrics in 25 years? How would someone from, say, Iraq interpret these lyrics? In other words, is the socio-historic context important to interpretation? Well these are the questions central to hermeneutics. Hermeneutics, which is rooted in the search for truth of and within scripture, has developed into a theory (and method) that recognizes that 'truth' is not locked in the words on a page or in the charcoal of a sketch. Rather, truth is recognized as a product of various relationships, such as between the author and his/her socio-historic reality, the audience and its reality, and author and audience. Interpretation is just that, interpretative, and hermeneutics explores the construction of meaning and the complexities of 'truth'. But back to *Green Day...* so what *do* these lyrics mean? Billie Joe Armstrong has publicly stated that the song was written about his father, who died of throat cancer in September 1982. But given the timing of the release and the context of the album, *American Idiot*, the overwhelming public interpretation was related to 9/11 and the seemingly endless war it spawned. In fact, so compelling was this interpretation that the band recognized its authenticity and decided to reflect this meaning in its video.

Debates and controversies

The standard for scientific discovery is objective truth and the hermeneutic theory/approach searches for relativistic truth (see *relativism*) that allows for multiple authentic interpretations – so it's bound to cause controversy. But as

110

we come to recognize the difficulty in understanding a world that is socially constructed (see social constructivism) yet still acts to 'construct' us, I'd argue it's a controversy we need.

Practical application

As well as a theory, hermeneutics is a method of *qualitative* data analysis that involves cycling between texts and various viewpoints in order to develop as rich an understanding as possible. Often called a hermeneutic circle or spiral, the aim is to understand the text (or the part) in relation to the socio-historic reality (the whole) and to understand that reality (or the whole) by exploring the text (the part).

Key figures

Key figures here include Wilhelm Dilthey, Max Weber, Martin Heidegger, Karl Mannheim, and more recently Edmund Husserl, Hans-Georg Gadamer and Paul Ricœur. These theorists recognize that texts are embedded in social context and that, unlike the natural sciences, interpretation needs to be undertaken in light of the socio-historic realities of both author and audience.

> *Every reader ... reads himself into the book, and amalgamates his thoughts with those of the author.*
>
> **Johann Wolfgang von Goethe** (1749–1832)
> German poet, philosopher – attributed

Recommended readings

Some good choices here include *Truth and Method* (Gadamer *1960* 2005), *Introduction to Philosophical Hermeneutics* (Grondin and Weinsheimer 1997), *Hermeneutics and the Human Sciences* (Ricœur 1981), and *Research Conversations and Narrative* (Herda 1999).

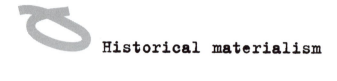 Historical materialism

Core definition

A major tenet or philosophical doctrine of *Marxist* theory that sees modes of production as the determining factor in the development of a society's social, political, intellectual, philosophical, and spiritual character.

Longer explanation

Why is any particular *society* the way it is? Why do societies shift, change, evolve, develop? Is the shape and form of our society dictated by God, fate, *ideology*, or even *state* policy? For Marx and Engels, the answer is none of the above. For them, understanding history is all about understanding 'modes of production'. Marx and Engels believed that the manner in which goods are produced determines social relationships, and these relationships will come to have influence, both overtly and subtlety, over all cultural and institutional features of a society. As Marx said: 'It is not the consciousness of men that determines their existence, but, on the contrary, their social existence determines their consciousness' (1859). This change in consciousness may happen smoothly and lead to stability, or it may be met with resistance and lead to conflict, *revolution* and political upheaval (Marx and Engels' prediction when exploring the rise of *capitalism*).

Debates and controversies

As a cornerstone of *Marxism*, there's bound to be debate. Three general critiques are: (1) Marx and Engels got it wrong – whether it's the intellect, God, biology, or ideology that's premised, many believe modes of production are a product, and not the cause, of change; (2) it's too simplistic – and this may well be the case, but in their later writings Marx and Engels continued to premise material forces, but also acknowledged the complexity of social relationships and interrelationships that drive change; and (3) historical materialism may hold up as a reflection of the rise of capitalism, but it's not shown itself to be a valid general theory of history.

Practical application

Understanding how history unfolds will always be a key theme in the social sciences. As nations around the globe continue to *industrialize*, it's interesting to explore whether changes in modes of production are, as Marx and Engels hypothesize, responsible for shifts in the social fabric, or whether ideological and political changes have laid a path for different modes of production. If only cause and effect were completely independent and easy to detach!

Key figures

As I'm sure you've gathered from the above, the key figures here are Marx and Engels, who as both social theorists and political activists predicted that the demise of capitalism would be brought about by its modes of production. This reflection was then generalized as an explanation for historical change.

> The mode of production in material life determines the general character of the social, political and spiritual processes of life.
>
> **Karl Marx** (1818–1883) German political/social philosopher – in *Contribution to the Critique of Political Economy* (1859)

Recommended readings

A good choice here is *Historical Materialism and the Economics of Karl Marx* (Croce 2004). I also like *Democracy against Capitalism: Renewing Historical Materialism* (Wood 1995), which argues for the applicability of the concept in the current age, and *Making History: Agency, Structure, and Change in Social Theory* (Callinicos 2004), which looks at the evolution of history in relation to both Marxist and non-Marxist theory. Marx's clearest articulation of historical materialism can be found in *Contribution to the Critique of Political Economy* (*1859* 1979).

 **Historicism**

Core definition

A term with two distinct meanings: (1) a belief that any period in history can only be understood in relation to its own time and place; (2) a belief in discoverable laws of historical change that can be used to predict the future.

Longer explanation

Let's start with the first meaning – historical periods can only be understood in relation to their own time and place. Sounds reasonable… cultures change, values and *norms* change, the world, and those in it, change. But in practice, we're quick to forget and quicker to judge. Most of us have a hard time believing 'good' men once owned slaves, or that we'd condone burning witches at the stake. But when our time and place is judged by others, some of our accepted practices may be considered barbaric. This version of historicism, 'relativistic' historicism, reminds us that historians weren't socialized into the worlds they explore. Without strong empathetic grasp of the conditions that create any historical phenomenon, judging it against current norms/values (or other cultures) is fraught with peril.

On to the second meaning – discoverable laws of historical change can be used to predict the future. In other words, a belief that if X happens, it will lead to Y. For example, the *Marxist* belief that *capitalism* will inevitably lead to political upheaval and eventually *socialism/communism* (which has now been disproved). This take on historicism, let's call it 'predictive' historicism, suggests there are rhythms or patterns in history that allow us to predict its evolution.

Debates and controversies

Can we truly know the past? Can we use the past to predict the future? Well, historicism is all about caution. 'Relativistic' historicism critiques any historical analysis that forgets that the historian's worldview helps paint the historical picture. Karl Popper redefined the term and put forward an attack of 'predictive' historicism. He warned of the perils of using the past to predict futures that have many unknowns, including the possibility to create new knowledge. For Popper, the future is not predetermined or predictable. It's one of unlimited possibility.

Practical application

The funny thing about worldviews is that we don't always remember we have one, yet we apply it in all our understandings. Historicism and its critiques can help us remember how culturally and historically biased we are. In fact, historicism is experiencing something of a renaissance in *cultural studies* and literary criticism. Labelled 'new historicism', it explores texts as products of a particular time and place.

Key figures

Hegel is most closely associated with 'relativistic' historicism and believed phenomena are meaningless outside their historical context. Karl Popper wrote a scathing attack of historicism in 1961, but his version of historicism, 'predictive' historicism, varied greatly from Hegel's even though he made reference to Hegel in this work. Popper's definition is now as common as the original.

> *People see themselves as the center of the universe and judge everything as it relates to them.*
>
> **Peace Pilgrim** (1908–1981)
> American pacifist and peace
> activist – attributed

Recommended readings

For a good introduction to 'relativistic' historicism, try *Historicism* (Hamilton 1996). If you're interested in Popper's critique of 'predictive' historicism try, *The Poverty of Historicism* (*1961* 2002). If your interest is in 'new historicism' (how confusing can one term be!), try *Practicing New Historicism* (Gallagher and Greenblatt 2001).

Human/social ecology

Core definition

Ecology is the study of relationships between living organisms and their environment. Human ecology specifically concentrates on the relationship between humans and their environment. Social ecology also looks at the relationships between humans and their environment, but specifically explores humans as social and cultural (not just biological) beings.

Longer explanation

As a branch of biological study, ecology recognizes the importance of exploring interactions and relationships among and between the non-living environment (i.e. air, water, soil) and its living components (i.e. bacteria, fungi, plants, animals). But in this bid to understand ecosystems, what wasn't always made explicit was the role of that biological entity called 'human' – enter human ecology. Human ecology explicitly recognizes the impact of humans (and their tendency to develop urban centres, mine, farm, log, fish, hunt, and develop industry) on the environment as well as the impact of the environment on humans. But humans are a complex bunch – not only do we have a direct relationship with the environment at a biophysical level, we also create social, cultural, and political *ideologies* and institutions that directly and indirectly affect how we interact with our environment. This complex and interdisciplinary area is the playground of social ecology. Social ecology explores all aspects of *society/culture* that affect relationships with, and the management of, ecosystems, for example modes of economic production, political and legal systems, cultural *norms* and values, dominant ideologies, spirituality and *ethics*. It tends to be quite political in nature and is not afraid of critiquing social/political systems that are seen as ecological threats.

Debates and controversies

Theoretically, no one really debates the need to work towards a sound ecosystem. No one denies that humans have had a huge impact on the environment. There's little disagreement that our socio-political structures work against environmental sustainability. The challenge is converting such beliefs into action in a world where development and wealth-building are the priorities.

Practical application

Many believe an ecological crisis (a shortage of fresh water, mass deforestation, global warming) is at our doorstep. Human/social ecology can not only help us understand some of the complexities that have acted to create these crises, but may also offer an inroad to sustainable solutions.

Key figures

Human ecology came into the fore in the 1920s through the work of Robert E. Park and Ernest Burgess, who were the first to study systematically the relationship between humans and the urban environment. The roots of social ecology can be traced to Murray Bookchin, who believed *capitalism* was a key cause of ecological degradation and introduced social ecology as a means for political change.

> *Modern society will find no solution to the ecological problem unless it takes a serious look at its lifestyles.*
>
> ***Pope John Paul II*** *(1920–2005) Polish ecclesiastic – in Pope John Paul II's New Year's Address (1990)*

Recommended readings

For an introduction to human ecology, try *Human Ecology: Following Nature's Lead* (Steiner 2002). If you're interested in social ecology, you can turn to *An Introduction to Cultural Ecology* (Sutton 2004). I also like the practical and applied nature of *Linking Social and Ecological Systems: Management Practices and Social Mechanisms for Building Resilience* (Colding and Berkes 2000).

 **Humanism**

Core definition

Various intellectual/ethical positionings that focus on the importance of human life, the significance of human experience, and the capacity of individuals to understand their worth and develop their potential.

Longer explanation

Where does ultimate *power* lie? With God, with spirits, with nature, – or with ordinary people? For humanists the answer is clear. It lies with ordinary people. We can't turn to God to solve our problems. It's up to us to recognize both our responsibilities and our worth. Humanism actually comes in many forms (and people can engage in humanism at different levels – some broadly accept it's ideals, while others embrace it as a sort of quasi-religion) but there are some basic tenants that give the concept coherence: (1) morality is not revealed by a higher *authority* but is based on *knowledge* drawn from human experience; (2) knowledge comes from human logic/investigation and through open discussion; (3) people are responsible to themselves and each other for improving the quality of life; (4) people can find fulfilment through self-development; (5) individuals all have worth; (6) there is a common humanity that overrides divisions of race, ethnicity, gender or belief; (7) most humanists are atheists, but even those who believe in God or a supernatural entity still look to human responsibility and effort to make a better world.

Debates and controversies

While the goals of humanism seem pretty intellectually and ethically sound, we're talking major controversy since humanism goes right to the heart of people's belief systems. 'There is an evil under the sun lurking amongst mankind known as humanism … an insane form of thinking that invades the human mind convincing it of it's superiority over God and His Word' (David J. Stewart on www.jesus-is-savior.com).

Practical application

Humanism is a great window for exploring fundamental concepts such as morality, *ethics*, knowledge, responsibility, worth, capacity, and fulfilment, and is particularly relevant in a **secularizing** world less and less dependent on God. But humanism, and the reaction it can provoke, is equally fascinating in the exploration of **fundamentalism**, religious tensions, and religious bigotry.

Key figures

The historical roots of humanism go back to ancient Greece and can be traced through the Renaissance and the Enlightenment. In fact, as scientific answers began to compete with religious myths (i.e. evolution vs. creationism), humanism took greater hold in public consciousness. Many key thinkers, such as Protagoras, Cicero, Voltaire, John Stuart Mill, Charles Darwin, Thomas Huxley, Marie Curie, Albert Einstein, Isaac Asimov, Bertrand Russell, Gloria Steinem, Simone de Beauvoir, and Mary Wollstonecraft have contributed to humanism's evolution.

> Man is the measure of all things.
>
> **Protagoras** (481–411 BC) Greek sophist,
> cited by Plato – in Smith, T.
> *Philosophers Speak*
> *for Themselves* (1934)

Recommended readings

To get a handle on humanist philosophy, turn to *On Humanism* (Norman 2004), *Humanism: An Introduction* (Herrick 2005), *Humanism* (Davies 1996) or *Meditations for the Humanist: Ethics for a Secular Age* (Grayling 2003). Another good choice here is *Humanist Anthology: From Confucius to Attenborough* (Knight 1995), which does an excellent job of engaging key thinkers.

 Hybridity

Core definition
A complicated entanglement of language, *culture*, ethnicity, and race that leads to new transcultural forms of being and is the product of forces such as migration, *colonization*, and *globalization*.

Longer explanation
Us and them… that's how we understand ourselves, others, and, in fact, the world. But contact, interactions, and exchanges can leave the boundary between us and them, while not necessarily eradicated, certainly blurred or softened. So who are we now? What does it mean to be Chinese in colonized Hong Kong? What does it mean to be Irish, if you've never been to Ireland? What is the identity of Australian aborigines post-invasion? As globalization invades the far reaches of the globe, will being a 'native' ever be the same? Hybridity addresses such questions and suggests that migration, colonization, and globalization – in other words our shrinking world – has not eliminated difference, but has created new cultural realities that involves a softening of cultural boundaries and an unsettling of identity. Hybridity questions the notion of 'pure' culture and 'pure' race and suggests we are all mongrels of a sort.

Debates and controversies
Biologically, hybridity can be seen as a threat to racial purity; 'half-breeds' are often thought of as inferior and certainly not desired. This is also the case with hybrid cultural and linguistic forms. People can be threatened by the thought of having their language, culture and even food 'tainted'. But hybridity can also be reflected on as a global reality that allows cultural exchange and growth, helps bridge difference, and can even break down traditional barriers that have been central to *discrimination* (see *prejudice/discrimination*) and oppression. The notion of supremacy is certainly threatened if purity of race and culture is just a myth.

Practical application
The world has become unbelievably smaller in the past 150 years. In the 1800s we travelled the globe at about 16 kilometres per hour. Today we do about 950

kilometres per hour. And we take advantage of this – we migrate, we invade, we trade, we tour, we go to war – and people, cultures, and races are never the same. Traces of other cultures exist in every culture, and exploring hybridity provides us with an opportunity to re-examine notions of *identity* as who we are takes new shape.

Key figures

Key theorists here include Homi Bhabha, who stresses the interdependence of colonizer and colonized, Stuart Hall, who explores the importance of hybrid identity within *communities*, Paul Gilroy, who fights against notions of purity, and James Clifford, who explores the relationship between 'roots' and 'routes' in a world where global travel is the norm.

> *Traditions co-exist with the emergence of new, hybrid and cross-over cultural forms of tremendous vitality and innovation.*
>
> ***Stuart Hall*** (1932–) Cultural theorist – in 'Un-settling the Heritage', Address to *Whose Heritage?* Conference, November 1999

Recommended readings

A modern classic here is Bhabha's *The Location of Culture* (2004). The writing, however, can be difficult. Other good choices include *Debating Cultural Hybridity: Multi-Cultural Identities and the Politics of Anti-Racism* (Werbner and Modood 1997), *Globalization and Culture* (Pieterse 2003), and *Hybridity, or The Cultural Logic of Globalization* (Kraidy 2005).

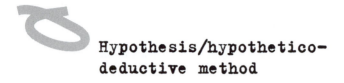

Hypothesis/hypothetico-deductive method

Core definition

A <u>hypothesis</u> is a logical conjecture or educated guess about the relationship between two or more variables expressed as a testable statement. In the <u>hypothetico-deductive method</u>, hypotheses are deduced from theory and evidence is gathered in order to test these hypotheses.

Longer explanation

In the world of science, there's an accepted formula for conducting research. You engage with **theory**, use that theory to deduce specific propositions or hypotheses, then gather data (in **social science research** this might involve experiments, surveys, interviews, observation or document analysis) in order to see if your hypothesis is supported or unsupported (see **scientific method**). For example, say you're interested in divorce and believe that changing marital roles puts pressure on marriages (your theory). More specifically, you formulate a hypothesis, 'a dual burden of full-time work and child-rearing causes martial discontent in women'. You now have a logical conjecture about the relationship between two variables (dual burden and discontent) that can be tested. Or you might decide to formulate a *null hypothesis,* in which you speculate that there's no relationship between your variables (i.e. 'a dual burden of full-time work and child-rearing does not cause martial discontent in women'). You then design your methods so you can refute your null hypothesis.

Debates and controversies

Is there an alternative to the use of hypotheses and the hypothetico-deductive methods in the social sciences? Therein lies the debate. **Positivists** believe hypotheses are the cornerstone of true science and that hypothetico-deductive methods define rigorous research. More **post-positivist** researchers, however, believe such deductive models constrain social research and do not allow for broader exploration and theory building.

Practical application

Whether the hypothetico-deductive method is appropriate for your own research depends on the nature of your inquiry. If you want to test aspects of a theory and are looking at relationships between particular variables, then this is a method worth exploring. But not all social science research is suited to this approach. For example, your study might seek to build broad understandings – your goal might be to offer rich descriptions of a phenomenon (see *phenomenology*) or cultural group (see ethnography). Alternatively, you may wish to engage in, and research, the process of collaborative change (see *action research*). In these cases you may not have preconceived hypotheses or even defined variables. In fact, in the social sciences there are plenty of instances where the hypothetico-deductive method simply doesn't fit.

Key figures

William Whewell, who wrote extensively on the philosophy of science in the early nineteenth century, was one of the first theorists to articulate the hypothetico-deductive method. But the method is most closely associated with Charles Sanders Peirce and Karl Popper, who were dedicated to 'true' rigorous science and proposed criteria for 'scientific' hypotheses.

> The great tragedy of science:
> the slaying of a beautiful hypothesis
> by an ugly fact.
>
> **Thomas Henry Huxley** (1825–1895)
> British biologist and educator –
> in Huxley, H.A. *Aphorisms and Reflections* (1907)

Recommended readings

There are a number of works on the hypothetico-deductive method, including *Scientific Method in Practice* (Gauch 2002), *Testing Statistical Hypotheses* (Lehmann and Romano 2005) and *Hypothesis Testing Behaviour* (Poletiek 2001). To dip into a classic, try Popper's *The Logic of Scientific Discovery* (*1959* 2002).

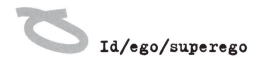 **Id/ego/superego**

Core definition

The id, ego, and superego are Freud's representation of the three structures of the mind. The <u>id</u> is the primal urges, primitive needs, and uncivilized passion we are born with. The <u>superego</u> is the 'moral' part of the mind that internalizes and embodies parental and societal values. The <u>ego</u> is the mediator between the two that attempts to balance primitive drives and socialized morality.

Longer explanation

Basically, the id is the naughty little pleasure-seeking devil on your shoulder who says, 'go ahead, you know you want to', while the superego is the equally annoying goody-two-shoes angel on the other shoulder reminding you 'to do what's right' and that 'you know better'. Stuck in the middle is the poor ego, torn between urges and morals, between pleasure and guilt. It's the ego's job to live in the real world and remember 'you can't always get what you want'. It needs to strike a balance between self-gratification and societal expectation. Negotiating the id and superego is central to the formation of **self**. If the id is too strong, it can lead to self-centredness. An over-developed superego can mean high levels of guilt and anxiety, while a strong ego can lead to over-rationality and a lack of spontaneity.

Debates and controversies

Sigmund Freud is one of the most controversial theorists of the twentieth century. Debates rage over whether or not his science was rigorous, his theories are correct, his therapies are useful, and if his character was stable. But regardless of these debates, the influence of his work, including his conceptions of the mind, are undeniable. His work has had a major influence on psychiatric practice as well as our common understandings of self.

Practical application

So why have I included these psych terms here? Well, how societal expectations are internalized or embodied in the self is a central question in psychology, philosophy, and sociology. Freud's structures of the mind, particularly his conception of the superego, folds the **norms**, mores, values, and **ideologies** of society into the development of *identity*, character and **personality**, and as such opens a fascinating window for exploring constructs such as **cognitive dissonance**, **ethics**, and **socialization**.

Key figures

While others have continued to develop work in this area (see the Recommended reading by Blanck and Blanck), the key figure and founding father here is clearly Sigmund Freud, who articulated his conception of the structure of the mind in *The Ego and the Id* (1923).

> The poor ego ... has to serve three harsh masters, and it has to do its best to reconcile demands of all three. ... The three tyrants are the external world, the superego, and the id.
>
> **Sigmund Freud** (1856–1939) Austrian psychiatrist – in *The New Introductory Lectures on Psychoanalysis* (1932)

Recommended readings

A good way into this area is through *The Politics of Psychoanalysis: An Introduction to Freudian and Post-Freudian Theory* (Frosh 1999) and *Ego Psychology* (Blanck and Blanck 1992). You can also attempt Freud's classic, *The Ego and the Id* (*1923* 1962). If you're interested in critiques of Freud, a highly controversial work is *Why Freud Was Wrong: Sin, Science and Psychoanalysis* (Webster 1996).

 **Idealism**

Core definition

Philosophical positionings in which the external world can only be experienced through the mind. What is 'real' is either constructed by the mind or is only given meaning through the mind.

Longer explanation

Have you seen *The Matrix*? In it, the notion of reality is turned on its head. The lives that people live, as in idealism, are lived solely though the mind (albeit no version of idealism talks about bodies being used by computers as batteries). Nonetheless, the movie makes us ask if an external world is really out there, or if it's all a dream, a figment of your own imagination. As Morpheus asks Neo in *The Matrix*: 'Have you ever had a dream, Neo, that you were so sure was real? What if you were unable to wake from that dream? How would you know the difference between the dream world and the real world?'

Debates and controversies

Try convincing someone that the pile of dog poop they just stepped in is only in their mind. My guess is that you won't get very far. The concept of reality is absolutely fundamental and talk of a world in which it doesn't exist seems crazy (unless you've been doing a lot of drugs, are a philosophy major, or better yet – both). Several theorists, for example G. E. Moore, David Stove, and John Searle, have all defended the notion of reality and the absurdity of a world confined to the mind.

Practical application

Deep stuff here... but this philosophical construct can also have a stronger, and arguably more grounded, sociological focus. The premise here is that 'thoughts' take priority over anything material. This can translate to **theory** before evidence, that is the notion that in research we need to theorize before we can seek proof of that theory. It can also refer to **ideology** before the material conditions, that is the notion that our ideologies and worldviews determine the structures of our society. Marxists often critique this notion of idealism since they believe the material world, in particular its modes of production, determine its ideology (see *historical materialism*).

Key figures

Plato, who believed that ideals and not individual things are real, is generally considered the first idealist philosopher. In the eighteenth century, George Berkeley stated that *knowledge* is based on perceptions and that perceptions can exist only in the mind. Therefore, only perceptions of objects (not objects themselves) are real. Similarly, Immanuel Kant held that all we can ever hold is mental impressions. In the nineteenth century, Georg Hegel postulated that since reality is a product of the mind, a greater mind or spirit must be at work in the universe.

> If real is what you can feel, smell, taste and see, then 'real' is simply electrical signals interpreted by your brain.
>
> **Morpheus** (*The Matrix* 1999)

Recommended readings

For a good overview of idealist thought, try *The Innovations of Idealism* (Bubner 2003). I also like *The Cambridge Companion to German Idealism* (Ameriks 2000). For an even more specific focus, turn to *Routledge Philosophy Guidebook to Berkeley and the Principles of Human Knowledge* (Fogelin 2001). If you're interested in exploring more sociological aspects of idealism, have a look at *Materialism vs. Idealism* (Kingsland 2005).

 Identity

Core definition

Our sense of *self*, which makes us unique (provides us with personal character) and yet makes us recognizable as a part of a social group (i.e. male, Asian, working-class).

Longer explanation

Who am I? This is a question that's getting harder and harder to answer. I'll get personal for a minute. I know my gender – luckily that's never been a source of confusion for me – but that's about all I know. My mother's Korean and my father is American of Irish decent – my ethnicity is blurred. I was born in the USA, but have lived in Australia for the past 18 years – so I annoy my kids when I'm not sure who to support during the Olympics. And my answer to the question 'what do you do?' often depends on who I am talking to – a mother, academic, author, lecturer, sociologist, researcher, consultant … ? And I'm not alone. We live in a world where identity is no longer stable. Race, ethnicity, *class*, nationality, gender, occupation, sources of identity that have traditionally defined a 'stable' self, are becoming ever more fluid. Mixed or *hybrid* races, *social mobility*, *globalization*, transsexualism, and unending career changes have made the answer to the question, 'who am I?' highly complex, and unlikely to be static.

Debates and controversies

Traditional theories see identity as relatively stable after childhood, with the exception of possible identity crises in adolescence and mid-life. But more recent theorists highlight the instability of identity that seems to exist in a *postmodern* (see *postmodernity*) world. So what do we make of this? Does instability offer unlimited possibilities in the construction of self? Can it help us reach self-actualization free from the confines of *culture*, religion, or tradition? Or are we headed for mass estrangement, meaninglessness and *anomie*? Are we lost souls suffering from unending identity crises?

Practical application

As the world changes and concepts of identity get tossed about, there can be tremendous value in exploring how we come to understand ourselves and our place in the world. Whether you're interested in personal opportunities/threats that travel with shifting and complex identities or you're interested in understanding the personal and political empowerment that can come from identification with others, how we come to negotiate identity will be a central question in *cultural studies* for some time to come.

Key figures

Key figures here include George Mead, an early social-psychologist who articulated the distinction between I, the outer presentation of self, and me, the inner reflection of self, and Erik Erikson, a psychologist who identified eight developmental stages of 'man' and coined the term 'identity crisis'. Erving Goffman, who explored the presentation of self, is also interesting here. More contemporary theorists exploring postmodern challenges to traditional concepts of identity include Anthony Giddens, Peter Berger, and Stuart Hall.

> Identity is such a crucial affair
> that one shouldn't rush into it.
>
> David Quammen (1948-) Science,
> nature and travel writer - attributed

Recommended readings

Works that address contemporary issues in identity include *Questions of Cultural Identity* (Hall and du Gay 1996) and *Reclaiming Identity: Realist Theory and the Predicament of Postmodernism* (Moya and Hames-Garcia 2000). For seminal works, turn to Mead's *Mind, Self, and Society* (*1934* 1967), Erikson's *Identity and the Life Cycle* (*1959* 1994) or Goffman's *The Presentation of Self in Everyday Life* (1959).

 Ideology

Core definition

Pervasive sets of belief that permeate the public conscious and help individuals interpret the world and their place within it.

Longer explanation

This can be a highly confusing term because there are at least three different uses. The first is highly specific – particular sets of mainly political, but also social and economic, beliefs or 'isms' (i.e. *fascism*, *capitalism* and *communism*). The second use is *Marxist* and quite negative – the belief systems of the ruling class that are imposed in various ways on the masses, such that the masses are 'duped' and accept and even reproduce the current political, social and economic order. Finally, the term is often used in a way that is both broad and neutral – the belief systems/worldviews that are embedded within any socio-historic period.

Debates and controversies

We know there are ideologies in operation. And we know that we're necessarily *socialized* into a societal framework with particular worldviews. But that doesn't tell us if we're the victims of ideological manipulation by the ruling class. Perhaps the ruling class is as much a victim of ideological forces as everyone else? And besides, in a world were accessibility to alternative ways of thinking abounds, is it possible that the adoption of ideological frameworks might be more at our discretion than ever before?

Practical application

Ideological battles are happening all the time. We defend capitalism and fight communism. We protect our freedoms to the death. We've even been drawn into a *jihad* or holy war. And yes, it's important that those in power socialize us so that we hold the same beliefs dear, making ideologies central to who we are, what we believe in, and what we live and die for. As such, exploring the adoption and negotiation of ideologies is a fascinating area of the social sciences.

Key figures

Karl Marx believed that the ruling class creates intellectual and cultural realities, or ideologies, that help maintain the existing social order. Antonio Gramsci suggested that this requires more than coercion and relies on **hegemony**, where the dominant group's values are transmitted and shared in ways that make them seem like an inevitable part of the natural order. Louis Althusser outlined the mechanism by which this occurs and named the family, church, education and legal systems, and even mass culture, as part of the ideological state apparatus that disseminates ruling ideology. Karl Mannheim also saw ideology as a filter to objective **knowledge** and argued that the goal of the social sciences is to be impartial to any particular ideological perspective. Meanwhile, Clifford Geertz viewed ideology as a much more neutral and essential cultural symbolic system.

> Ideology ... is indispensable in any
> society if men are to be formed,
> transformed and equipped to respond
> to the demands of their
> conditions of existence.
>
> **Louis Althusser** (1918–1990) Marxist
> philosopher – in *For Marx* (1965)

Recommended readings

There are some good introductory books here. I'd recommend *Ideology: A Very Short Introduction* (Freeden 2003) and *Ideology* (Hawkes 2003). For a broad reader that covers a range of key thinkers, try *Ideals and Ideologies: A Reader* (Ball and Dagger 2003). Marx and Engel's *The German Ideology* (*1845* 1998) is also worth an attempt.

 **Imperialism**

Longer explanation

Over 2000 years ago Caesar helped build the Roman Empire by using military might to invade and conquer his neighbours. In the late 1700s/early 1800s France's Napoleon attempted to conquer continental Europe in much the same way. Fast forward 100 years to the height of the British Empire and you'll find that rather than military siege of neighbouring nations, the British established *colonies* across the globe in order to bring riches to the homeland. In the 1920s British colonies could be found in Europe, Asia, the Pacific Islands, North America, Australia, and Africa. Today the USA is the superpower that some are calling an empire. While conquests may not be seen to be as brazen as Caesar's, and the USA may not have a host of 'colonies', many feel that US intervention, the presence of military bases and multinational corporations, and even foreign aid, exerts tremendous political, economic, and cultural control over a host of nations.

Debates and controversies

So why is the concept of empire building so fundamental in the history of global politics? Undeniably, the answer lies in two of the greatest motivators ever known to humankind – power and money. But it's not quite that simple. The quest for empires is also built on the back of belief systems and *ideologies* that people live and die for. Whether these ideologies revolve around religious values, racial integrity, extended benefits of civilization, *democracy*, liberty, (see *liberalism*) freedom, or free trade, building empires is tied to impassioned principles.

Practical application

It's true that many nations have 'decolonized' and gained independence from past empires, but few nations stand alone. We're a much more *globalized* world than we once were. New forms of imperialism, in other words the economic, political, cultural, and ideological forces that create dependence and can control the shape of nations, offers unending avenues for social science exploration.

Key figures

While imperialism can be traced back thousands of years and across a wide diversity of cultures, theories of imperialism did not appear until the turn of the twentieth century and tended to focus on Western economic perspectives. In particular, they explored the need for imperialist expansion (cheap labour and resources, new markets) under *capitalism*. In 1902, John Hobson argued that imperialist expansion was necessary to secure markets for the overproduction of goods. Vladimir Lenin further argued that imperialism is the highest (and last) stage of capitalism. Joseph Schumpeter, however, saw imperialism as irrational in capitalist economies and viewed it as a throwback to militaristic *nationalism*.

> *The truth is that neither British nor American imperialism was or is idealistic. It has always been driven by economic or strategic interests.*
>
> **Charley Reese** (1937–)
> American syndicated columnist –
> in *Kipling's Back*, 16 August 2004

Recommended readings

Have a look at *Culture and Imperialism* (Said 1994) or *The New Imperialism* (Harvey 2005), which explores more subtle forms of imperialism that many argue operate in US politics. To delve into the classics, turn to Hobson's *Imperialism* (*1902* 1965) or Lenin's *Imperialism the Highest Stage of Capitalism* (*1916* 1969).

Individualism

Core definition
Social/political doctrines or philosophies that hold an individual's rights and responsibilities to be of the highest importance.

Longer explanation
What motivates us to do good or to succeed? Do we watch out for number one, or do we do it for the team? Whose fault is it if we fail? Do we blame ourselves, or do we blame the system? And what about the system? Should governments mind their own business and simply protect our civil liberties, or should they have a bigger hand in directing our lives for the good of all? Well, individualism premises free choice, independence, self-reliance, self-interest, personal responsibility and governments whose role is to protect individual rights and liberties (see *liberalism*) . So rather than stress social welfare or the collective good, individualism justifies private over public interests. This doesn't necessarily mean that societies with strong individualist tendencies are unregulated or unstructured. Rather, the direction these societies take suits particular types of political and economic reality. In fact, individualism sits so well with the free trade and independent nature of *capitalist* economies, it's sometimes referred to as the 'spirit of capitalism'.

Debates and controversies
A tension in all governments is balancing public good with individual freedoms. Countries (and individuals) with strong individualistic tendencies are quick to condemn unprotected civil liberties, high levels of government intervention, and things like free tertiary education if it comes at the price of high taxes. On the other hand, criticism is just as sharp when individual liberties come at the expense of public welfare and/or community *solidarity*, such as the right to bear arms costing innocent lives or the need for private medical insurance to cover basic medical needs.

Practical application
There are strong cultural and ideological belief systems at work that underpin our societies' structures. Where cultural groups sit in relation to the tension

between individual liberties and striving for the collective good is a large part of these beliefs. In a *globalizing* world, it's interesting to explore how changes in political and economic landscapes are effected by, and come to affect, notions of individualism.

Key figures

Individualism is a powerful philosophy in the 'West', and nowhere stronger than in the USA, where individual liberties where captured in the 1700s by George Mason, who authored the *Bill of Rights.* Around this same period, English social philosophers, Jeremy Bentham and John Stuart Mill, argued for a range of individual and economic freedoms, including the separation of church and state (see *secularism*), freedom of expression, equal rights and free trade. In the 1800s, Herbert Spencer advocated a 'law of equal liberty', in which individuals are allowed to do as they wish, as long as it doesn't infringe on the rights of another person.

> *A nation is only an individual multiplied.*
>
> **Mark Twain** (1835-1910) US author – in 'The Turning Point of my Life', Harper's Bazaar, 44.2 (1910)

Recommended readings

For a good range of key readings, try *Communitarianism and Individualism* (Avineri and de-Shalit 1992). Other good choices here include *Capitalism and Individualism* (Machan 2002) and *Individualization: Institutionalized Individualism and Its Social and Political Consequences* (Beck and Beck-Gernsheim 2002).

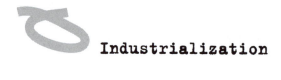
Industrialization

Core definition

Process of social and economic change which sees societies shift from agriculturally based subsistence economies to economies reliant on large-scale production and mass manufacturing.

Longer explanation

How different must the world have been when your vegetable patch was your main source of food, when you were reliant on wind and water for power, when the only tools you had were ones you could hold in your hands, when there were no clocks, only the sun and when there were no bosses, just your own need to survive. Well, up until about 200 years ago this was the reality. But things have definitely shifted in the West and are continuing to shift in the developing world. We now live in industrial societies where *technological* innovations and mass production of energy has reshaped our world and who we are within it. The agriculture sector has shrunk with the few now able to provide for the many. Mechanized factories are commonplace. We accept divisions of labour. We get our rewards from pay cheques and an ability to create wealth. We've learned to deal with *bureaucracy*, we've moved into *urban* areas, and we expect scientific knowledge to aid problem-solving.

Debates and controversies

Industrialization has impacted just about everything in our world. It's lead to profound *ideological*, *cultural*, economic, political, and personal transformations. In fact, changes heralded by industrialization triggered the development of sociology as a discipline. Concern over a new world order in which both the natural world and labourers were at risk of exploitation, where *capitalism* thrived on industrial production, where *community* ties were weakened, and where women were relegated to the 'private', opened a new world of social debate.

Practical application

In an ever-*globalizing* world, social scientists continue to be interested in how industrialization (as well as more recent moves in the West to a *post-industrial* order) affects various aspects of our world, including the political landscape, standards of living, environmental and ecological integrity, community and family life, and women's roles in society.

Key figures

Auguste Comte, who coined the term sociology, predicted the impacts of industrialization to be both positive and profound. He believed that the creation of affluence would bring global peace and that false ideas of religion would be replaced by a religion of humanity. Later thinkers were not so optimistic. Durkheim saw the potential for social equilibrium under industrialization, but also stressed the suicidal tendencies that could result from a loss of community *solidarity* (see *anomie*). Marx saw industrialization, particularly under a capitalist paradigm, as something that would lead to the severe *alienation* of workers, while Weber stressed the increasing level of *bureaucracy* that's endemic to industrial production.

> We must recognize the dangers inherent
> in a frenzied, unheedful push
> towards that would-be Golden Age
> or Utopia which supporters of
> mechanization and industrialization
> suggest is attainable.
>
> **Alexander B. Campbell** (1933-) Former
> Canadian premier - in the Empire
> Club Address, 8 November 1973

Recommended readings

Historical overviews such as *Industry and Empire* (Hobsbawn 1999) and *The Industrial Revolution in World History* (Sterns 1998) are a good place to start. But also worth a look are works that link industrialization with pressing social phenomenon, for example *Repositioning Class: Social Inequality in Industrial Societies* (Marshall 1997) and *Industrialisation and Globalisation* (Weiss 2002).

Instrumentalism

Core definition

Belief that the value of any particular theory does not lie in its ability to capture truth, but lies in its usefulness for understanding and predicting phenomena.

Longer explanation

You know some of the world's most influential social scientists (and natural scientists) have been wrong. We're still waiting for Comte's religion of humanity to arise from *industrialization*. And Marx's prediction of a *communist* utopia never quite came about. But does this take away from the power of such *theories*? For instrumentalists, the answer is no. Theories are best seen as 'instruments' that help us make our way through a world that's constantly changing. To judge theories by their ability to capture 'truth' is a tough standard if you're trying to hit a moving target. What counts is the ability of theory to shed light; value is in a theory's end contribution. In fact, the word 'instrumental' is often used as an adjective indicating an orientation to 'end results' over 'processes'. For example, someone with an instrumental orientation to education would gain rewards from grades received rather than *knowledge* attained. And rather than an appeal to intrinsic or higher values, 'what is right' in instrumental morality is what satisfies particular needs. In instrumental politics, political systems need not be viewed as intrinsically good or bad. Rather, they should be judged according to what they offer citizens.

Debates and controversies

We're definitely instrumental since we constantly revise our theories in order to meet the challenges of our world. And we're definitely results-oriented – not many of us would go to work if there were no pay cheque. But we also search for truth and seek processes that have inherent value, such as the joy of learning (stop laughing!) or the empowerment that should accompany democratic processes. Debate arises when people believe that one orientation has greater value than the other and should be the standard for the production of knowledge, behaviour, and morality.

Practical application

As the world becomes more *postmodern* (see *postmodernity*) and *post-structural* (see *structuralism/poststructuralism*), there's a growing appreciation of the socially constructed (see *social constructionism*) nature of our world and how difficult it can be to capture 'truth', if truth exists at all. Instrumentalism reminds us that truth is not the only standard we might work towards. Theories can be judged according to their utility and their ability to enlighten and affect change.

Key figures

Key figures go back as far as Aristotle, who believed that 'end results' were a fundamental consideration in human action (see *teleology*). Max Weber warned against instrumental rationalization or reliance on the most technically efficient means for reaching an end purpose. In the mid-twentieth century, American philosopher John Dewey argued that political/cultural ideas should not be judged on truth-value, but by the ends they serve.

> *Truth is what works.*
>
> **William James** (1842-1910)
> US philosopher, psychologist –
> in *What is Pragmatism?* (1904)

Recommended readings

A good place to start is *A Companion to Pragmatism* (Shook and Margolis 2006). If your library has a copy of *The Chicago School of Pragmatism* (Shook 2003), this comprehensive four-volume set covers many of instrumentalism's key tenets and is worth a look. Other good choices are *Transforming Experience: John Dewey's Cultural Instrumentalism* (Eldridge 1998) or William James' work, *Pragmatism* (*1931* 2005).

 **Justice**

Core definition

What is considered fair or equitable in relation to rights, rewards, resources, punishments and sanctions.

Longer explanation

We all want a just world. We actually scream for justice from the moment we can talk – 'That's not fair!' Whether the cry comes from the toddler who believes his sibling's piece of chocolate is slightly bigger than his, or it's said with venom by the teenager who feels she did NOT deserve to be grounded, our desire for justice runs deep. In fact, it's a central moral standard in social life. Whether it's distributive justice that looks at the allocation of benefits and burdens, or retributive justice that looks at the fairness of social/legal sanctions, the concept is fundamental across the social sciences.

Debates and controversies

But what constitutes justice? Should we turn to political *ideologies*, religious beliefs, *ethics* and values, majority opinion, logic, the law? Should there be an objective standard for justice or should it be something that is culturally relative? For example, in the West many believe it's better for ten guilty people to go free than have one innocent person punished. But in other *cultures* the punishment of the occasional innocent is a small price if it means the guilty will definitely pay. And then there's the tension between personal and social justice, for example is it just to allow 18 year-olds to go to war but not have a drink? Or is this fair and just because it's for the social good? As long as such questions are debated, justice will remain a highly contested social science concept.

Practical application

A country's form of government, political party platforms, economic systems, foreign policy, policies related to healthcare and education, criminal justice systems, religion, laws, *norms*, mores, morals, ethics and values all sit on foundations of 'justice', making it an invaluable window in social science exploration.

Key figures

The concept of justice has been addressed by any number of social, philosophical and political theorists. One of the first was Aristotle, who identified three types of justice that are still referred to in the literature: distributive, corrective, and equitable. More recently, John Rawls, a twentieth-century philosopher, specifically addressed justice and argued that inequity in resource distribution is justified only if it advantages the most marginalized social groups. Robert Nozick disagreed and argued that any distribution of goods (even unbalanced ones) are just if it's brought about by non-exploitative free exchange. A good example here is Kyle Macdonald, who in July 2005 attempted to trade up from a single red paperclip to a house – he achieved this in just under 12 months. Another recent theorist to contribute to the debate is Nancy Fraser, who argues that the complexity of justice demands it be understood along three interrelated dimensions: distribution of resources; recognition of varying contributions of different groups; and it's representation in language.

> The administration of justice is the
> firmest pillar of government.
>
> *George Washington* (1732-1799) First US
> president, *Letter to US Attorney
> General Edmund Randolph* (1789)

Recommended readings

I like the political contribution of Barry, which asks *Why Social Justice Matters* (2005), Fraser's *Justice Interruptus* (1997) and *A Short History of Distributive Justice* (Fleischacker 2005). Also worth a look are Rawls's *A Theory of Justice* (*1971* 1999) and Nozick's *Anarchy, State and Utopia* (1977).

 Knowledge

> **Core definition**
> Awareness or understanding of a condition, act, fact, or truth.

Longer explanation

There are statements of personal opinion or speculation for which you don't need to be right, for example, 'I think I'll be reincarnated when I die'. There are also statements of faith that don't need to be justified, for example, 'I believe in reincarnation'. But there are also knowledge statements that need to be based on evidence. In fact, for thoughts to be considered 'knowledge', most philosophers agree they need to be believed, true, and justified, which is why the knowledge statement 'I know we're all going to be reincarnated' is likely to be met with 'How in the world would you know that?' The study of how we come to have 'legitimate' knowledge is called *epistemology*, but I won't say much about that since it has its own entry. What I will mention are common categories of knowledge: *propositional or explicit knowledge* – statements based on facts (e.g. the sky is blue); *procedural knowledge* – knowing how to do something such as riding a bike; *personal or tacit knowledge* – based on experience, like personally knowing the pain of childbirth; and *situated or local knowledge* – knowledge that is highly contextual and embedded in language, culture, or traditions, (e.g. aboriginal creation 'myths').

Debates and controversies

What do we know? How do we know it? What counts as knowledge? Can we know anything outside ourselves? Can we know ourselves? Who has a right to create knowledge? What impact do knowledge producers have on knowledge itself? Are we manipulated through knowledge? Is knowledge *power*? Why are certain types of knowledge marginalized and others legitimated? Given the centrality of knowing to humankind, it shouldn't be surprising to find no end of debates related to this contentious concept.

Practical application

We tend to take knowledge for granted. We accept facts, data, and information that have an evidentiary basis, generally a scientific one, as knowledge. But we live in a particular time and place in history. What constitutes the production of legitimate knowledge now (say, science), differs from the past (the Gods) and is likely differ in the future. Understanding the *social construction* of knowledge reminds us to question just about every assumption we hold.

Key figures

A number of theorists have explored knowledge and its relation to *society*. Karl Marx argued that societal knowledge is a product of social structures (see *ideology*). Emile Durkheim believed that the mental categories we use to understand the world stem from the organization of society. Karl Mannheim argued that various social positions determine differing forms of knowledge that all have equal truth-value. Michel Foucault explored the intersection of knowledge and power.

> If confusion is the first step to knowledge, I must be a genius.
>
> Larry Leissner (1901-1990) French anthropologist, author - attributed

Recommended readings

A number of recent works explore theories of knowledge: *Experience and Prediction: An Analysis of the Foundations and the Structure of Knowledge* (Reichenbach 2006), *Theory of Knowledge* (Alchin 2006), and *An Introduction to the Theory of Knowledge* (O'Brien 2006). I also like *Tracking Truth: Knowledge, Evidence, and Science* (Roush 2006). For recommendations on various ways knowledge is generated, see Recommended readings listed under *epistemology*.

Labelling theory

Longer explanation

What impact would it have on your psyche if everyone around you – your family, *community*, school, and even the legal system – labelled you a delinquent? Or what if you knew someone who grew up constantly being called stupid? Any chance it would limit intellectual growth? Well labelling theory suggests that the labels attached to us can be instrumental in forming our self-perception. In fact, labels can act as a self-fulfilling prophecy. If people see you and talk about you in a certain way, you're likely to come to see yourself in that way, to think that way, and eventually act in ways that make the label true.

Debates and controversies

Traditional theories of *deviance* tend to emphasize an individual's inherent personality traits and their free will in breaking social norms. But labelling theory, which focuses on ways in which societal interactions affect the construction of self, offers an alternative. Many, however, feel that labelling theory provides an excuse for unacceptable behaviour and relieves 'deviants' of all responsibility. Others feel it doesn't get at primary psychological or structural causes of deviance. Labelling theory is also criticized for being too *deterministic* in that it does not recognize the ability of individuals to make conscious choices in controlling their own lives.

Practical application

Labelling theory is important in understanding deviant behaviour, but its social science application is actually much broader. For example, labels, particularly those applied early in life, can be a determining factor in how one sees opportunities. If parents see and label their child as talented, they're likely to foster those talents and the child is likely to internalize those beliefs and continue to develop those talents throughout their life course. Another example is school tracking where children are segregated according to perceived academic ability. Teacher, peer, and self-expectations vary dramatically between top and bottom tracks. And to either the advantage or disadvantage of these children, they get sent down particular paths.

Key figures

George Herbert Mead, a *symbolic interactionist*, recognized the importance of others in the formation of identity. For him, identity is continuously constructed and reconstructed though interpersonal relationships. Labelling theory derives from Mead's work and was first applied to the study of deviance by Edwin Lemert, who made a distinction between primary deviance and secondary deviance attributable to societal perceptions. The actual term 'labelling theory', however, was coined in the 1960s by Howard Becker, who argued that systems of social control cause criminalized identities to become part of self-identity.

> What I really resent most about people sticking labels on you is that it cuts off all the other elements of what you are.
>
> *Siouxsie Sioux* (1957–) Lead singer of *Siouxsie & the Banshees*, *Uncut* interview, 29 November 2004

Recommended readings

I'd start with Mead's seminal work, *Mind, Self and Society* (*1934* 1967), but if you're more comfortable with a contemporary reading, try *The Ethics of Identity* (Appiah 2004). For readings more specific to deviant behaviour, try Becker's seminal work, *Outsiders* (*1963* 1997), or *Creating Deviance: An Interactionist Approach* (Dotter 2004).

 **Labour**

Core definition

The work that humans engage in. Labour is considered one of the four basic factors of production (the others being *capital*, land, and enterprise).

Longer explanation

Labour, as defined by Marx, is the paid work that the masses are forced to sell to the owners of the means of production in capitalist systems. That's a mouthful, so to put it in other words, you don't sell the bread you bake or the shirt you tailor to those who will eat it or wear it. Under *capitalism*, what the masses sell is their ability to work for others (i.e. factory owners). These owners then sell the products of your labour in order to make profits for themselves. If they can get more labour for less money, profits increase. Now this conception has been central to nineteenth- and twentieth-century Western economic, political and social theories, and is reflected in the doctrine of international labour parties dedicated to protecting worker rights. But this is actually a somewhat narrow view of the term. In *post-industrial* societies, labour is not relegated to factory work or manual labour. Human efforts are often more technical, service-oriented or managerial. And we don't always get paid for it either. Unpaid domestic labour is often left out of economic theories and has acted to *marginalize* the economic and political position of women.

Debates and controversies

Everyone wants to be fairly compensated for what they do. But there has yet to be a political or economic system that has been fair, equitable, just, or non-exploitative. Finding the system that brings the greatest benefit to the masses – in the face of a human drive for power and riches – is a challenge not met by *capitalism*, *socialism*, *communism*, or any socio-political system searching for ways to empower and justly compensate us for our labour.

Practical application

Perhaps one of the greatest challenges in a *globalizing* world is working towards equity and social *justice*. As *developing countries* build an *industrial* workforce and *developed countries* move labour-intensive industries offshore, the need to manage labour in ways that are just and avoid the tendency for exploitation is as important now as it was a the dawn of the industrial revolution.

Key figures

While many social, economic, and political theorists have explored the concept of labour, no one's had more influence than Karl Marx. Marx believed the only way to maximize profits in capitalist systems was to squeeze labour costs, leaving workers highly vulnerable. Now, Marx actually believed that capitalism would come to be replaced by communism, but capitalism survives and even thrives. And while labour conditions in the developed world have arguably improved, the battle for worker rights continues in both capitalist and non-capitalist economies across the globe.

> *All wealth is the product of labour.*
>
> ***John Locke*** *(1632-1704) British philosopher - attributed*

Recommended readings

This is a broad area, so I'm recommending a mixed bag starting with *Globalisation, State and Labour* (Fairbrother and Rainnie 2006), *From the Folks Who Brought You the Weekend: A Short, Illustrated History of Labor in the United States* (Murolo and Chitty 2003) and for a more feminist perspective, *Doing the Dirty Work?: The Global Politics of Domestic Labour* (Anderson 2000). For Marx's seminal thoughts, try *Wage Labor and Capital* (*1891* 2004).

 **Leadership**

Core definition
The ability to influence and inspire others towards the achievement of common goals.

Longer explanation

There are plenty of people who tell us what to do in an attempt to manage or control us. But how many actually inspire us to follow? How many have the vision and skills necessary to unite and motivate us in ways that help us work towards a common purpose? Well, this is the true nature of leadership. While some have positions of **authority** and, along with it, the ability to enforce sanctions for non-compliance, true leaders, whether or not they have formal authority, are seen as inspirational motivators whom others choose to follow. Now leaders can vary in behaviours, personality, style, and can be born or made, but there are certain traits that define leaders and leadership. So in contrast to, say, managers, who tend to concentrate on tasks, watch the bottom line, exercise power and control, and have short-term goals, leaders tend to concentrate on people, watch the horizon, motivate and encourage, and have a clear, shared vision.

Debates and controversies

The above is the ideal but, naturally, the reality falls short. Even the best leaders fail to motivate everyone, particularly when leadership arises from the majority and fails to represent those in the margins. And rarely are we 100% happy with our leaders – there's always something we find frustrating. Perhaps this is because we forget that our leaders generally have to work within, or at least negotiate, a world in which all the inspiration, motivation, and vision you can muster can still have a hard time overcoming a need to answer to bottom lines and short-term goals. It's also important to recognize that leaders can have visions that are far from humanitarian. Some of the most charismatic leaders have been or are responsible for unthinkable atrocities.

Practical application

Things are changing at an extraordinarily fast rate. Nothing is stable. Families in turmoil, downsized workplaces, the overthrow of governments, global warming, *globalization* – we face consistent crises of change. And no matter what the scale, we tend to look to our leaders, both formal and informal, for guidance and inspiration. Understanding what determines effective leadership has never been more important.

Key figures

The figure most closely associated with the construct of leadership and authority is Weber, who articulated three leadership types: legal/rational, traditional, and charismatic (see *authority*). More recent writers, however, sometimes use alternate classifications. An example is Patricia Pitcher, who characterizes leaders as inspirational 'artists', sensible 'craftsmen' or detail-oriented 'technocrats'.

> All of the great leaders have had
> one characteristic in common: the
> willingness to confront unequivocally
> the major anxiety of their people
> in their time. This ... is the
> essence of leadership.
>
> *John Kenneth Galbraith* (1908–2006)
> US economist – in *The Age
> of Uncertainty* (1977)

Recommended readings

Good choices here are *Contemporary Issues in Leadership* (Rosenbach and Taylor 2006) and *Theory and Practice of Leadership* (Gill 2006). Also worth a look is *Enlightened Power: How Women are Transforming the Practice of Leadership* (Coughlin et al. 2005). Pitcher's classification can be found in *The Drama of Leadership* (1997), while Weber's work on authority can be found in *Economy and Society* (pt I, ch 3) (*1921–22* 1978).

 **Liberalism**

Core definition

Political doctrine or *ideology* that premises liberty and individual rights, such as freedom of thought/religion, equality of opportunity, and the right to own property. Because self-determination is seen as key to concepts of liberty, liberalism tends to advocate free competition and free markets.

Longer explanation

What rights do individual citizens have and what responsibility do governments have in protecting these rights? Well, liberalism contends that all individuals have the right to life, liberty, and property, or, as expressed in the *US Declaration of Independence*, 'life, liberty and the pursuit of happiness'. Put simply, liberalism puts liberty at the heart of its political, social and economic ideology. As such, liberal governments are responsible for establishing and protecting individual liberty and a right to self-determination. Elections are generally fair and unbiased, individual rights are made explicit, and citizens are equally protected under the law. Economic policy tends to be based on the premise that competition between entrepreneurs is not only the right of individuals, but that it builds a strong economy. Government intervention is thus kept at a minimum.

Debates and controversies

This can be a highly confusing term because it covers a wide range of political orientations and political parties that can premise anything from human/individual rights (see *humanism*) to a strong belief in free-market *capitalism* (sometimes referred to, in contemporary politics, as neo-liberalism). But it's not just the range of orientations within liberalism that can be an issue. There's actually a fundamental tension in liberalism – a need to protect individual rights versus a 'laissez-faire' orientation that limits government intervention. For example, a debate across liberal camps might be: Should governments enact legislation to protect workers' rights or should it let market forces, and therefore employers, rule?

Practical application

It's interesting to explore how governments around the world balance the tension between basic rights and the right to self-determination. In an ideal world, where there might be equal opportunity, protecting an individual's ability to get ahead is easy to justify. But in the real world, even in the most democratic and liberal societies, inequality is a reality. Negotiating the welfare of everyone, or at least the disadvantaged, in ways that don't impinge on individual rights is a huge challenge.

Key figures

Enlightenment thinkers such as John Locke and Baron Montesquieu believed political powers must be limited in order to protect individual rights. Revolutionaries in the American colonies, that is Ben Franklin, Thomas Jefferson, and James Madison, based the *Declaration of Independence*, *The Constitution*, and *Bill of Rights* on these beliefs. Other thinkers include Adam Smith and David Ricardo, who argued the value of competition in free markets, and John Stuart Mill, who fought for liberty for all, including women.

> If one is going to err, one should err on
> the side of liberty and freedom.
>
> **Kofi Annan** (1938–) Seventh secretary-general
> of the United Nations – attributed

Recommended readings

For a concise introduction, try *Liberalism* (Gray 1995). For a bit more depth, I like *Contemporary Theories of Liberalism: Public Reason as a Post-Enlightenment Project* (Gaus 2003). For more on economic aspects, try *Liberalism Against Liberalism* (Javier 2006). Finally, to delve into classical theory, look at *Mill's Radical Liberalism: An Essay in Retrieval* (Riley 2006) or Mill's *On Liberty* (*1859* 2006).

 **Marginalization**

Core definition

The process by which individuals, social groups, and even ideas are made peripheral to the mainstream by relegating or confining them to the outer edges or margins of *society*.

Longer explanation

Every society has a mainstream *culture*, a dominant *ideology* and social or cultural groups that help define that particular society. But rarely does this represent the diversity likely to exist within a society's boundaries. There are always people, groups and ideas that are pushed to the margins and kept there by both subtle and overt processes (see *hegemony*). Take African-Americans as an example. In addition to blatant racism and discrimination (see *predjudice/discrimination*), subtle cultural realities reinforced a marginal position. For years, African-Americans could not buy 'black' dolls for their children. And while Crayola changed its 'flesh' coloured crayon to 'peach' in 1962 to recognize skin colour diversity, you can still find 'nude' stockings that only look nude on 'white' people. Sexist language accomplishes a similar task. The constant use of 'he' in literature was a subtle, yet effective, way of keeping women at the margins of intellectual thought. The exclusion of domestic labour in our economic calculations similarly acts in marginalizing ways by keeping the contribution of, say mothers, from being recognized, and fully valued.

Debates and controversies

Marginalization keeps 'others' from threatening the ideological, cultural, economic and political *power* of the dominant, and is therefore extremely effective in maintaining the status quo. But at what cost? Some say marginalization is functional since it helps maintain cultures and even equilibrium. But the psychological, social, political and economic costs to those at the margins, who can even suffer from social exclusion, can be extraordinarily high. And of course, there's also the range of costs borne by societies unwilling to capitalize on the value that cultural and intellectual diversity can offer.

Practical application

Looking at the mainstream, the status quo, and the dominant is important in all studies of culture, but it won't give you the full story. Exploring the margins, particularly exploring the relationship between the dominant and the marginalized, can expose key cultural values often hidden among political/cultural rhetoric.

Key figures

A number of contemporary writers have explored the concept of marginalization across various contexts. Homi Bhabha explores marginalization as a legacy of *colonialism*, Trinh T. Minh-Ha articulates the marginalization of both migrants and women, while bell hooks explores how relationships between race, *class*, and gender can produce and perpetuate oppression and domination.

> There's a new movement which sees corporate power, government power and police power as merging together to marginalize the rights of indigenous peoples, the powerless and workers.
>
> **Don White** Protest organizer for the Democratic National Convention 2000 – quoted in the *Los Angeles Times*, 23 June 2000

Recommended readings

Marginalization is a reality for individuals and cultural groups across the globe, so it's worth exploring a range of works that covers the various dimensions. I'd start by looking at *Marginalized Places and Populations: A Structurationist Agenda* (Wilson and Huff 1994), *Out There: Marginalization and Contemporary Culture* (Ferguson et al. 1992), and *Global Institutions, Marginalization and Development* (Murphy 2004)

 **Marxism**

Core definition

Political, economic and sociological philosophy associated with Karl Marx and his collaborator Frederich Engels.

Longer explanation

Marx and Engels weren't just political, economic or social theorists. They were social activists and political revolutionaries determined to fight the threat of *capitalism* – a system they saw as extraordinarily exploitative of, and detrimental to, the working *class*. The legacy of their mission has been extremely broad, with 'Marxism' penetrating the political, social and *cultural* fabric of countries across the globe. Some key tenets of Marxism are that: (1) capitalism alienates workers by stripping their creativity and exploiting their *labour* (see *alienation*); (2) workers will (and should) revolt against capitalist exploitation; and (3) *revolutions* (brought on by the inherent contradictions of *capitalism*) will see it replaced by *socialism,* where the distribution of goods is in accordance with individual contributions, and ultimately *communism,* where each gives according to their ability and receives according to their need. Marx and Engels also generalized their theories at a historical level arguing that (1) modes of production determine a society's social, political, intellectual, philosophical, and spiritual character (see *historical materialism*); and (2) the history of society is the history of class struggle – revolutions are needed to create historical change.

Debates and controversies

Have Marxist theories accurately predicted the progress of history? Well no, *capitalism* marches on and *communism* struggles. Marxist theories may have merit, but real-world application has fallen short of the ideal. But ask if Marxism was and still is highly influential, and the answer is a definitive yes. Not only have all communist nations been based on some level of Marxist philosophy, the influence within capitalist societies is also undeniable. Modern conceptions of things like welfare, labour conditions, and trade unions (not to mention academic disciplines across the social sciences) owe much to Marxist thought.

Practical application

Throughout the world workers feel alienated, labour is exploited, and class struggle continues. *Globalization* may have moved much of this out of the developed world's view, but as long as the desire for social and economic *justice* butts heads with the needs of capitalist development, Marxism will remain relevant and applicable.

Key figures

Marx and Engels are obviously key here, but they drew on theorists such as Georg Hegel, Henri de Saint-Simon, and David Ricardo. Famous Marxists, post Marx and Engel, include communist leaders Vladimir Lenin, Leon Trotsky, Joseph Stalin, and Mao Zedong, and political, economic and social theorists including Karl Kautsky, György Lukács, Antonio Gramsci, Theodor Adorno, Max Horkheimer, Erich Fromm, Herbert Marcuse, and Jean-Paul Sartre, and Louis Althusser, to name just a few.

> Let the ruling classes tremble
> at a Communistic revolution.
> The proletarians have nothing to
> lose but their chains.
> Working Men of All Countries, Unite!
>
> **Karl Marx** (1818–1883) and
> **Friedrich Engels** (1820–1895)
> German political/social philosophers –
> in *The Communist Manifesto* (1848)

Recommended readings

For a contemporary overview, I'd turn to *The Meaning of Marxism* (D'Amato 2006) or *Main Currents of Marxism: The Founders, The Golden Age, The Breakdown* (Kolakowski *1978* 2005). While all Marx and Engels' original works are relevant, I'd definitely have a look at *The Communist Manifesto* (*1848* 2004) and explore *Das Kapital* (*1867* 1999).

 **Materialism**

Core definition

A term with three distinct, yet overlapping, meanings: (1) belief that everything that exists is material in nature; (2) that material conditions (economic and technological realities) are central in creating social/cultural realities; and (3) the excessive regard for material possessions or wealth.

Longer explanation

With three distinct meanings, no wonder this is a confusing term. Let's start with the common denominator – all three definitions premise material things over phenomena such as ideas or values. The first definition, which is philosophical, is the broadest and suggests that only material things (things that actually exist in time and space) are real, and that everything else, including thoughts, feelings, and mental states, can be explained as the result of material interactions. You've heard of 'mind over matter', well with materialism, it's matter over mind. The second definition, which is **Marxist**, also premises the material world but focuses on 'material conditions' such as modes of production and technology, and sees them as key to the development of a **society's** social, political, intellectual, philosophical, and spiritual character (see **historical materialism**). For Marx, ideas don't create the material world, the material world creates ideas. The final definition relates to the prioritization of material goods over anything else. As they say, he who dies with the most toys, wins!

Debates and controversies

There's a fundamental debate here about what's real, what's important and what counts. There are those who believe that what's real is what is constructed by the mind (see **idealism**); what's important is ideas and **theories**; and what counts are values and **ethics**. But then there are the materialists who believe that what's real is what we can touch; what's important is the system that surrounds us; and what counts is what we own. The debate will continue…

Practical application

Whether you're interested in larger philosophical questions about the nature of reality, or the relationship between the material world and the world of ideas, or you can't decide between giving to charity and buying a new iPod, understanding materialism can help you both ground and expand your thinking.

Key figures

Philosophers who've expounded the materialist argument include Thomas Hobbes and Ludwig Feuerbach. The notion that material conditions are key to the development of the social fabric comes from the work of Karl Marx and Friedrich Engels. Thorstein Veblen is the economist most closely associated with early theories on materialism in a consumer-oriented world.

> If you want me to believe in God,
> you must make me touch him.
> **Denis Diderot** (1713-1784)
> French philosopher – attributed

> Men's ideas are the most direct
> emanations of their material state.
> **Karl Marx** (1818-1883) German
> political/social philosopher – attributed

> You know that we are living in a material
> world and I am a material girl. **Madonna**
> (1959-) US singer – Lyrics,
> Material Girl (1985)

Recommended readings

To delve into philosophical materialism, turn to *Materialism vs. Idealism* (Kingsland 2005). For the Marxist take, try *Historical Materialism and the Economics of Karl Marx* (Croce 2004) and the preface to *Contribution to the Critique of Political Economy* (Marx *1859* 1979). Finally, *Born to Buy: The Commercialized Child and the New Consumer Culture* (Schor 2004) provides an interesting read on our societal obsession with material possessions.

 McDonaldization

Longer explanation

According to George Ritzer, author of *The McDonaldization of Society* (1995 2004), the McDonald's formula is efficiency – finding optimal methods for accomplishing tasks; calculability – emphasizing quantity in relation to products sold and service time; predictability – customers know what they're getting; and control – making tasks standardized and repetitive so employees are effectively and uniformly managed. And there's no doubt this formula has been successful in the fast-food world (there are over 31,000 McDonald's in 119 countries on six continents). The worry is that this 'fast-food formula' is becoming standard across a range of societal institutions, including the church, the prison system, theme parks, the sex industry, the family, the police service, and higher education.

Debates and controversies

If we were only after economic 'success', the application of a fast-food formula across various sectors of our society wouldn't be a problem. But for all the efficiencies, there are a host of concerns related to how scientific management and rationalization disempowers workers and lowers our general standards. At the employee level, the fear is that McDonaldization represents dehumanization, deprofessionalization, deskilling, and the non-recognition and non-utilization of human capital. As a society, the fear is that we'll come to accept quantity over quality (the desire for bigger and fatter), superficial relationships (employees being forced to ask 'how are you today?' at the supermarket checkout), environmental degradation (huge amounts of waste), and a lack of diversity (malls are malls all over the world).

Practical application

While drawing from the early twentieth-century efficiency developed in Fordism (attributed to the car assembly line production of Henry Ford) and the scientific labour management of Taylorism, McDonaldization is a relatively new term that, as indicated by over 172,000 Google hits, is finding broad application. If you try to think of an example of McDonaldization within established institutions, you'll find it quite thought-provoking. For example, if you apply McDonaldization to higher education, you'd need to ask if rationalization is forcing degrees to be 'sold'. Or whether the benchmark for decision-making is quality education or profit? It's also interesting to explore McDonaldization in relation to *globalization* and the impact rationalization and scientific management are having on the developing world.

Key figures

Critiques of bureaucratic rationalization, which underlies McDonaldization, can be traced to Max Weber, who outlined the problems associated with a move from traditional to rational modes of thought in the modern *bureaucracy*. George Ritzer has applied this quite cleverly to the realities of late *modernity* and has given Weber's classic theories contemporary significance.

> It's the Land of
> McDonald's - mediocrity rules.
>
> **Alex Winter** (1965-) Actor, director,
> and film writer - attributed

Recommended readings

There are several McDonaldization works by Ritzer, including *The McDonaldization of Society* (*1995* 2004). *The McDonaldization Thesis* (1998) and *McDonaldization: The Reader* (2002). Also worth exploring is *Resisting McDonaldization* (Smart 1999). I'd also recommend Weber's thesis on rationalization, which can be found in *Economy and Society* (pt 2 ch 7, 11) (*1921–22* 1978) and Taylor's seminal work, *The Principles of Scientific Management* (*1911* 2006).

 **Metanarratives**

Core definition

Also referred to as grand narratives, these are overarching or all-encompassing accounts, philosophies, *theories*, or stories that provide 'truths' and link our smaller stories together.

Longer explanation

I'll start with some examples: we're all sinners but we can work towards forgiveness and earn our place in heaven; the truth is out there and science can provide the answers; history is the story of progress from the primitive to the civilized. These are some of the stories or metanarratives of *modernity* that attempt to capture universal truths and provide frameworks for ordering our thoughts and experiences. Metanarratives such as these therefore serve a purpose. They provide common frames of reference and take away uncertainty. And what's interesting about them is that they can often go unseen and unquestioned. We tend to accept them without much reflection. But *postmodern* theorists (see *postmodernity*) theorists suggest that we are becoming more and more sceptical. Not only do we question the truth of particular metanarratives, we're also beginning to question the whole notion of metanarratives, which are increasingly recognized as political *ideologies* that legitimize particular versions of truth. The alternative here is to accept a range of theoretical standpoints that acknowledge local contexts as well as the diversity of human experience.

Debates and controversies

The concept of truth is always controversial, so there's bound to be debate around the 'truth' of any particular narrative. But I think the larger debate here is about the nature of metanarratives in a postmodern world. For example, are we increasingly incredulous about metanarratives or are they still accepted without much reflection? And if we are losing faith in them, are the implications positive (metanarratives are, after all, narrow and constraining) or negative (metanarratives do provide common understandings). Finally, isn't the theory of the demise of metanarratives in a postmodern world, a postmodern metanarrative?

Practical application

We all live under the spectre of metanarratives. It's impossible not to when they run so deeply in our societies and are consistently reinforced by social institutions such as the family, church, schools, and government. But the world keeps getting smaller, affording us the opportunity to understand our experiences under the rubric of alternate metanarratives – thereby perhaps breaking metanarratives into 'micronarratives'. But at the same time, a globalizing world also provides opportunities for the imposition of Western metanarratives over local knowledge.

Key figures

The key figure here is definitely Jean-François Lyotard, who was determined to resist and oppose any universals or metanarratives. He saw them as highly limited and limiting since they don't acknowledge difference, diversity, the local, chaos, or irrationality. For these reasons, Lyotard saw value in the proliferation of micro or local narratives.

> Simplifying to the extreme,
> I define postmodern as incredulity
> towards metanarratives.
>
> Jean-François Lyotard (1924-1998)
> French philosopher – in
> The Postmodern Condition: A Report
> on Knowledge (1984)

Recommended readings

Lyotard explores this area more explicitly than any other postmodern theorist. Have a look at *The Postmodern Condition: A Report on Knowledge* (1984) and *Postmodern Fables* (1999). If you'd rather start with a Lyotard overview, try *Lyotard and the End of Grand Narratives* (Browning 2000).

 Methodology

Core definition
The principals of reasoning by which valid *knowledge* is obtained.

Longer explanation
Not long ago, social science methodology followed the rules of *scientific method*. Objects of inquiry might differ – a *cultural* group instead of, say, a cluster of cells – but research was united by a common belief in the power and truth of science and the *hypothetico-deductive method*. The assumptions here are that the world is knowable, predictable, and singular in truth; researchers are objective experts; methods are *deductive* and *hypothesis*-driven; and findings are *quantitative*, statistically significant, and generalizable. Enter the latter half of the twentieth century, however, and many of these *positivist* assumptions began to be questioned, critiqued, and even denigrated, creating a space for a whole new world of social science methodologies. These 'new' *post-positivist* methodologies premised an ambiguous, variable world with multiple truths; subjective researchers who might be both participative and collaborative; *inductive* (see *deductive/inductive reasoning*) and exploratory methods; and findings that tend to be *qualitative* and often idiographic. Examples of such methodologies include *action research*, *ethnography*, *ethnomethodology* and *phenomenology*.

Debates and controversies
Not much sparks a heated debate like asking a group of academics what research methodologies are most appropriate in the social sciences. Academics tend to use, rely on, believe in, and even be devoted to, particular methodological approaches. In fact, defending particular methodologies is sometimes prioritized over getting credible answers to research questions. Researchers who might see themselves in this description should recognize that methodologies are simply constructed tools for finding answers and not answers themselves. Methodologies should only be judged by their ability to credibly answer the research questions at hand.

Practical application

Conducting research is a huge part of the social sciences. And while debate over appropriate methodologies is likely to be ongoing, I'd argue that once you're familiar with the various methodologies and the assumptions they're premised upon, there's no need to be pigeonholed. Each research question and research situation is unique and various methodologies will all offer something of value. The trick is to be open to finding the approach that best addresses your particular research goals in a particular research context.

Key figures

Classic thinkers like Weber and Durkheim explored ways and means for studying the social, while Karl Popper and Paul Lazarsfeld, two highly influential twentieth-century philosophers of science/social science, developed rigorous methodological protocols. Meanwhile, theorists such as Clifford Geertz (see *ethnography*), Alfred Schütz (see *phenomeonology*), and Michel Foucault (see *genealogy*) have all made significant contributions to social science methodologies post-positivism.

> Who knows the minds of men and how they reason and what their methodology is?
>
> **Walter Martin** (1928-1989)
> US Evangelical minister,
> founder of the *Christian Research Institute* – attributed

Recommended readings

For key works on the development of various social science methodologies, I'd recommend the readings offerred in *Philosophies of Social Science* (Delanty and Strydom 2003). To get into the nitty-gritty of various methodologies, turn to the entires on *action research*, *ethnography*, *ethnometholodolgy*, *hypothesis/hypothetico-deductive method*, *phenomenology*, and *scientific method*.

 **Methods**

Longer explanation

Say you suspect your partner's cheating, but you need to know for sure. Well the methods you might use to gather your evidence actually corresponds to typical data collection methods used in the social sciences. For example, you might conduct a *survey* by getting on the phone and asking your friends if they think it's true. You might *interview* (or interrogate!) your partner. You might also engage in *observation* or use more *unobtrusive methods* like rifling through belongings. And as a last resort you might conduct a little *experiment*, such as setting them up to see if they take the bait. And just like in rigorous *social science research*, each method will have its pros and cons and bring something a bit different to the table. So you need to weigh up which method or methods will give you the most accurate information, which are within your capability, which are morally, ethically, and legally acceptable, and which are most practical for your particular context. Now in our little scenario, you'd probably analyse your data in your head. But in more rigorous social science research, data pools are generally too large, leaving you with a need to use statistics to analyse your quantitative data and developing some thematic schema for working your qualitative data.

Debates and controversies

What every research student wants to know is which data collection method is best and which should they use? Well without a doubt, the selection of methods is research question- and context-specific. And while each method has its strengths and limitations (some being better suited to collecting quantitative data from the masses while others are better suited to collecting rich qualitative data in a more intimate way), one is not inherently better than another. Some researchers might be tied to particular methods, but each method requires rigorous and conscious decision-making if the process is to be managed in ways that lead to credible findings.

Practical application

Research is central to the social sciences. Being familiar with, and gaining experience in, the collection and analysis of data is essential in helping you move from someone who learns knowledge to someone capable of producing it.

> *It is a capital mistake to theorize before one has data.*
>
> **Sherlock Holmes** (Sir Arthur Conan Doyle, 1859–1930)

Recommended readings

Almost all social science methods texts, including my own – *The Essential Guide to Doing Research* (O'Leary 2004) and *Researching Real-World Problems* (O'Leary 2005) – cover methods of data collection and analysis. But for a bit more depth on each approach, I'd recommend *Survey Research Methods* (Fowler 2001), *Survey Methodology* (Groves et al. 2004), *Handbook of Interview Research* (Gubrium and Holstein 2001), *Qualitative Interviewing* (Rubin and Rubin 2004), *The Power of Observation* (Jablon et al. 1999), *Analyzing Social Settings: A Guide to Qualitative Observation and Analysis* (Lofland and Lofland 2003); *Unobtrusive Methods in Social Research* (Lee 2000), *Using Documents in Social Research* (Prior 2003), *An Introduction to Design of Experiments* (Barrentine 1999) and *Experimental Methodology* (Christensen 2000).

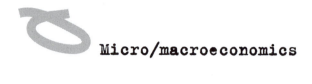

Micro/macroeconomics

Longer explanation

Economics is often referred to at either micro or macro levels. Microeconomics looks at individuals as both suppliers of *labour* and as consumers. It explores supply and demand, and the factors that determine levels of production and price setting. I'll give you an example… there's simply no way an ugly doll sold in the 1980s (the Cabbage Patch Kid) was worth more than US$25, but in 1983, a Christmas craze and a shortage of supply saw people waiting for hours for the privilege of spending ten times that amount. As soon as supply was increased and a crazed demand decreased, prices dropped dramatically.

On to macroeconomics… my youngest daughter recently asked me, 'If the country's so broke, why doesn't the government just print more money?' My somewhat dismissive answer (I was tired…) was, 'It just doesn't work that way'. Well, macroeconomics investigates how the larger system does work. It explores various sectors of the economy, such as the gross domestic product, inflation, trade balances, interest rates and the interrelationship between such sectors. For example, macroeconomics can explore relationships between interest rates and unemployment, or say, exchange rates and trade. It also looks at how the economy influences government policy and how government policy affects the economy.

Debates and controversies

When it comes to finances and money we like to be precise, but as Paul A. Samuelson, professor of economics at MIT, once said: 'Economics has never been a science, and it is even less now than a few years ago.' Economics is an ever-evolving area of study, with *theories* constantly being developed, refined, trashed, and rediscovered. And as it stands, no school of economic thought perfectly captures the complexities of ever-shifting economies.

Practical application

At both implicit and explicit levels, economics sits at the heart of many, many social science issues. After all, money makes the world go round. Knowing the basics of our economic system, and, at a minimum, being familiar with the major tenets of micro and macroeconomics should be a prerequisite for almost all social science exploration.

Key figures

There are several theorists who've contributed to our understandings of the economy, for example, William Petty, Adam Smith, David Ricardo, Karl Marx, William Stanley Jevons, Carl Menger, Léon Walras, Alfred Marshall, John Maynard Keynes, Joseph Schumpeter and Piero Sraffa to name a few. Roncaglia's work (see Recommended reading) provides good coverage of these thinkers.

> The first lesson of economics
> is scarcity:
> There is never enough of anything
> to satisfy all those who want it.
>
> Thomas Sowell (1930-) US
> economist - attributed

Recommended readings

If you want to go right to the basics, try *Economics for Dummies* (Flynn 2005). I also like *Microeconomics Demystified* (Depken 2005) and *Macroeconomics Demystified* (Swanenberg 2005). If you're looking for more theoretical depth and coverage of key thinkers, try *The Wealth of Ideas: A History of Economic Thought* (Roncaglia 2005).

Modernism/postmodernism

Core definition

Modernism – A late nineteenth- and early twentieth-century *aesthetic* approach in Western art, architecture and literature that marks a deliberate departure from tradition. Postmodernism – a late twentieth- and early twenty-first-century aesthetic approach to Western art, architecture, and literature that reacts against earlier principles and practices of modernism. *(In addition to these 'aesthetic' definitions, modernism and postmodernism are often used more broadly as synonyms for the conditions of **modernity** and **postmodernity**.)*

Longer explanation

At every point in history there's been a convention or a 'proper' way to write, to design, to paint, to compose, and modernism was a deliberate reaction to the Western conventions that marked the nineteenth century. It was a time when creative minds felt stifled by the rules of creativity and decided to ignore or subvert them. So artists went about redefining creative enterprise. Now you can try to capture some of the characteristics of modernism, but it's difficult because the conventions that modernists were reacting to differed in architecture, literature, art, and music. So while modern art might be characterized by, say, cubism, modern architecture could be represented by the New York City skyline, and literature by a Virginia Woolf novel that highlights the tragedy of human fragmentation.

And so it was through the mid-twentieth century, until it was time for another reactionary stance. Postmodernism reacted to the earnestness, value, and high culture associated with modern art, but that doesn't mean it was diametrically opposed to modernism. In fact, postmodernism sometimes takes modernism to an extreme, or simply 'plays' with it. It emphasizes pastiche, parody, and playfulness, and rejects boundaries between high and low art (a trip to the Eiffel Tower or a visit to the Great Pyramids – both in Las Vegas – will give you some perspective here). Postmodernism also accepts mass reproduction of art and music where authenticity no longer holds special value.

Debates and controversies

We *really* need a new naming convention. When people first started to use the term 'modern' to indicate a break from tradition in things like art, architecture, music, film, literature, and society it would have made sense. But as we attempted to 'capture' it as its own genre, we discovered that it's an ever-moving, multifaceted target. Postmodernism is worse. In fact, it's probably one of the least stable terms around, with it being used to describe anything from defined styles of architecture to life in virtual reality. But wait for it... I just Googled 'post-postmodern' and got 845,000 hits!

Practical application

While modernity and postmodernity have a more direct significance to social science students, understanding the basic tenets of modernism and postmodernism is important because it can help diffuse the confusion that occurs when there terms are used interchangeably. Also significant is that these avant-garde aesthetic movements do not sit outside broader cultural realities. We live in times of rapid social transition – our media, communications, **technology**, politics, economic systems, and ideology are constantly shifting and it's interesting to see how this is reflected in the arts.

> The postmodern reply to the modern consists of recognizing that the past, since it cannot really be destroyed, ... must be revisited: but with irony.
>
> **Umberto Eco** (1932–) Italian semiologist, novelist – in 'Postmodernism, Irony, the Enjoyable', *Reflections on the Name of the Rose* (1983)

Recommended readings

A couple of good choices for delving into modernism are *Modernism* (Childs 2000) and *Modernism: An Anthology of Sources and Documents* (Kolocotroni et al. 1999). When it comes to postmodernism, two introductory works I'd recommend are *Postmodernism: A Very Short Introduction* (Butler 2003) and *Postmodernism for Beginners* (Powell 1998).

 Modernity

Core definition

A historical period associated with the European Enlightenment (mid-eighteenth century) that captures the shift from traditional 'Middle Age' societies to contemporary societies that characterize an *industrialized* world.

Longer explanation

I think modernity is best characterized by the notion that 'We've got it all figured out' (as compared to *postmodernity* when we realized, 'Hey, maybe we don't know much at all'). Modernity is when we became 'enlightened' and knew the answers – or at least had defined methods for finding answers. When it came to self, we were unambiguous. We knew who we were and had pride in our sexual, ethnic, cultural and religious identity. We had a defined set of morals and values tied to family, church, *community* and nation. And the family, which consisted of dad, mum, and 2.3 children, was our core social unit. It may have been hierarchical, but so was the rest of society. Modernity's also a time when we believed in progress, the opportunities inherent in *capitalism*, and the benefits of *industrialization*. We even had faith in our political systems. When it came to knowledge, we believed in reason, rationality, objectivity, and mastery… and put our faith in science. We also believed in *metanarratives*, or big answers, for example that the truth is out there and science will help us find it. In a nutshell, modernity is a period of minimal cultural confusion.

Debates and controversies

Okay, I might have just presented what looks like a clear depiction of modernity, but it's really just a sense of some of the things that theorists claim characterize the modern. And this is certainly not without debate. There's little agreement on the precise characteristics of this period, and whether we've moved beyond it. Perhaps this is because modernity is such a confusing historical label. It means not old, or not antiquity. It means 'now' but has been used to capture 'now' at various times (and for various cultural forms) since the eighteenth century.

Practical application

There's growing recognition that what we know, what we believe, in fact our orientation to everything, is a product of socio-historical realities. So modernity, which gives much of the world its frame of reference, should be of great interest. This is particularly true as social scientists attempt to capture, analyse, critique and even free us from its confines (see **postmodernity**).

Key figures

The social sciences are actually founded on the economic, social, political and cultural opportunities and threats associated with modernity. So a list of key figures reads like a who's who of social, philosophical and political theory. Parker and Sim (1998) (see Recommended reading below) overviews 100 modern theorists.

> Modernity exists in the form of a desire to wipe out whatever came earlier, in the hope of reaching at least a point that could be called a true present, a point of origin that marks a new departure.
>
> **Paul de Man** (1919–1983) Belgian-born US literary critic – in 'Literary History and Literary Modernity', *Blindness and Insight* (1971)

Recommended readings

Modernity: An Introduction to Modern Societies (Hall et al. 1996) or Gidden's contemporary classic *The Consequences of Modernity* (1991) offer good starting points. Also worth a look are *A Singular Modernity: Essays on the Ontology of the Present* (Jameson 2002), which provides a critical exploration of modernity and *A–Z Guide to Modern Social and Political Theorists* (Parker and Sim 1998).

Multiculturalism

Longer explanation

How do we build or maintain a sense of national identity when we live in a world of migrants? How can we define our culture when 'others' keep entering the picture? At one stage, our answer was assimilation – throwing migrants into the 'melting pot' until we ended up with a homogeneous brew. But as Jesse Jackson, the black civil rights activist, once said: 'I hear that melting-pot stuff a lot, and all I can say is that we haven't melted.' Jane Elliott, a famous diversity trainer, agrees. She says: 'We don't need a melting pot... We need a salad bowl. In a salad bowl you want the vegetables – the lettuce, the cucumbers, the onions, the green peppers – to maintain their identity. You appreciate differences.' And it's not a bad analogy. Multiculturalism is an approach to managing cultural diversity that stresses acceptance and mutual respect for cultural difference.

Debates and controversies

So is multiculturalism the answer for managing cultural diversity? Well, as a public policy, multiculturalism is hotly contested. Yes, it's advocated as a way of caring for cultural groups and enhancing a nation's cultural profile. But those who want to protect the mainstream argue that it threatens the stability of national identity; can alter or weaken the moral fabric of society; and might even lead to the tolerance of gender-based, religious, or ethnic discrimination inherent within certain cultures. There are also concerns that by slowing social integration, multiculturalism actually disadvantages the cultural groups it aims to protect. The result is difficulties in schooling, economic hardships, and an inability to participate in political processes. This leads some advocates of multiculturalism to support a certain level of structural assimilation in which migrant groups are encouraged to, at a minimum, learn the dominant language. Finally, it's argued that some governments embrace multiculturalism at only superficial levels, and this acts to mask the power of dominant groups.

Practical application

In an ever-**globalizing** world, managing cultural diversity will stay high on the agenda with no easy answers in sight. Yes, we're often ready to embrace the easy end of multiculturalism… great food, exotic festivals, fantastic clothing. But when the dominant culture feels threatened, it's a whole other story. Whether or not fears are legitimate, tendencies towards racism are much more common than we'd like to admit. I think Apu Nahasapeemapetilon (everyone's favourite Kwik-E-Mart manager) plays on this in quite a confronting way when he quips: 'Yes! I am a citizen! Now which way to the welfare office? I'm kidding, I'm kidding, I work, I work.'

> We become not a melting pot
> but a beautiful mosaic. Different
> people, different beliefs, different
> yearnings, different hopes,
> different dreams.
>
> *Jimmy Carter* (1924–) 39th US
> president – speech, Pittsburgh,
> Pennsylvania 27 October 1976

Recommended readings

There are a number of recent works that will give you a good introduction to the key issues and controversies surrounding multiculturalism. Have a look at *Multiculturalism* (Kukathas and Schott 2006), *Multiculturalism: A Critical Introduction* (Shachar 2006), *An Introduction to Multiculturalism* (Pritchard 2006) or *Diversity and Community: An Interdisciplinary Reader* (Alperson 2002).

Nationalism

Longer explanation

Who am I? The answer, in part, is likely to involve national identity – I'm British, French, Australian. We identify with our nation and have pride in our national symbols whether they're hot dogs, kiwis, bulldogs or meat pies. We celebrate our national literature, folklore, food, music, religion, and in fact national myths of all sorts. And it moves us. We believe in the values on which our nation is founded and are even willing to pick up arms to protect it. Lee Greenwood, in his song *God Bless the USA*, captures this really well:

> And I'm proud to be an American where at least I know I'm free.
> And I won't forget the men who died, who gave that right to me.
> And I'd gladly stand up next to you and defend her still today.
> 'Cause there ain't no doubt I love this land, God bless the USA.

So here in this one chorus we have concepts of pride, values, history, sacrifice, brotherhood, the privilege to protect, territory, and even religion – key components in nationalist identity and, together, quite powerful in strengthening national unity.

Debates and controversies

So what's the problem with a bit of nationhood? Well, how nations come to be legitimately formed, and what they come to represent, is almost always contested. Nations are created political entities that can be based on ethnic groups, language, culture, geographic boundaries, and/or religion. But rarely is there uniformity within these boundaries. Groups within (and those left outside) nations can be highly *marginalized*. This can lead, and has led, to limits on 'foreign' populations within nations, limits on immigration, racism, and even ethnic cleansing/genocide. Nationalism can also create a climate of cultural *conservatism*, xenophobia, and international hostility. Creating (and maintaining) a nation is not without conflict. Whether it's the American Revolution, the rise and fall of British Empire, South African apartheid, conflict between Northern Ireland and the Republic, coups between Indo and indigenous Fijians, the dissolution of the Soviet Union, or the ongoing Israeli–Palestinian conflict, we're not short of examples of nationalism tied to intense struggle.

Practical application

Arthur Clarke, author of *2001: Space Odyssey,* one said: 'It is not easy to see how extreme forms of nationalism can long survive when men have seen the Earth in its true perspective as a single small globe against the stars.' Nonetheless, we seem unable to move away from our nationalistic orientations towards more cosmopolitan positioning. Nationalism at the level of both individual loyalties and *states*' rights will continue to play a key role in national and international politics.

```
Who is here so vile, that will
     not love his country?

William Shakespeare (1564-1616)
English dramatist, poet - in
     Julius Caesar (1599)
```

Recommended readings

For solid coverage of nationalism's key tenets, have a look at *Nationalism: Theory, Ideology, History* (Smith 2001), *Imagined Communities: Reflections on the Origin and Spread of Nationalism* (Anderson 2006), *Nationalism in the New World* (Doyle and Pamplona 2006), and *Rethinking Nationalism: A Critical Introduction* (Hearn 2006).

Nominalism

Core definition

The view that abstract concepts have no corresponding realities and do not exist outside the mind. In fact, the only thing that a particular group of entities have in common is the mutual name we give them.

Longer explanation

So what do 'white' people have in common? A realist would say there's a universal conception or archetypal standard for a white person and that any person defined as white matches or falls under that universal category (see *realism*). But a nominalist would disagree. A nominalist would say there is no universal white person – it's only an abstract concept of the mind and doesn't exist in reality, for if it did, you'd be able to point to this universal icon of whiteness. Now, nominalism comes in various forms, from moderate to extreme. An extreme nominalist (or a predicate nominalist) would argue that the only thing white folk have in common is that we've given them the same name (after all, they're certainly not that colour). Language, rather than independent reality, is the only thing that provides similarity. A more moderate nominalist (a resemblance nominalist or conceptualist) would still argue that universals are nothing more than concepts of the mind, but would accept that abstract conceptions can express real similarities among individual entities ('white' people tend to be lighter than 'black' people).

Debates and controversies

There are some entities where labels might seem inconsequential and debates over universals less significant. Take a rose as an example. Whether the concept of rose is 'real' or exists in name only doesn't change the price you have to pay for them on Valentine's Day. But it's a different story when you're dealing with people and cultural groups where labels can be extraordinarily powerful. Whether or not our naming conventions are arbitrary becomes highly significant.

Practical application

To be called black, Jewish, Aboriginal, etc. not only creates a sense of *identity*, it creates a sense of identity that's strongly tied to life opportunities. And this gives tremendous power to the labels we assign to ourselves and others. Whether labelling conventions are based in reality or they are nominal and arbitrary takes on increased significance in a highly global and mobile world in which racial and ethnic purity is arguably becoming more myth than truth (see **hybridity**).

Key figures

While the problem of universals goes back to likes of Plato and Aristotle, the debate between realism and nominalism was a key feature of medieval philosophy. Roscellinus, an eleventh-century French philosopher and theologian, is generally regarded as the founder of nominalism and was the first to articulate how language creates reality. In the fourteenth century, English Franciscan philosopher/nominalist William of Occam argued against universals or essences, stating that only individuals, and what they create in their minds, exist.

What's in a name?

That which we call a rose by any other name would smell as sweet.

William Shakespeare (1564-1616)
English dramatist, poet - in
Romeo and Juliet (1597)

Recommended readings

Some good choices here include *The Nature of Properties: Nominalism, Realism, and Trope Theory* (Tooley 1999), *Resemblance Nominalism: A Solution to the Problem of Universals* (Rodriguez-Pereyra 2002), and *Deflating Existential Consequence: A Case for Nominalism* (Azzouni 2006), which explores nominalism and its impact on scientific/mathematical theory.

 Norms

> **Core definition**
> Culturally established and socially enforced expectations of appropriate social behaviour.

Longer explanation

We're surrounded by norms. Some profound (incest is wrong), some ridiculous (platform shoes are out), some religious (do unto others as you would have them do unto you), some nonsensical (asking God to bless a sneezer), some rational (stay away from racial humour), some that are made into law (rape and murder), and some are based in custom (bringing your host a gift). And people tend to abide by these social norms, and not just those that are punishable by the legal system. People tend to follow norms even if the sanction is simply being labelled rude, ignorant or eccentric. You see, norms aren't just somebody else's rules we're told to follow. Norms are actually ours in the sense that they're *socialized* and internalized into us and become part of how we assess others and ourselves. In fact, norms and normative behaviours are so ingrained that we don't often recognize how arbitrary or ridiculous they can be.

Debates and controversies

So what's the function of a norm? Well, when it comes to norms that have been ensconced in law and are there to protect the welfare of individuals, the function is obvious and generally appreciated. But what about the more arbitrary norms that define a *culture*'s social behaviour? Do they create a society of mindless sheep as well as a static model of social interaction? Or do they give us a sense of cultural belonging as well as allowing us to have fairly accurate expectations of others? The answer is all of the above. The trick is for individuals (and even societies) to develop the *reflexivity* necessary to challenge societal norms that are limiting or even dysfunctional.

Practical application

Every *society* has norms. For the most part they are deeply internalized (which is when norms can become the values we hold so dear) and are often adopted without too much reflection. But in an age of mass media, **globalization**, international travel, and migration, the norms that define a society are becoming more transparent. This offers us two opportunities: (1) to question some of the rules that dictate our own behaviour; and (2) to understand and respect the norms of 'other' cultures.

Key figures

Durkheim believed that norms are essential in giving individuals boundaries. He argued that individuals living without a defined set of norms can often feel helpless, lost, and even suicidal (see **anomie**). Talcott Parsons also argues the value of norms, saying that they're essential because they allow individuals to predict what others will do.

> We are in the process of creating
> what deserves to be called the
> idiot culture ... the weird and
> the stupid and the coarse are
> becoming our cultural norm.
>
> *Carl Bernstein* (1944–) US journalist –
> quoted in *The Guardian*,
> London, 3 June 1992

Recommended readings

For a broad introduction, try *The Grammar of Society: The Nature and Dynamics of Social Norms* (Bicchieri 2005) or *Social Norms* (Hechter and Opp 2001). For a slightly different approach, you might like *Multicultural Manners: Essential Rules of Etiquette for the 21st Century* (Dresser 2005), which explores the diverse array of norms in our **multicultural** world. Durkheim's writing on social norms are contained in *The Rules of Sociological Method* (*1895* 1982) and *Suicide* (*1897* 1997).

 **Ontology**

Core definition
Branch of philosophy concerned with the study of what exists, and how things that exist are understood and categorized.

Longer explanation
The main question addressed by ontology is 'what types of things actually exist?' And you may be surprised by the debate this generates. You see, there are different ways of knowing (see **epistemology**), and therefore different conceptions of 'real'. For example, take the category of physical or concrete objects. We live in a world where **knowledge** tends to come from our senses (see **empiricism**), so things we can see or touch are generally thought to exist. But what about abstract things we tend to know about and even use, but can't touch? Are they real, or just constructs of the mind? And if they are just constructs of the mind, are they any less real? Take, for example, properties like softness or pinkness. The ontological question here is whether these things exist independently of any particular examples of them (would pinkness exist if there was nothing in the world the colour pink?). Another ontological category is abstract entities like time, space, and numbers – things we can conceptualize but can't put in our pocket. There are a number of other difficult ontological cases. Some examples here are constructed things, say for example, doughnuts (would 'doughnuts' be real if all doughnuts were destroyed never to be made again?); the mind (do you agree with 'I think therefore I am'?); relationships (the concept of near or far); and of course, God (is faith enough to create existence?).

Debates and controversies
So who gets to say what's real? Well empiricists, who believe that all knowledge is limited to what can be observed by the senses, would have a difficult time acknowledging anything other than concrete objects. But there are competing epistemologies (other ways of knowing). Those with religious epistemologies would say that God is real, while those with indigenous ways of knowing would accept myths and legends. The postmodernist (see **postmodernity**), however, might question whether knowledge is ever anything more than political.

Practical application

Believe it or not, this philosophical construct does impact on the social scientist's world. Researchers, for example, increasingly recognize the limitations inherent in a *positivist* worldview, in which the only things we can know are external and physically observable. *Post-positivist* researchers acknowledge that humans play a large part in the 'construction' of knowledge, and truth may be more ambiguous and fluid than once thought.

Key figures

While ontological debates go as far back as Plato and Aristotle, a number of more recent key philosophers, such as Descartes, Spinoza, Kant, Hegel, Heidegger, Husserl, and Wittgenstein, have argued various ontological positions and debated which categories of being should be considered fundamental.

> The first law of reason is what
> exists, exists; what is, is;
> and from this irreducible
> bedrock principle all knowledge
> is built.
>
> *Terry Goodkind* (1948–) US author –
> in *Faith of the Fallen* (2000)

Recommended readings

To get your head into this philosophical quagmire, I'd try *Riddles of Existence: A Guided Tour of Metaphysics* (Conee and Sider 2005), *Ontology* (Jacquette 2002) or the readings offered in *Metaphysics: An Anthology* (Kim and Sosa 1999). Another interesting choice here is *Four-Dimensionalism: An Ontology of Persistence and Time* (Sider 2003).

 Other

Core definition

What a person considers to be utterly outside their self-image, but is nonetheless a factor in the constitution of that self-image.

Longer explanation

So how do you develop a sense of *self*? Well, it definitely comes from knowing 'what' you are, that is American, Christian, white male. These characteristics, however, only take shape by contrasting them to what they're not. In other words, what they're opposed to or different from, that is not from the 'third world', definitely not those other religions like Islam or Buddhism or whatever that one is where they believe in reincarnation, definitely not 'black', and absolutely not female. So identity is defined, at least in part, by what is considered foreign or alien – what is classed as 'other'. In fact, many *cultural* units, for example people, ideas, social groups and organizations, are what they are, and stay what they are, by processes of exclusion and opposition – or 'othering'.

Debates and controversies

The process of 'othering' can be ugly and narrow-minded. And since the process not only defines the self, but can actually define dominant and minority groups, it's generally detrimental to those labelled 'other' (e.g. natives in *colonized* lands). Another example here is the tendency for Australians to talk about 'real' Australians (ironically not aboriginals, but descendants of English blood) as opposed to 'wogs' (a derogatory term that once stood for 'westernized oriental gentleman'). Or consider titles. All men are 'Mr', while women are labelled not on their own accord, but in relation to men: married 'Mrs', or available 'Miss'. Now this process is often internalized by those labelled as 'other'. The upshot can be ethnic minorities that feel more allegiance to faraway lands than the country where they were born, or women who still feel their biggest potential contribution is what they can offer their family, rather than *society*.

Practical application

We simply can't fight *globalization* – the world is no longer geographically dispersed and culturally segregated. Things like mass media, the internet, travel, tourism, and international sport are putting cultural diversity and 'others' in a shared space. How this impacts on the negotiation of power and the construction of personal and national *identity*, patriotism, notions of supremacy, *multiculturalism* and cultural diversity should be of great interest to contemporary social scientists.

Key figures

The notion that we need 'others' to construct the self has been taken up by several key thinkers, including philosophers such as Hegel, Kierkegaard, Nietzsche, Sartre, Foucault and Levinas, linguists such as de Saussure, and psychoanalysts such as Jacques Lacan.

> Not only were we constructed as different and other ... they had the power to make us see and experience ourselves as 'Other'.
>
> Stuart Hall (1932-) Cultural theorist - in 'Cultural Identity and Diaspora', Colonial Discourse and Postcolonial Theory: A Reader (1993)

Recommended readings

For a broad introduction, I'd try *Social Cognition: Understanding Self and Others* (Moskowitz 2004) or *Identity: Community, Culture and Difference* (Rutherford 2003). *The Myth of the Other: Lacan, Foucault, Deleuze, Bataille* (Rella 1994) will introduce you to key theorists, while Hegel's work can be found in *Hegel and the Other: A Study of the Phenomenology of Spirit* (Kain 2005).

 **Paradigm**

Core definition

A pattern of thinking based on shared assumptions or **collective** awareness that is predominant in a society and affects the way individuals perceive and respond to the world.

Longer explanation

It can be difficult to see what surrounds us. In fact, just as fish have no need to contemplate water unless they're removed from it, we often accept our world without contemplation... that is until we come face to face with other ways of knowing and being. So yes, when you live in a foreign land you will be able to 'see' its **culture** and maybe even begin to appreciate it. But perhaps even more interesting, is that when you step outside your own world, it can bring its hidden paradigms to light. Now paradigms underline all cultural forms and every society has a dominant paradigm or a system of thought that is broadly accepted and seen as standard. But paradigms are often specifically referred to in relation to science and scientific ways of knowing. Scientists who share a particular paradigm have a common way of understanding, practising and evaluating science.

Debates and controversies

When it comes to science, paradigms can be thought of as current 'rules of the game'. They define how science should be conducted (see **positivism** and **post-positivism**) and set boundaries for the legitimate production of **knowledge**. Scientific paradigms are therefore instrumental to rigorous inquiry, but they can also limit our ability to 'think outside the box'. Broader cultural paradigms are similar. They offer common frameworks for knowing, but can exclude other ways of knowing and being, thereby marginalizing those whose beliefs and values sit outside the dominant framework.

Practical application

Two major cultural shifts are bringing the notions 'paradigm clash' and 'paradigm shift' to the fore and make this a central social science construct. The first is the move from **modernity** to **postmodernity**, in which many of the assumptions underpinning the Western world are being brought into question. The second is **globalization** where traditional/local paradigms are coming head to head with the dominant Western frameworks.

Key figures

Thomas Kuhn introduced the term 'paradigm' in the 1960s and argued that science sits under larger cultural frameworks. When anomalies that don't fit within the current framework grow too numerous, a new way of seeing and understanding scientific phenomena begins to develop. Since the 1960s philosophers and social theorists, such as Immanuel Wallerstein, have applied the term at broader cultural levels.

> The historian of science may be tempted to exclaim that when paradigms change, the world itself changes with them.
>
> **Thomas Kuhn** (1922–1996)
> US philosopher, historian of science – in *The Structure of Scientific Revolutions* (1962)

Recommended readings

The seminal reading here is Kuhn's *The Structure of Scientific Revolutions (1962* 1996). For a contemporary response to Kuhn, try *Paradigms Explained: Rethinking Thomas Kuhn's Philosophy of Science* (von Dietze 2001). *The Paradigm Dialog* (Guba 1990) offers a discussion of paradigms more specific to social science research, while *Unthinking Social Science: The Limits of Nineteenth-Century Paradigms* (Wallerstein 2001) explores the notion of paradigms at broader cultural levels.

 **Patriarchy**

Core definition

Traditionally, a system of household organization in which fathers have **authority** and dominance over their wives and children. Households, however, are now considered only one form of patriarchy with the term more broadly applied to a range of social systems (and the **ideology)** that supports male domination.

Longer explanation

Do we live in a patriarchal world? Do men dominate? Well there are actually a number of societal sectors we can look at here. First is the household. Yes, there are examples of equality within the home, but if our sitcoms are anything to go by, father's still rule, while mothers provide (often unpaid) support. Even Homer Simpson has the right to put his foot down: 'Marge, the foot has spoken!' In the public sector, there are still gaps in wages and job opportunities, and women are definitely under-represented in politics. Violence against women continues, and in certain parts of the world, women have little control over their **sexuality** or even reproduction. Now in its broadest sense, patriarchy functions as an ideology that explains and justifies this dominance and subsequent inequity. Such explanations range from inherent biological factors that exist independently of social processes to **social constructions** of gender that have nothing to do with biological characteristics.

Debates and controversies

There are definitely inherent biological differences between men and women. And as long as these differences remain, there's likely to be an unequal division of labour in both the private and public sectors. As long as women bear children and make milk it's hard to be on an level playing field. But does this lead to some inherent right of one gender to dominate another? Isn't there a way to honour difference without the traditional patriarchal structures of the past or the separatist notions of radical **feminists**? We'll be debating this one for some time to come.

Practical application

In an *industrial* world, it could be argued that the patriarchal family actually made some sense. Husbands went off to do paid labour and wives ran the home and raised the children. But the world is changing. Most Western societies are becoming *post-industrial* and service sector-oriented. More and more women have joined the workforce and men have developed 'domestic talents'. How such structural changes will impact family and other social units will be of interest to any social scientist wishing to explore contemporary society.

Key figures

A wide range of feminist scholars, for example Kate Millet, Riane Eisler, Mary Clark, Mark Kann, Shulamith Firestone, Mary Daly, and Sylvia Walby have explored the origins, impacts, and alternatives to patriarchy. A range of key works associated with these and other theorists are offered in Biaggi (2006) (see Recommended reading below).

> Patriarchy is the homeland of
> males; it is Father Land;
> and men are its agents.
>
> Mary Daly (1928-) US feminist,
> educator, writer – in Gyn/Ecology:
> The Metaethics of
> Radical Feminism (1990)

Recommended readings

Some good choices here include *History Matters: Patriarchy and the Challenge of Feminism* (Bennett 2006), *The Gender Knot: Unravelling Our Patriarchal Legacy* (Johnson 1997), and *The Rule of Mars: Readings on the Origins, History and Impact of Patriarchy* (Biaggi 2006). I also like the the short multicultural stories and essays offered in *Women in Patriarchy: Cross-Cultural Readings* (Jain 2005).

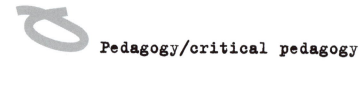

Pedagogy/critical pedagogy

Core definition

<u>Pedagogy</u> focuses on strategies, techniques, and approaches used to facilitate learning. <u>Critical pedagogy</u> is also interested in learning facilitation, but is primarily concerned with exposing the interests involved in the production and dissemination of knowledge.

Longer explanation

Rows of desks facing forward. *Authority* and *knowledge* at the front of the room. Teachers teaching what they know is important, in ways they're told are most efficient. As for students, the rules are: don't question – just listen; don't argue – just accept; don't think – just memorize. Yes, examples of more liberal pedagogical approaches can certainly be found, but this conservative approach is often standard. And many would argue that it comes at a great cost. As Paul Simon said in *Kodachrome*: 'When I think back on all the crap I learned in high school, it's a wonder I can think at all.' Enter critical pedagogy, which encourages students to question social *norms* and dominant beliefs/practices and become independently *critical*. Critical pedagogy explores the relationship between *power* and knowledge and asks if standard educational practices serve dominant interests. Critical curriculum therefore views history as a particular construction of the past that affects our understandings of things like race, gender and ethnicity, and acknowledges the importance of culturally distinct knowledge. It attempts to create broader interdisciplinary ways of knowing.

Debates and controversies

Controversy here centres on critical pedagogy, with detractors stating that critical teachers are anti-status quo and don't actually want students to think for themselves, but to think like them. They also stress that if criticality takes away from tradition, creates distrust in government, and leads to subversive students who are cynical towards the mainstream, it can be quite detrimental, not only to society, but to students themselves.

Practical application

Pedagogy, whether it be mainstream, liberal or critical, should be of interest to anyone who sees gaps (often huge) between (1) the vast array of knowledge that exists in the world and the content politically chosen to be in the school curriculum; and (2) the virtually unlimited ways people can and do learn and the extraordinarily narrow means schools rely on in teaching.

Key figures

While several thinkers, such as Henry Giroux, Donaldo Macedo, Peter McClaren, Michael Apple, bell hooks, and Michelle Fine, have argued that education should be more than just the transmission of fact, Paulo Freire, author of *Pedagogy of the Opressed*, is the most famous proponent of critical pedagogy. Freire argued that traditional education systems, which see students as empty accounts to be filled by the teacher, is not only unproductive, but incorrect. Freire believed in student empowerment and argued against teacher–student *dichotomies*.

> That's two independent thought alarms
> in one day. Willie, the children are
> over-stimulated. Remove all the
> colored chalk from the classrooms.
>
> **Principal Skinner** *(The Simpsons)*

Recommended readings

For a solid introduction to critical pedagogy, try *Critical Pedagogy: Notes from the Real World* (Wink 2004) *or Life in Schools: An Introduction to Critical Pedagogy in the Foundations of Education* (McLaren 2006). To delve into original readings of key thinkers, try *The Critical Pedagogy Reader* (Darder et al. 2002) or Friere's classic, *Pedagogy of the Oppressed (1970* 2000).

 **Personality**

Core definition

Behavioural, emotional, and mental characteristics of an individual that produce consistent patterns of thought, feeling and behaviour and distinguishes that person from any other.

Longer explanation

So what makes me, me and nobody else? There's no shortage of *theories* here. For example, some argue the centrality of traits – that is characteristics such as openness, agreeability, conscientiousness, introversion, extroversion, or neuroticism; Type A vs. Type B; or thinking vs. feeling – are what determines thoughts, feelings and behaviours. But others argue the importance of the sub-conscious and see personality as the product of tensions between primal urges and social norms, or in Freudian psycho-analytic terms, interactions of the *id*, *ego*, and *superego*. Then there are *behaviourists*, who argue that personality is contingent on the environment and developed through conditioning and external stimuli. Social learning theorists also argue for the importance of the environment, but suggest that the environment needs to be considered alongside memories and feelings. *Humanists* agree that feelings are central and argue for the importance of subjective experiences and free will in determining behaviour and personality. And finally, on a different track altogether, are those who argue along neurological lines and focus on the relationship between brain function and personality.

Debates and controversies

I think the main debate here is whether people do have consistent patterns of thoughts, feelings and behaviours, that make up a core personality. At times we've all had thoughts like, 'I would have never ever expected that of him/her' or 'Ever since they started hanging around with ____, they're like a different person'. The argument here is that inconsistency in behaviour undermines just about all personality theories. If environmental, psychological, biological and neurological factors can change an individual's personality throughout the life course, what, if anything, is at our core?

Practical application

We know personality is central in psychology, but how important is it in the broader social sciences? Well, social scientists sometimes sideline issues of personality in lieu of more socio-cultural constructs. But the real world is not nearly as discrete as the one created by academic disciplines. In fact, I'd argue that understanding the connection between personality and the workings of the social world is crucial to holistic knowing.

Key figures

Trait theorists include psychologists such as Gordon Allport, Raymond Cattell, Isabel Briggs Myers, and Katharine C. Briggs. Sigmund Freud would be the father of psycho-analytic theories of personality, while behaviourism owes much to the work of B. F. Skinner and Ivan Pavlov. Albert Bandura would be the most prominent social learning theorist exploring personality development, while Abraham Maslow and Carl Rogers advocated a humanistic approach.

> We continue to shape our personality
> all our life. If we knew ourselves
> perfectly, we should die.
>
> Albert Camus (1913-1960) French-Algerian
> philosopher, author - in
> Notebooks 1935-1942 (1962)

Recommended readings

Two solid introductory works, both entitled *An Introduction to Theories of Personality*, are offered by Hergenhahn and Olson (2006) and Ewen (2003). Other good choices include *Developmental Psychology: A Reader* (Messer and Dockrell 1998) and *Current Directions in Personality Psychology Reader* (American Psychological Society 2004).

 Phenomenology

Longer explanation

Is a rat (1) a long-tailed rodent of the genus *Rattus*; (2) a plague-carrying rodent responsible for countless deaths; (3) a disgusting creature that freaks me out; or (4) the best pet, and friend, you could possibly have? Well, (1) is an 'objective' dictionary definition, while (2) provides historical context. Phenomenology would have little interest in either of these. Phenomenologists would only be interested in the third and fourth options, or the individual, lived experience of rats (which, as in this case, can vary dramatically). In fact, phenomenologists would argue that 'objective' knowing or truth should be 'bracketed' or put aside so that the focus can be on internal processes of consciousness. They would further argue that direct awareness, as in (3) and (4), are the only things we really can know, since all knowing depends on individual perceptions. Phenomenologists believe that reality is always socially constructed (see **social constructionism**) rather than natural, and is therefore unavoidably ambiguous and plural.

Debates and controversies

So is there an objective truth attached to an object (what philosophers refer to as 'noumena')? And if there is, can we ever know it? Or can we only ever know phenomena, or the world, as we experience it? Is reality strictly subjective? This debate is particularly significant in scientific/social investigation where the search for 'objective truth' is directly at odds with first-person phenomenological approaches to knowing that premise perception.

Practical application

Taken to its philosophical extreme, the value of phenomenology might be understanding consciousness, pure truth, or **existential** knowing. But phenomenological approaches can also be quite grounded and offer much to *social science research*. For example, capturing the essence of what it's like to live with AIDS would add much to the literature and be invaluable to both the recently diagnosed and their carers.

Key figures

In the early nineteenth century Georg Hegel argued that the exploration of phenomena is necessary if we're to grasp the pure spirit that underlies all phenomena. But it's Edmund Husserl, the twentieth-century philosopher who argued that phenomena are the necessary starting points for understanding the essential features of any experience, who is most closely associated with modern phenomenology. Other key figures include Maurice Merleau-Ponty, Martin Heidegger, Jean-Paul Sartre and Alfred Schütz.

> *Pure phenomenology is the science of pure consciousness.*
>
> **Edmund Husserl** (1859–1938) German philosopher – inaugural lecture at Freiburg im Breisgau (1917)

Recommended readings

Introduction to Phenomenology (Moran 2000) and *Introduction to Phenomenology* (Sokolowski 2000) are both good entry points for getting your head around this construct. To engage with the writing of key phenomenological philosophers, try *The Phenomenology Reader* (Moran and Mooney 2002). To go further into the work of Husserl, turn to *The Phenomenology of Husserl: Selected Critical Readings* (2003).

Pluralism

Core definition
The recognition and acceptance of multiplicity and diversity.

Longer explanation

Do we get farther with a single answer, a united vision, and a common voice or are we better off with a multiplicity of explanations, a range of views, and a chorus of voices? Well pluralism, while used somewhat distinctly in a number of disciplines, is about diversity, with proponents arguing the strengths associated with broadened horizons. In philosophy, pluralism refers to a belief that reality consists of more than one kind of fundamental substance or element. So things like the mind, physical matter, an higher energy all exist rather than the world consisting of only one such element. In socio-cultural terms, pluralism still refers to the acceptance of multiplicity, but is more specifically tied to respect for individual and group differences. Differences are recognized as enriching the social fabric and members of diverse ethnic, racial, religious, or social groups aim to fruitfully coexist and interact without *prejudice* or conflict. Pluralism here is closely related to *multiculturalism*. In political science, pluralism becomes even more specific and refers to the dispersion of power to varied individuals/interest groups in order to ensure that democratic processes reflect broad concerns rather that just the agenda of the dominant. Political pluralists believe that dispersion of *power* and open negotiation are the most effective means of attaining common good.

Debates and controversies

In philosophy, pluralism is challenged by both monism and dualism, which argue that the world exists of only one (monism) or two (dualism) fundamental elements. At a socio-cultural level, pluralists need to defend the intolerance, prejudice, discrimination and even ethnic cleansing and genocide that have been outcomes in some plural societies. Finally, in political science, the argument is that democratic pluralism is a sham. Power sits with the wealthy and well-educated, and those in power give undue privileges to the dominant of society. Only lip service is paid to minority groups.

Practical application

At the socio-cultural level, **globalization** and migration have seen plurality become the norm in many societies around the world. Understanding plurality's positive association with cultural tolerance/appreciation and open **democratic** processes, as well as its negative association with **marginalization, discrimination,** (see **prejudice/discrimination**) and oppression, should be fertile ground for any social scientist.

Key figures

Key philosophers who continue to debate the metaphysical nature of our world include Hilary Putnam, W. V. O. Quine, and Ludwig Wittgenstein. Horace Kallen, an American philosopher, is credited with coining the term 'cultural pluralism'. Debates over political pluralism can be traced to Plato and Aristotle. More contemporary political philosophers who advocate a pluralist view include Isaiah Berlin, Stuart Hampshire and Bernard Williams.

> We're deeply committed to the
> idea of pluralism. ... A bird needs
> two wings to fly: a left wing
> and a right wing.
>
> Tom Kahn President of the Washington
> chapter of the American Jewish
> Committee — Rahman reception,
> 9 September 2005

Recommended readings

To delve into debates surrounding philosophical pluralism, try *Truth in Context: An Essay on Pluralism and Objectivity* (Lynch 1998). To delve into socio-cultural pluralism, turn to *Emancipating Cultural Pluralism* (Toffolo 2003) or *A World Beyond Difference: Cultural Identity in the Age of Globalization* (Niezen 2005). For a more specific introduction to political pluralism, try *Pluralism* (Connolly 2005).

 Positivism

Longer explanation

Can science answer all the mysteries of the universe? Can it unravel the complexity of the social? Can it make sense of the human mind? For positivists, the answer is a definitive yes. Positivists firmly believe in the scientific method and see the goal of research as describing sensory data through observation and measurement (see *empiricism*). And just like the natural sciences, the social is seen as an object that can be studied 'scientifically'. Inherent in this belief are a number of assumptions about both the world and the nature of knowing. For example, positivists believe the world is a fixed entity whose mysteries are not beyond human comprehension. It is knowable, subject to laws and theories, (e.g. the law of gravity) and singular in truth and reality. In relation to *knowledge*, positivists believe true knowledge is gathered through rigorous, unbiased, scientific, and generally empirical methods. Knowledge that is not verifiable (i.e. knowledge that is theological, theoretical, metaphysical) is not seen as valid.

Debates and controversies

Positivists believe that this rigorous and systematic approach to knowing is the 'proper' way to get at universal truth. But while positivism has certainly shaped sociological research and has been the benchmark for *research credibility*, there is growing appreciation of the authenticity of the local and particular as well as growing recognition of the politics of knowledge creation. Many social scientists now see the world as highly variable and ambiguous, and understand that knowing involves recognition of things like intuition, *subjectivity*, *power*, and worldview.

Practical application

Positivist approaches to knowing still have quite a stronghold in the social sciences, let alone the natural sciences. So even though more *post-positivist* forms of discovery (i.e. *ethnography*, *ethnomethodology*, and *phenomenology*) have gained much credibility over the past 30 years, *social science research* quite often relies on scientific method based on *hypothesis* testing and empirical fact-gathering.

Key figures

While the foundations of positivist knowing were articulated by early social thinkers like Francis Bacon, George Berkeley, and David Hume, the term was actually coined by the man considered the founding father of sociology, Auguste Comte. Comte's doctrine of positivism emphasized the need for science to be standardized and rigorous, reliant on observed facts, and free from all value judgements.

> There can be no real knowledge but that which is based on observed facts.
>
> **Auguste Comte** (1798–1857) French theorist who coined the term 'sociology' – in *Course of Positive Philosophy* (1830)

Recommended readings

If you'd like to jump in and start with the founding father himself, you can attempt Comte's *Positive Philosophy of Auguste Comte* (*1855* 2003). For a broad array of more contemporary readings, turn to *Readings in the Philosophy of Science: From Positivism to Postmodern* (Schick 1999). I also like *The Politics of Method in the Human Sciences: Positivism and Its Epistemological Others* (Steinmetz 2005). Finally, if you're interested in the nitty-gritty of scientific method, turn to the Recommended readings listed under *scientific method* and *hypothesis/hypothetico-deductive method*.

Postmodernity

Longer explanation

There's really no way around it, to understand postmodernity you have to get your head around modernity – so that's where you need to start. But let's assume you have some sense of modernity. Well, postmodernity takes the 'certainties' and assumptions of modernity and turns them on their head. So if the modern self is unambiguous, the postmodern self accepts diversity, *plurality* and even contradiction – gender isn't even sacred. The family has changed as well. The nuclear family has made way for a host of alternatives with values likely to be drawn from a range of *secular*, religious and quasi-religious areas. At a more macro level, there's a profound questioning of the benefits of *capitalist* development, as well as a shift from a goods to service economy. But perhaps the biggest change comes in our orientation to *knowledge*. In the age of the Web, experts have lost their mystique – knowledge is everywhere. And we no longer have blind faith in reason, rationality, objectivity, or even science. In fact, grand truths or *metanarratives* are looked at with scepticism. We accept that truth may be something we actually construct as we make our way through the world (see *social constructionism*). Basically, in a postmodern world, the need for certainty is replaced with an acceptance of chaos, complexity, the unknown, incompleteness, diversity, plurality, fragmentation and multiple realities.

Debates and controversies

There's considerable debate around conceptions of modernity, so pinpointing postmodernity is a tough task. It's without a defined start date or a historical perspective that allows for the retrospective examination of its tenants. In fact, it's a moving target – and one that is sometimes accused of being inconsistent. For example, postmodern theorists argue against *theory*, rationality and reason, but then use these tools to make their arguments. They also argue the death of the metanarrative, which is arguably a metanarrative in itself!

Practical application

There is growing recognition of the emergence of a Western postmodern age that's reaching into all facets of human activity (i.e. economic systems, means of intellectualization, social relationships, creation of *identity*). And this makes understanding postmodernity (and its inherent critiques of modernity) essential for any contemporary social scientist.

Key figures

Key figures include Jean-François Lyotard, who argues against metanarratives and all encompassing accounts of *culture*, Jean Baudrillard, who believes we live in a world of images where authenticity has little meaning, Jacques Derrida, who problematizes reason, truth, and knowledge, Michel Foucault, who explores 'truth' as a historical construct, and Frederic Jameson, who sees postmodernity as a reflection of late capitalism.

> What is meant by 'postmodern'?
> Even to ask the question is to
> beg it, for the meanings given to
> the postmodern are plural and diverse,
> and some would define the enterprise
> as beyond definition.
>
> **Peter Beilharz** (1953–) Author,
> professor of sociology – attributed

Recommended readings

For a good introduction, try *Postmodernity* (Lyon 1999) or *Postmodern Theory* (Best and Kellner 1991). Lyotard's *The Postmodern Condition* (1984) is also worth working through, as is Jameson's *Postmodernism, or The Cultural Logic of Late Capitalism* (1992).

Post-industrial

Core definition

Developmental stage that follows *industrialization* characterized by a shrinking manufacturing labour force, rapid growth of information *technology*, and the service sector, and *knowledge* as a key source of *capital.*

Longer explanation

It wasn't long ago that we moved from agriculturally-based subsistence economies to economies reliant on large-scale production and mass manufacturing (i.e. industrialization). But Western societies continue to shift and as quickly as we moved from the farm to the factory, we're moving from the factory to the office. No longer is the emphasis on the production of tangible goods, but on the provision of services and the production of information and knowledge. We've entered an age where university education is commonplace and often required, an age where you can pick up a computer for a couple of week's wages, an age where the information superhighway – the internet – is available at local libraries, cafés, your home, and even on your mobile phone.

Debates and controversies

As with any change in economic and social structures, there are those who benefit and those who suffer. The loss of domestic manufacturing has decimated many industrial towns and has left more than a few labourers with a need to re-skill. Manufacturing has also moved offshore, with industrialization key to shifting economies in *developing countries*. But if labour-intensive manufacturing cannot be offset by technology or displaced to even less developed countries, the question is whether newly industrialized nations can ever move to a post-industrial state. But it's not all bad. The growth of IT and the service sector means that worker options are no longer limited to the factory floor. And for many countries, such as India and Ireland, the growth of IT has been a huge economic boon.

Practical application

A huge agenda of the social sciences is dealing with change (see *social change*), attempting to understand its implications, to defend against it, to embrace and work towards it, and to predict it. As the developed world moves towards a post-industrial economic and social order, the exploration of causes and effects will provide social scientists with unlimited opportunities for exploration across both social institutions and the *self*.

Key figures

In 1976, sociologist Daniel Bell wrote *The Coming of the Post-Industrial Society*, in which he predicted a shift towards societies that are highly technological, and information- and service-oriented. Around the same time, Alvin Toffler, a theorist/futurist, described a 'third wave' of civilization in which societies would be characterized by diversity in lifestyles, fluidity in organizations, information as a key *commodity*, and an ability to adapt to change.

> The concept of post-industrial deals primarily with the techno-economic realm, and its impacts are vast.
>
> Daniel Bell (1919-) US sociologist – in *The Coming of Post-Industrial Society* (1976)

Recommended readings

I'm going to recommend two modern classics here: Bell's *The Coming of Post-Industrial Society* (*1976* 2001) and Toffler's *The Third Wave* (1984). I'd also look at *The Party's Over: Oil, War and the Fate of Industrial Societies* (Heinberg 2005) and *From Post-Industrial to Post-Modern Society: New Theories of The Contemporary World* (Kumar 2005).

Post-positivism

Core definition
Critique, opposition, and/or rejection of *positivism*'s central tenets.

Longer explanation
Positivism asserts that the natural and social worlds can be understood through application of *scientific method*. Inherent in this are a clear set of assumptions about the world and the nature of knowing. But post-positivists reject these assumptions and question just about everything the positivists 'know' to be true. For example, post-positivists don't believe the world is know-able or predictable. Rather it is ambiguous, infinitely complex, variable and open to interpretation. And in such a chaotic system, positivist approaches to knowing (i.e. objective, scientific, empirical methods) (see *empiricism*) are not only seen as limited, but as inappropriate and incapable of generating authen-tic accounts of a world that we are constantly constructing through our actions and interactions (see *social constructionism*). In a nutshell, post-positivism rejects the very foundations of modern science and in doing so attempts to open up alternate possibilities for knowing.

Debates and controversies
Thirty or 40 years ago, *social science research* was an unambiguous enter-prise that followed the rules of scientific method. The goal was the objective collection and analysis of generally *quantitative* data. But enter the 1960s and 1970s and there began to be a growing recognition of things like the fallibility of objective science as conducted by *subjective* humans; the constructed nature of our world; the inconsistent and variable nature of the social; the impact of researcher worldview on inquiry; the value of the *qualitative*; the lim-its of top-down approaches to knowing; and the political nature of *knowledge* production. And while this has opened up new approaches to knowing, it has also led to a major and often unproductive divide in social science inquiry (see *qualitative/quantitative*).

Practical application

There are a number of post-positive approaches to inquiry that attempt to work within an ambiguous, variable, and constructed world and call the premise of objectivity into question. Sometimes referred to, in an overly simplistic way, as qualitative methodologies, a few approaches to become familiar with include *ethnography*, *ethnomethodology*, and *phenomenology*.

Key figures

Any number of *feminists* (who see positivism as tied to *patriarchal* ways of knowing), social/philosophical theorists, and 'qualitative' researchers have contributed to the development of post-positivism. Some early theorists who led the way in developing alternative modes of inquiry include anthropologist and father of ethnography Clifford Geertz, phenomenologist Alfred Schütz, and ethnomethodologists Harold Garfinkel and Harvey Sacks.

> Philosophers say a great deal about
> what is absolutely necessary for
> science, and it is always,
> so far as one can see, rather
> naïve, and probably wrong.
>
> **Richard Feynman** (1918–1988) US
> educator, physicist – in *Lectures*
> *on Physics* (1970)

Recommended readings

To delve into the debate between positivism and post-positivism, try *Knowledge and the World: Challenges Beyond the Science Wars* (Carrier et al. 2004). If you're more interested in an introduction to the theory and practice of post-positive methods in social science inquiry, try *Research Method in the Postmodern* (Scheurich 1997), *Mindful Inquiry in Social Research* (Bentz and Shapiro 1998) and *The Landscape of Qualitative Research: Theories and Issues* (Denzin and Lincoln 2003).

 **Power**

Core definition
The capacity of individuals or institutions to achieve their goals despite opposition from others.

Longer explanation
When it comes to power there are three things worth considering: (1) the nature of power; (2) who has it; and (3) how it's wielded. So what is the nature of power? Well, since power can bring about both positive and negative change, it has the potential to be both constraining and enabling. It's also considered both relational and reciprocal. Someone with power has that power over someone else, therefore making it relational. And generally both parties have some (albeit often unequal) level of power. For example, teachers can exercise power over students through things like humiliation, detention, and suspension. But students are not powerless. In fact, they can reciprocate by making the life of a teacher a living hell. So does this mean everyone has power? Well, we tend to think of the powerful as those with legitimate *authority* (e.g. government officers, police, teachers and parents). Power is also seen to rest with the elite or ruling *class* as well as with those with certain skills, expertise, and *knowledge*. But if power is relational and reciprocal, then through various means of resistance everyone (e.g. general citizens, the working class, students, and children) can exercise a degree of power and control. As Foucault said, 'Power is everywhere … because it comes from everywhere' (1980). Perhaps this is because power can be wielded in so many ways (i.e. violence, coercion, manipulation, guilt, shame, money, persuasion, tradition, charisma, rewards, discourse and knowledge).

Debates and controversies
Traditional notions of power have centred on top-down means of control over others. But our understanding of power has shifted and, in fact, broadened. Power is now understood as something that is exchanged in just about every interaction within our complex social order.

Practical application

Nothing is more central to understanding social interaction than power. From the power of an infant's scream, to the power a nation has in going to war, the complexity of all social interactions cannot be understood without deep exploration of this central construct.

Key figures

Key figures here include Weber, who saw power as key to understanding **social stratification** and the organization of social action, C. Wright Mills, who explored societies' power elite (those at the helm of government, business and trade), Gramsci, who explored the exercise of power through the dissemination of particular **ideologies** (see **hegemony**), Talcott Parsons, who explored the enabling side of power, Foucault, who explored the relationship between power and knowledge and saw power as a complex strategic exchange, and Steven Lukes, who argues that control comes from decision-making power, non-decision-making power and ideological power.

> To deny we need and want power is
> to deny that we hope to be effective.
>
> **Liz Smith** (1923–) US journalist,
> gossip columnist – attributed

Recommended readings

Solid introductory works here are *Power* (Scott 2001) and *Power. A Reader* (Haugaard 2002). If you'd like to delve into particular theorists with more depth, you might like to have a look at Weber's *Economy and Society* (pt I, ch 3) (*1921–22* 1978), Mills' *The Power Elite* (*1956* 2000), Foucault's *Power/ Knowledge: Selected Interviews and Other Writings* (1980) *or Language and Hegemony in Gramsci* (Ives 2004).

Pragmatism

> ## Core definition
> A doctrine holding that truth and value can only be determined by practical application and consequences.

Longer explanation

Philosophy isn't usually described as 'down to earth', but pragmatism, which arose from the USA in the early twentieth century, attempts to get philosophers' heads out of the clouds and into the real world where consequences, and not abstract speculation, is what counts. In fact, William James, a founding father of pragmatism, expressed his frustration with philosophy's preoccupation with transcendent **knowledge** and questions that have no verifiable answer or practical application. He's said to have quipped, 'If a man's good for nothing else, he can at least teach philosophy'. Pragmatism attempts to be practical and asks why we should even consider an issue if its potential understanding won't make a difference in the real world. Pragmatism argues that significance, value and even truth are determined by consequences or utility. Truth is plural, contextual and relative to purposes of inquiry. In fact, for pragmatists, knowledge and truth are not ideal or fixed conceptions of reality, but a means for dealing with it effectively.

Debates and controversies

In addition to broad critiques of its supposed 'Americaness', the main point of controversy here is that pragmatism can justify any belief or action on the grounds of 'usefulness'. In fact, pragmatism has been cited as a justification for various acts of discrimination, aggression, and imperialism. Proponents of pragmatism, however, suggest that this only occurs due to misinterpretations of the doctrine and would argue that pragmatist goals should not go against the public good.

Practical application

Over the past decades, pragmatism has regained some of its popular appeal. In our **postmodern** (see **postmodernity**), **post-structural** world, there's a growing recognition of reality as complex, diverse, **plural**, fragmented, contextual and even constructed (see *social constructionism*). We no longer accept grand theories or *metanarratives* and we question traditional notions of truth – all of this sits quite well with pragmatist doctrine that premises the applied over the abstract.

Key figures

Generally seen as an American philosophical movement, founding fathers include Charles S. Peirce and William James, whose orientations to pragmatism were quite distinct. Peirce, who coined the term, was interested in developing a general theory of scientific knowledge and believed that theoretical claims should be tied to verification. James, on the other hand, was interested in the intersection of truth with other areas of human experience, such as beliefs and values. Other pragmatists include philosopher of education John Dewey and social psychologist George Herbert Mead.

> Europe, in legend, has always been the home of subtle philosophical discussion; America was the land of grubby pragmatism.
>
> *Daniel Bell* (1919-) US sociologist – in *The End of Ideology* (1960)

Recommended readings

There are several excellent readers that can introduce you to this philosophical area and its key theorists. Try *Pragmatism: A Reader* (Menand 1997), *Pragmatism, Old and New: Selected Writings* (Haack 2006) *and A Companion to Pragmatism* (Shook and Margolis 2006). If you're interested in the theory of William James, his key work, *Pragmatism* (*1931* 2005), is actually quite accessible.

Praxis

Core definition

The process by which a *theory* becomes part of lived experience and empowers individuals to become *critically* conscious beings.

Longer explanation

Marx once said, 'philosophers have only interpreted the world … the point, however, is to change it' (1845). And this is precisely the goal of praxis – to bridge the gap between knowledge and action. Praxis takes theory beyond intellectualization and reflectively grounds it in experience. In *Marxist* theory, praxis is considered creative activity (as distinct from exploited *labour*) that helps construct an individual's world. The capacity for praxis is seen as central to human liberation. Marxists therefore argue that praxis should be the goal of all philosophy. Praxis is also central in education where it's used to denote learning that goes beyond rote memorization and simple concept understanding. The goal of educational praxis is to engage in experiential leaning where theories are 'lived', reflected upon, and modified in ongoing cycles. At its most *radical* (see *critical/radical*), educational praxis leads to personal transformation which develops *critical* perspectives, self-determination, and liberation. Finally, in the religious sector, praxis refers to the lived or felt experience of God or the divine, and not just intellectual understanding.

Debates and controversies

It's hard to deny the importance of praxis. Of course theory needs to be grounded in the real world. What good is intellectualization if we don't live it, or if it makes absolutely no difference to the human condition? But then again, if the need for praxis is so evident, why are we surrounded by so much empty theory, such as endless political rhetoric, education systems based on rote memorization, and churches full of hypocrisy?

Practical application

The social sciences are certainly not short of theory. And while action and change may be the end goal, it doesn't always happen. Ironically, this makes praxis itself easier in theory than in practice. Nowhere is this more evident than in *social science research* where the aim of generated **knowledge** is often problem alleviation or situation improvement. Inquiry, however, often stops at the building of knowledge without feasible change strategies or commitment to action. Dedication to praxis, designed to bridge this gap, is a worthwhile goal in all inquiry.

Key figures

While Aristotle was one of the first theorists to recognize various types of knowledge, including theoretical (which leads to truth), poetical (which leads to production) and practical (which leads to action), Marx is most closely associated with attempts to link theory with political action. Paulo Freire is also instrumental here, particularly in his quest for **critical pedagogy** (see **pedagogy/critical pedagogy**), where education has the potential to lead to human liberation.

> However much you are read in theory,
> if thou hast no practice
> thou art ignorant.
>
> **Muslih-uddin Sa'di** (1184-1292) Persian
> poet, author – in *The Gulistan* (1256)

Recommended readings

For a good introduction to various philosophical theories of praxis, including those of Marx, turn to *The Praxis and Action: Contemporary Philosophies of Human Activity* (Bernstein 1999). For more on educational praxis, try Freire's *Pedagogy of the Oppressed* (*1970* 2000) or *Liberating Praxis: Paulo Freire's Legacy for Radical Education and Politics* (Mayo 2004). If you're interested in the link between social science inquiry and action, try *Transforming Social Inquiry, Transforming Social Action* (Sherman and Torbert 2000).

Prejudice/discrimination

Core definition

Prejudice refers to judgements (usually adverse) about an individual or group based on limited **knowledge** and/or stereotypes. Discrimination is the unfair treatment of a person or group based on such prejudice.

Longer explanation

The easiest people to understand, the easiest to have empathy for, and the easiest to get along with tend to be those who are most like us. For any number reasons (e.g. fear of others, the need to elevate our own status, **socialization**, perceived/actual threat, quests for **power**, competition, patriotism/national pride, and religious conviction), we humans categorize, generalize, stereotype, and discriminate against any individual or group we've been able to label and externalize. The history of humanity is thus riddled with prejudice based on race, gender, **class**, age, appearance, religion, ethnicity, and **sexuality** with discriminatory practices ranging from avoidance to genocide.

Debates and controversies

There's no doubt that tremendous amounts of human suffering can be traced to prejudice and discrimination, but can we manage to make our way through the complexity of the social world without the short-cuts offered to us by our prejudices? For example, remember/imagine the first time you walked into a large lecture theatre. It's simply impossible to gather the data necessary to judge each and every person on their merits, so you cast your eye over the crowd and quickly (and generally without malice) judge your peers on the basis of external characteristic like age, gender, race, class, and appearance. And you do this in order to decide where to sit, who to talk to, and who to get to know. Such discriminatory practices happen everyday, often at an unconscious level. So perhaps rather than calls to eradicate prejudice and discrimination, there's a need to manage our use of these 'short-cuts' in ways that avoid/minimize human suffering.

Practical application

When it comes to prejudice and discrimination a *globalizing* world is a two-edged sword. On one edge, a variety of fluid boundaries hopefully means we can become less fearful of '*others*'. On the flip side, however, a shrinking world means that our ability to come into contact and conflict with '*others*' increases. Given this rapid *social change*, the management of prejudice and discrimination continues to be one of the biggest social challenges we face.

Key figures

While theorists such as Gordon Allport have directly contributed to our knowledge of prejudice and discrimination, these themes are quite foundational in the social sciences. To that end, any number of theorists, including Enlightenment thinkers, *Marxists*, colonial theorists, *cultural theorists*, *feminists*, queer theorists and *post-structuralists* (see *structuralism/post-structuralism*) have all contributed to our understanding of these pervasive concepts.

> Oh look. It's Mr. Homer, my favorite
> customer. Please feel free to flip
> through my Playdudes and eat my
> raw bacon and tell me to go back
> to some country I'm not actually from.
>
> **Apu Nahasapeemapetilon** (*The Simpsons*)

Recommended readings

A good way into this topic is through anthologies or readers. I'd recommend *Understanding Prejudice and Discrimination* (Plous 2002), *Stereotypes and Prejudice: Essential Readings* (Stangor 2000), and *On the Nature of Prejudice: Fifty Years after Allport* (Dovido et al. 2005). *The Psychology of Prejudice and Discrimination* (Whitley and Kite 2005) also provides a good overview of these concepts.

Protestant ethic

Core definition

Principles of Protestantism (particularly Calvinism) that emerged in the 1600s and stressed a disciplined work ethic, thrift, *individualism*, this-worldly concerns, and rational orientation to life.

Longer explanation

There's no doubt that one of the most crucial turning points in modern history was the shift from traditional economic barter systems to *capitalism*. But what exactly allowed this shift to occur? How was it that societies were able to let go of tradition and accept a whole new orientation to economic gain? Well, Weber argued that religious ideas can help develop an economic system's ethos and actually facilitate the system's evolution. In particular, he believed that the Protestant ethic was instrumental in encouraging individuals to apply themselves rationally to capitalist work. For example, a key tenet of Protestantism is predestination or that only a small number of people are chosen for salvation. Protestants felt that hard work in the service of God was a way of assuring they were indeed predestined for salvation. Any wealth accumulated through this work, as long as it was not squandered hedonistically, was seen as just reward for one's efforts. Protestants also believed that God assigns occupations, and that pursuing one's calling demands a methodical and disciplined approach to life. For Weber, this valuing of *rationalism* along with a material orientation are central to a capitalist spirit. In fact, Weber argued that early capitalist development was more successful in Protestant nations than those dominated by the Catholic faith where there was a completely different orientation to both work and wealth.

Debates and controversies

Weber's thesis on the rise of capitalism is often contrasted with *Marxist* theories on *social change* – that change is the product of conflict of opposites (*dialectic* processes), and that economic systems are what define a society's *cultural* and religious forms (economic *determinism*). But while Weber did put forth a distinct and controversial approach to understanding the psychological preconditions fundamental to economic change, he saw capitalism as a product of multiple forces and argued against any simple reductionist accounts of its development.

Practical application
Developing countries are relying on capitalism to take them to **developed nation** status. Weber reminds us that the imposition of any economic system needs to occur in conjunction with consideration of cultural and religious forces. Understanding the ethos of a culture and how that ethos can impact on shifting economic realities is as current in our developing world as it was in Weber's time.

Key figures
The key figure here is unquestionably Max Weber, whose work *The Protestant Ethic and the Spirit of Capitalism* (*1905* 2003) articulated his thesis on capitalism's origins.

> The three great elements of modern civilization: gunpowder, printing, and the Protestant religion.
>
> **Thomas Carlyle** (1795–1881) Scottish essayist, historian – in *The State of German Literature* (1827)

Recommended readings
A good place to start is *The Protestant Ethic Turns 100: Essays on the Centenary of the Weber Thesis* (Swatos and Kaelber 2005) or *Weber's Protestant Ethic: Origins, Evidence, Contexts* (Lehman and Roth 1995). I also like Tawney's classic historical overview *Religion and the Rise of Capitalism* (*1926* 1998) or the more contemporary *Religion and the Transformations of Capitalism* (Roberts 1995). Of course Weber's original thesis, *The Protestant Ethic and the Spirit of Capitalism* (*1905* 2003) is also worth a look.

Qualitative/quantitative

Core definition

Qualitative refers to descriptive characteristics rather than numerical measurements. Quantitative refers to numerical measurements rather than descriptive characteristics.

Longer explanation

One of the greatest divides in *social science research* is the one that exists between the qualitative and quantitative. Now I'd argue that these terms can be useful in helping us distinguish types of data and their corresponding modes of analysis, that is qualitative data – data represented through words, pictures and icons, analysed using various modes of thematic exploration – and quantitative data – data that is represented through numbers and analysed using statistics. But the words 'quantitative' and 'qualitative' do more than distinguish types of data, and are, in fact, used to describe distinct orientations to social science research. For example, research labelled quantitative tends to sit under a *positivist* framework and describes an objective search for singular truth reliant on things like *hypotheses* and variables. On the other hand, qualitative research generally sits under a *post-positivist* umbrella and is seen as subjective, value laden, and accepting of multiple realities. So beyond descriptors of various data types, the terms qualitative and quantitative often define quite distinct and divided approaches to *knowledge* acquisition.

Debates and controversies

Quantitative and qualitative research approaches are often *dichotomized* in methods literature. But I'd argue that this division actually limits our ability to produce holistic knowledge. The world is indeed complex and the need to see it through only one window is surely limiting. I'd also argue that the division is highly artificial. For example, think about quantitative data. Most quantitative data starts out as word-based qualitative concepts (i.e. religious affiliation, gender, level of satisfaction). These words then get coded numerically (quantified) and treated statistically. But even in this quantified form they still represent real knowledge about real people.

Practical application

It's easy to become either a qualitative or quantitative researcher, but I'd argue that it's of much greater value to work from research questions out. Some questions will lead you down a positivist path and perhaps a preponderance of quantitative data, but other questions should have you considering post-positivist approaches to research and see you dealing with levels of complexity that might be best captured through qualitative data. Of course another logical possibility is recognizing that is doesn't have to be either/or. You have the option of combining the power of words with the authority of numbers.

> *Not everything that can be counted counts, and not everything that counts can be counted.*
>
> ***Albert Einstein*** (1879–1955)
> German-born US theoretical physicist –
> sign hanging on Einstein's office
> door at Princeton

Recommended readings

To delve into qualitative approaches in social science research, try *The Sage Handbook of Qualitative Research* (Denzin and Lincoln 2005) or *Designing Qualitative Research* (Marshall and Rossman 2006). For an introduction to quantitative approaches, see *Quantitative Research Methods in the Social Sciences* (Maxim 1999) or *Quantitative Methods in Social Science* (Gorard 2003). To explore mixed methods, try *Research Design: Qualitative, Quantitative, and Mixed Methods Approaches* (Creswell 2002) or *Designing and Conducting Mixed Methods Research* (Creswell and Plano Clark 2006). Finally, if you'd like to delve into the debate on the qualitative/quantitative divide, have a look at *The Science Wars: Debating Scientific Knowledge and Technology* (Parson 2003).

 **Rationalism**

Core definition
A philosophical doctrine that emphasizes reason as the basis for *knowledge*.

Longer explanation
We humans have an insatiable curiosity about our world. But we don't always agree on the correct ways for discovering and creating knowledge. Only a few hundred years ago, we answered our questions by looking to things like God, scriptures, myths, stories, and legends. But in a *modern* world (see *modernity*), most believe that knowledge is scientific and derived from sensory experiences (see *empiricism*). Well, rationalism offers an alternative to these positions and argues that reason drives knowledge and that truth is found through intellectual logical processes rather than myth or sensory experience. Mathematical knowledge is often given as a prime example (how *do* we know pi equals 3.14159265?) At its most extreme, rationalists argue that reason is the only path to knowledge, but more moderate rationalists simply argue that reason has precedence over other ways of knowing. Some moderate rationalists even argue that reason may work in theory, but empiricism may be necessary in practice.

Debates and controversies
So where does the answer lie? With God, with science, or with our capacity for reason? Well, as *postmodernists* (see *postmodernity*) would argue, knowledge is the product of particular socio-historic forces. So for those born into a religious community, God has the answer. For indigenous communities, the answers might lie in myth and legend. For those of us raised in the age of science, it is this that tends to gives us knowledge. But my question is whether these ways of knowing need to be mutually exclusive. Don't we need to use reason or rational thought in conjunction with all the above?

Practical application
Whether knowledge is derived from God, science, or reason, I'd argue that a major consideration of any social scientist should be the real-world application of knowledge. Rational thought, intellectualization, and reason really come to

the fore here, since the power of knowledge lies in our ability to use it in rational and informed decision-making aimed at improving the human condition.

Key figures

René Descartes, the seventeenth-century philosopher most closely associated with rationalism, once exclaimed, 'I think therefore I am'. Descartes argued that all truth relies on intuitive reasoning processes that are independent of the senses. Other key seventeenth-century rationalist philosophers include Baruch Spinoza, who believed that the universe operated according to rational principles, and Gottried Leibniz, whose rationalist philosophy drew on his work in mathematics.

> I do not feel obliged to believe that the same God who has endowed us with sense, reason, and intellect has intended us to forgo their use.
>
> **Galileo Galilei** (1564-1642) Italian mathematician, astronomer, physicist, philosopher – in *Letter to Christina of Tuscany* (1615)

Recommended readings

For a good introduction to rationalist arguments, try *In Defence of Pure Reason: A Rationalist Account of A Priori Justification* (BonJour 1997) or *Companion to Rationalism* (Nelson 2005). For a solid introduction to key theorists, I'd turn to *Rationalists: Descartes, Spinoza and Leibniz* (Phemsiter 2006) or *The Rationalists* (Cottingham 1988). If you're interested in the links between rationalism and other ways of knowing, I'd recommend *Realistic Rationalism* (Katz 1997).

 **Realism**

Core definition

There are two distinct meanings here. In philosophy, realism is the view that particular things exist independently of perception. In political science, realism stresses that a state's motivation is security, wealth and **power**, and not ethical ideals.

Longer explanation

Philosophical realism can be summed up by two questions. Question 1: If you destroyed every material example of things that are pink, would the colour pink still exist? For realists, the answer is yes. This type of realism asserts that universals, like colours, exist independently of any particular examples of them. Realism here is opposed to **nominalism**, which contends that universals like pink don't exist at all. In fact, what pink things have in common is that we've given them the same name. Question 2: If a tree fell in the woods and there was no one around to hear it, would it make a sound? Again realists would say yes and argue that things exist whether or not anyone is there to perceive them. Realism here is opposed to **idealism,** which argues that the external word exists only in the mind.

Political realism takes a different bent and is less about what's real than the need to 'get real'. Realism here is about recognizing that states often work in self-interested ways and that ethical or **ideological** positionings come second to the need for military and economic power. Realists maintain that negotiating any balance of power must recognize this 'reality'.

Debates and controversies

Debates over the nature of reality have been the soul food of philosophers since time immemorial. Yes, an independent reality may exist – but until we find a way of experiencing it without human consciousness or perception, it's a debate that is likely to continue. As far as realism in the political sciences goes, what some call realism, others call cynicism. Critics of political realism are quick to cite any number of examples where **states** have worked together cooperatively with little self-interest.

Practical application

The answers of *modern* science (see *modernity*) have given way to the endless questioning of *postmodernity*. So what was once taken for granted as 'real' is now up for examination. Whether it's the reality behind our morals and ethics, the reality that supports our political ideologies, or the reality of space, time or numbers, understanding what we accept as real reaches into every aspect of our social lifeworld.

Key figures

Philosophical realists go back as far as Plato and Aristotle, but more modern realists include British philosophers Bertrand Russell and Roy Bhaskar, American philosopher John Searle, and Australian philosopher David Stove. Key political science realists include British historian E. H. Carr, German international relations theorist Hans Morgenthau, and American diplomat Henry Kissinger.

> *Reality is that which, when you stop believing in it, doesn't go away.*
>
> **Philip K. Dick** (1928–1982) US science fiction writer – in 'How to Build a Universe that Doesn't Fall Apart Two Days Later', *I Hope I Shall Arrive Soon* (1986)

Recommended readings

For a solid introduction to philosophical realism, I'd turn to *Realism, Philosophy and Social Science* (Dean et al. 2006) or *The Nature of Properties: Nominalism, Realism, and Trope Theory* (Tooley 1999). I also like *Reason and Reality: Realism and Idealism in Pragmatic Perspective* (Rescher 2005). For an introduction to realism in the political arena, try *Realism and the Balancing of Power: A New Debate* (Vasquez and Elman 2002).

 **Reductionism**

Core definition

Strategies or *theories* that reduce the nature of complex phenomena, entities, structures, or theories to more fundamental or primary levels.

Longer explanation

What's the best way to understand complexity? Well, holists like Aristotle argue that the whole is more than the sum of its parts. So complex natural or social systems need to be explored *as* complex systems (see *systems theory*). But for reductionists, the best way to tackle complexity, whether it's in the physical, biological or social sciences, is to break things down to their basic components. For reductionists, it's parts that best explain the whole. Now, there are actually three types of reductionism: (1) ontological reductionism, which argues that reality is composed of a minimum number of kinds of entities or substances (i.e. molecules, or alternately, consciousness); (2) methodological reductionism, which argues that the most fundamental understandings of our world sit at the level of the smallest possible entities (i.e. DNA, atoms and quarks); and (3) theoretical reductionism, which argues that rather than new theories replacing old ones, theories actually go through a process of reduction, with the endpoint being a potential 'grand theory' that can explain all the sciences. As Einstein once said: 'The grand aim of all science is to cover the greatest number of empirical facts by logical deduction from the smallest number of hypotheses or axioms.'

Debates and controversies

In our *postmodern* (see *postmodernity*) world, critiques of reductionism abound. In fact reductionism, which has been instrumental in modern scientific discovery and continues to be influential in understanding complexity, has a quite negative connotation. Reductionism now infers a tendency to ignore chaos and complexity, to ignore context, to oversimplify, to deny the social and social-psychological, and in fact, to belittle what it means to be 'human'.

Practical application

While debates over reductionism can be seen as philosophical, it's actually a debate social science researchers engage in at the level of **methodology**. **Positivist** researchers, who follow the rules of **scientific method** or, more specifically, **hypothetico-deductive method**, are often critiqued as being overly reductionist. On the other hand, **post-positivist** researchers, who see the world as **socially constructed** and infinitely complex, are sometimes accused of being overly relativistic and adding little to theoretical **knowledge**.

Key figures

At a philosophical level, seventeenth-century theorist René Descartes used the metaphor of a clock to describe the workings of the world. Just as the clock could be understood by analysing its components, the world is best understood by exploring the entities of which it is composed. At a scientific level, any number of natural, biological, and social scientists might be described as reductionist, but it's not a label they would choose to have associated with them or their work.

> Science will never be able to reduce the value of a sunset to arithmetic. Nor can it reduce friendship ... to a formula.
>
> Dr Louis Orr Former President, American Medical Association – Commencement address at Emory University, Atlanta, 6 June 1960

Recommended readings

When exploring reductionism in relation to the generation of knowledge, a good pace to start is *Reductionism: Analysis and the Fullness of Reality* (Jones 2000) or *Reductionism and the Development of Knowledge* (Brown and Smith 2002). For a more sociological perspective, I'd recommend *The Retreat of the Social: The Rise and Rise of Reductionism* (Kapferer 2005).

 Reflexivity

Longer explanation

There are plenty of people who are oblivious – oblivious to who they are, to who they could be, and to how they affect others. But then there are those who choose to reflect – they're willing to learn from the mirror they hold up to themselves. Reflexivity actually takes this process of self-reflection a bit further and sets it within particular *ideological* frameworks. It allows us to explore ourselves as both products and creators of social order. At the level of personal development, reflexivity is self-examination that allows us to construct, reconstruct and fine-tune *identity*. We recognize ourselves as social actors with creative capability. *Ethnomethodologists* (who study the rules used to accomplish daily actions) make a similar argument in relation to social order. Rather than seeing social order as something that exists outside individuals, ethnomethodologists argue that through reflexivity – interactions and conversations actually create order. Now this ability to reflexively create the social is actually a dilemma in *social science research*. The nature of who we are, as well as our interactions within research settings, can actually shape research processes and outcomes. Reflexivity in research is the recognition of this dilemma as well as an attempt to work towards authentic interpretations that take the impact of researchers into account.

Debates and controversies

Reflexivity reminds us that humans are a messy lot, and understanding them (us) and their (our) world is fraught with internal difficulties. As we go through our travels we create ourselves, we create our social order, and more specifically, we create our research world. The question here is if this makes it impossible to step back and research/analyse what we are necessarily a part of.

Practical application

One of the main social science applications of reflexivity is when conducting research. Interestingly, this concept actually cuts two ways. On one side, reflexivity means we can't stand outside what we research, so objectivity is called into question. Yet, on the other side, being reflexive about how we impact research processes is the first step in attempting to control it.

Key figures

Key figures here include Anthony Giddens, who argued that society is becoming increasingly self-aware and that growing reflexivity sees individuals continually constructing their identity, Harold Garfinkel, who explored reflexivity in relation to the construction of social order, and Pierre Bourdieu, who argued that credible research requires social scientists to be reflexively aware of inherent biases.

> The reflexivity of modern social life
> consists in the fact that social practices
> are constantly examined and reformed
> in the light of incoming information about
> those very practices, thus constitutively
> altering their character.
>
> **Anthony Giddens** (1938–) British sociologist –
> in *The Consequences of Modernity* (1991)

Recommended readings

For a good general introduction, try *Reflexivity* (May 2006). To delve deeper into Giddens' arguments on the growth of reflexivity in **modernity**, turn to *Modernity and Self-Identity* (1991). To explore reflexivity in relation to the creation of social order, turn to Garfinkel's *Studies in Ethnomethodology* (1967). Finally, to explore the impacts of reflexivity on social research, try *An Invitation to Reflexive Sociology* (Bourdieu and Wacquant 1992) or *Reflexivity: A Practical Guide for Researchers in Health and Social Sciences* (Finlay and Gough 2003).

Reification

Core definition

The process by which abstract concepts are treated as if they're real material things.

Longer explanation

You might not think you're familiar with the process of reification, but taking the abstract and treating it as if it's real is actually something we come across every day. Consider the following statement: 'Mother Nature cares about all her creatures.' Here we're reifying Mother Nature by treating an idea as a real thing... with a name (note the capitalization), a gender (her), a relationship (mother) and a human characteristic (caring). The same is true when we say something like, 'Religion tries to repress *sexuality*'. Religion is a human-made belief system and, as such, can't 'try' to do anything. Another example is when we say something like, 'Why can't my family be more like the Simpsons?' or, 'Gee I wish I looked like Angelina Jolie'. Well, if your family were like the Simpsons, they'd be celluloid, and never forget that the reified Angelina Jolie we see in the media doesn't look like the Angelina Jolie Brad Pitt wakes up to (that's if they're still together). Finally, consider the statement, 'I work for my pay cheque'. In reality we usually work for employers, and *Marxists* would argue that reifying the relationship between things (labour and pay cheques) masks the real relationship, which is a social (and in the Marxist world, often exploitative) relationship between employee and employer.

Debates and controversies

For Marxists, reification is used somewhat narrowly to explain processes that mask exploitative relationships common under *capitalism* – it is therefore seen as negative. The term is now used more generally, but there's still concern that how we describe something influences what we believe about it. For example, if we believe IQ is really intelligence, and not just a socio-political measure of 'something', then we give the concept an awful lot of *power*. We need to use caution when holding ourselves up to ideas and ideals that don't actually exist.

Practical application

Our world is full of abstract concepts or ideological phenomena such as super-stars, the perfect body, marriage, or family; national identity; concepts of race and sexuality; or things like *globalization*. The reification of such constructs has immense influence on how we as individuals (and social groups) see and conduct ourselves at both personal and political levels.

Key figures

While Marx didn't actually write about reification, twentieth-century Marxist, Georg Lukács, introduced the term as a means of generalizing Marx's theory of commodity fetishism (when objects come to be worshipped – see *commodification*). In the non-Marxist tradition, Peter Berger and Thomas Luckmann explored reification as central in the *social construction* of reality.

> Escape the tendency to reify our
> constructs and treat them as if
> they were not constructs at all,
> but actually all the things that
> they were originally only
> intended to construe.
>
> *George Kelly* (1905–1967)
> US psychologist and educator –
> in *Clinical Psychology*
> *and Personality* (1969)

Recommended readings

Making Sense of Reification (Thomason 1982) is a good place to start. If you are after a more specific introduction to the Marxist treatise on reification, try Lukács' *History and Class Consciousness* (1972), while Berger and Luckmann's *The Social Construction of Reality* (1967) offers an excellent social constructivist account. Another interesting choice is *Reification: Or the Anxiety of Late Capitalism* (Bewes 2002).

 Relativism

Core definition

The view that there are no universals, and that things like truth, morals, and *culture* can only be understood in relation to their own the socio-historic context.

Longer explanation

You know what really frustrates me? Filling out questionnaires that force me to answer either yes/no or agree/disagree. For me, very few things are black and white and my answer is almost always 'it depends'. Context is everything. And this is certainly the case for relativists. For relativists, there are no absolutes or universals. Judging things like morals, *ethics*, values, truth, beauty, and cultural practices cannot be done without consideration of social, cultural, historic and even personal contexts. So what is beauty? For relativists, it's in the eye of the beholder (or as one student told me, the eye of the beer holder), and that beholder is undeniably influenced by his or her culture. But what about morals and values? Surely there are some universal standards here? Well, more extreme relativists argue that nothing exists that is abjectly wrong. More moderate relativists, however, do accept certain universals (e.g. incest is wrong), but argue that it's not possible to pass judgement on individuals or cultural groups who accept any practice if it's not deemed inappropriate within their cultural context. Cultural relativists argue that beliefs and actions can only be assessed in terms of an individual's own culture.

Debates and controversies

We humans like knowing where we stand. We like knowing what's right and what's wrong, what's true and what's false, what's good and what's bad. So relativism's rejection of absolutes can be unsettling. For example, for those who believe in the 'truth' of science, evolution and creationism should not be considered equal options. The same goes for morals and values: those who argue against relativism would question the meaning of humanity if there isn't any baseline for judging values and consequent actions.

Practical application

The concept of relativism can remind us of the importance of empathetic understanding. Remember, a key aim of the social sciences is to build broad understandings. But all of us, researchers included, carry cultural biases that can unwittingly lead us to use our own standards when judging other cultures. It's therefore important for researchers to engage in methodological relativism, where researchers attempt to bracket or control for cultural biases in a bid to build understandings that are true to local contexts.

Key figures

Numerous philosophers have argued the case of moral relativism, including ancient Greek philosophers Protagoras and Herodotus, Enlightenment philosopher David Hume, philosopher/anthropologist Edward Westermarck, existentialist Jean-Paul Sartre, and post-structuralist Michel Foucault. Cultural relativism is linked to the work of twentieth-century anthropologists Melville Herskovits and Franz Boas, and sociologist William Sumner.

> What kind of truth can that be that
> is bounded by these mountains, and that
> becomes a lie to the people on
> the other side of them?
>
> **Michel de Montaigne** (1533–1592)
> French essayist – in 'Apology for
> Raymond Sebond', *The Essays* (1595).

Recommended readings

For an overarching introduction, try *Relativism* (Baghramian 2004). To delve into more specific debates on the nature of universal truth, have a look at *Moral Relativism: A Reader* (Moser and Carson 2000), *Fear of Knowledge: Against Relativism and Constructivism* (Boghossian 2006), and *Social Science and the Challenge of Relativism: A Wilderness of Mirrors* (Hazelrigg 1989).

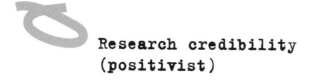

Research credibility (positivist)

Core definition
The ability of a research process to generate findings that elicit belief and trust.

Longer explanation

When it comes to **knowledge** we generally try to learn what other people have already discovered. But when doing research, the goal is to generate new knowledge, knowledge that other people will hopefully learn from and even base decisions upon. It therefore has to be credible – for without credibility, findings simply won't be accepted into a body of knowledge. Under a **positivist** framework, **social science research** follows the rules of the natural sciences with indicators premised around a knowable world that can be objectively and quantifiably measured through defined rules of inquiry (i.e. **scientific method**). Positivist indicators include:

- *Objectivity* – the conduct of research and conclusions drawn are based solely on observable phenomena and are not influenced by a researcher's emotions, personal prejudices, or **subjectivities**.
- *Reliability* – concerned with internal consistency; whether data/results collected, measured, or generated are the same under repeated trials.
- *Validity* – concerned with truth-value; whether research methods actually relate to what is being explored (internal validity).
- *Generalizability* – whether findings and/or conclusions from a sample, setting, or group are directly applicable to a larger population, a different setting, or to another group (also known as external validity).
- *Reproducibility* – whether results/conclusions would be supported if the same **methodology** were used in a different study with a similar context.
- *Ethicality* – refers to a professional 'code of practice' designed to protect the researched from unethical processes. Key ethical considerations include informed consent, causing no harm, and a right to privacy.

Debates and controversies

While positivism (and its relevant indicators) has set the benchmark for credible social science research, an ever-growing number of researchers now see the world as highly variable and ambiguous, and understand that knowledge production involves recognition of things like intuition, subjectivity, **power**, and worldview. With this set of alternative assumptions, the appropriateness of the above indicators comes under question. This has led to the establishment of new indicators for assessing credibility (see *research credibility (post-positivist)*).

Practical application

There are two main reasons for becoming familiar with indicators used in assessing research credibility. The first is so that you can place yourself in a position to critically analyse the research of others. Just because it's published doesn't mean findings should be taken as gospel. There are a lot of shoddy studies out there. The second is so that you are aware of what it will take for you own research to meet the criteria of credibility.

> *This is a rigorous process designed*
> *to demonstrate the technical*
> *credibility of the research*
> *that has been and will be conducted.*
>
> *Todd Wright* Director US science
> laboratory – Department of Energy
> press release, 2 May 2006

Recommended readings

Just about any research methods text, including my own, *The Essential Guide to Doing Research* (O'Leary 2004) and *Researching Real-World Problems* (O'Leary 2005), will take you through traditional research indicators. But for more statistical depth, try *Quantitative Research Methods in the Social Sciences* (Maxim 1999) or *Quantitative Methods in Social Science* (Gorard 2003).

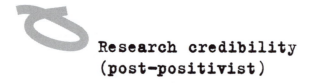

Research credibility (post-positivist)

Core definition
The ability of a research process to generate findings that elicit belief and trust.

Longer explanation
One of the great challenges for researchers who work under *qualitative* or *post-positivist* frameworks (i.e. they believe the world is ambiguous, complex, constructed and open to interpretation and that researchers are *subjective* beings) is having their work seen as credible, particularly by those comfortable with a *positivist* (scientific) paradigm. Yet credibility is essential since the goal of post-positivist research is the same as positivist research – to generate new knowledge that other people can learn from and even base decisions on. It is now recognized that an alternative set of indicators is more appropriate for research premised around a post-positivist world of infinite complexity and multiple truths. Post-positivist indicators include:

- *Transparent subjectivity* – acceptance and disclosure of subjective positioning and how it might impact on the research process/conclusions.
- *Dependability* – accepts that reliability in studies of the social may not be possible, but attests that *methods* are systematic, well documented, and designed to account for research subjectivities.
- *Authenticity* – concerned with truth-value, but recognizes that multiple truths may exist. It is also concerned with describing the deep structure of an experience or phenomenon in a manner that is 'true' to the experience or phenomenon.
- *Transferability* – whether findings and/or conclusions from a sample, setting, or group lead to 'lessons learned' that may be germane to a larger population, a different setting, or to another group.
- *Auditability* – accepts the importance of the research context and therefore seeks full explication of methods to allow others to see how and why the researchers arrived at their conclusions.

- *Utility* – concerned with the practical contribution a research process will have for relevant stakeholders.
- *Ethicality* – refers to a professional 'code of practice' designed to protect the researched from unethical processes. Key ethical considerations include informed consent, causing no harm, and a right to privacy.

Debates and controversies

Unfortunately there's quite a divide in **social science research** (see **qualitative/ quantitative**) that can limit holistic knowing. But I'd argue that **reflexive** researchers don't need to pigeonhole themselves into one camp or another. They should come to value the contributions of both positivist and post-positivist research.

Practical application

Thirty or 40 years ago, **social science research** was an unambiguous enterprise that relied on traditional indicators of credibility (see **research credibility (positivist)**), but new perspectives have created a need for new credibility criteria. Becoming familiar with such criteria allows you to assess appropriately research that sits under a post-positivist umbrella.

> Full information removes doubt and removes suspicion and creates authenticity and credibility.
>
> Lorry Lokey (1927–) Entrepreneur – on National Public Radio, 3 November 2005

Recommended readings

Works that focus on qualitative approaches to **social science research** are your best choices here. Turn to *Naturalistic Inquiry* (Lincoln and Guba 1985), *The Sage Handbook of Qualitative Research* (Denzin and Lincoln 2005), and *Designing Qualitative Research* (Marshall and Rossman 2006).

 **Revolution**

Core definition
Drastic and far-reaching change to social or political institutions that occurs over a relatively short period of time.

Longer explanation
Sometimes change is slow and unhurried, in other words it's evolutionary, but other times it seems to happen overnight and it's revolutionary. Suddenly we're faced with a new political regime, new economic system, new social order, new *epistemology* (way of knowing), or new *technological* realties. Now political revolutions generally refer to a change of government by citizens, often through violent overthrow (think American Revolution). The goal is to change not only the old guard, but the entire political system in order to *radically* (see *critical/radical*) transform society's *power* structure. By-products of political revolutions are often socio-cultural and economic revolutions. Examples here are *communist* revolutions where the overthrow of the political order is intertwined with goals that involve changing economic systems and dominant cultural *ideologies*. There are, however, examples of socio-cultural revolutions (think Renaissance or sexual revolution) and economic revolutions (the move from traditional to *capitalist* systems) that are not reliant on the overthrow of government. Revolutions also occur in how we understand the world (e.g. the scientific revolution) as well as in the technologies we rely on (e.g. the agricultural revolution, industrial revolution, and digital revolution).

Debates and controversies
Saul Alinsky once said: 'Change means movement. Movement means friction. Only in the frictionless vacuum of a nonexistent abstract world can movement or change occur without that abrasive friction of conflict' (*1971* 1989). In other words, all revolutions, come with a price. Whether changes are political, economic, cultural, epistemological, or technological, they all represent changes to structures of power. And while it might be argued that *society* is better off because of revolutions, there are always winners and losers.

Practical application

If I could use only one word to describe the subject matter of the social sciences, it would be 'change'. And revolutionary change, characterized by rapid onset and major consequences, is of particular interest, especially in a rapidly moving and *globalizing* world where nothing seems to stay the same for very long.

Key figures

While there are many social scientists who continue to explore revolutionary change, theorists as far back as Aristotle debated the causes of political and cultural revolutions. Karl Marx, however, is most commonly associated with revolutionary theory (as well as advocacy). Rather than a strict emphasis on political leaders/leadership, Marx's analysis centred on *class* conflict, and more specifically, on exploitative relationships caused by modes of production.

> All civilization has from time to time become a thin crust over a volcano of revolution.
>
> *Havelock Ellis* (1859–1939) British psychologist – in *Little Essays of Love and Virtue* (1922)

Recommended readings

For generalist overviews, try *Revolutions: Theoretical, Comparative, and Historical Studies* (Goldstone 2002), *Revolutions: A Worldwide Introduction to Political and Social Change* (Sanderson 2005) or *Social Revolutions in the Modern World* (Skocpol 1994). For a more global perspective, turn to *The Future of Revolutions: Rethinking Radical Change in the Age of Globalization* (Foran 2003). Finally, for an introduction to Marx's theories, try *Karl Marx's Theory of Revolution* (Draper and Haberkem 2005).

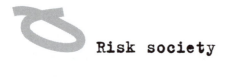

Risk society

Core definition

Societies in which risk (the chance of undesirable consequences) not only arises from hazards outside human control, but from human-made hazards, both of which are recognized as needing to be consciously negotiated and managed.

Longer explanation

Life has never come with a guarantee. Since the beginning of human history, we've needed to assess risk (the risk of our prey eating us, of disease, of jealous lovers) and decide whether to take our chances. But in modern societies, we face a new breed of risk. As well as natural hazards (tsunamis, earthquakes and droughts) and socially determined hazards outside our control (attacks and invasions) we now live in a world where hazards are consciously and deliberately created for the sake of perceived benefits. Examples here are risks related to *industrialization* (pollution, global warming), *technology* (cars, nuclear power, internet predators), scientific advances (genetically modified foods), medical advances (surgical procedures). The list goes on and on. And the need to deal with all this risk can actually create a climate of anxiety or depression. But many of the ways we deal with these states (de-stressing with drugs and alcohol or seeking a high by bungee jumping or skydiving) can in themselves be risky. Modern risk societies are thus characterized by the simultaneous manufacture and management of risk.

Debates and controversies

One debate here revolves around the equitable distribution of risk. Some theorists argue that risk producers do pay for the consequences of their actions. For example, those creating industrial pollutants pay via their air and water quality. Others, however, argue a strong correlation between risk and *socioeconomic status*. Those without wealth often live in the most polluted areas, have the riskiest jobs, are unable to purchase things like air conditioning systems or bottled water, and are even targeted by alcohol and cigarette advertising.

Practical application

There are lots of dimensions to explore here – for example, the government's public policy response to environmental or industrial risk, the idea of corporate responsibility/action, and the social psychology of risk aversion, risk management, and risk taking. Also interesting is how risk and its close cousin, fear, are manipulated by the government, industry, and the media in order to sell everything from elections, to the news, to goods that range from bike helmets to cleaning products that kill 99% of that germs that cause...

Key figures

As a social science construct, 'risk' is quite contemporary. Key figures include Mary Douglas, whose work with African tribes led to the development of a cultural theory of risk, sociologist Anthony Giddens, who argues that the logic of **modern** (see **modernity**) industrial societies is changing from one based on goods distribution to one based on risk distribution, and sociologist Ulrich Beck, who argues that modernization has produced hazards which societies need to deal with systematically.

> The risk climate of modernity is
> thus unsettling for everyone:
> no one escapes.
>
> **Anthony Giddens** (1938–) British
> sociologist – in Modernity
> and Self-Identity (1991)

Recommended readings

A good pace to start is with foundational works of Beck, *Risk Society: Towards a New Modernity* (1992), and Giddens, *The Consequences of Modernity* (1991). For an even more contemporary take, try *Risk and Society* (Denny 2005), *Beyond the Risk Society* (Mythen and Walklate 2006) or *The Risk Society and Beyond: Critical Issues for Social Theory* (Adam et al. 2000).

 **Role**

Core definition

Socially prescribed patterns of behaviour associated with an individual's societal position(s).

Longer explanation

Yes, you have a **personality** that makes you unique. But in our socially constructed world, you're still expected to play any number of roles where behaviours are shaped by normative expectations (see **norms**). As a student, a friend, a son or daughter, an employee, or an athlete, there are behavioural guidelines (sometimes complimentary, sometimes contradictory) that define these roles. Now a **functionalist** approach, which stresses the contribution of a social unit to larger society, argues that roles define (1) how you're supposed to act; (2) how others are supposed to act; and (3) how you're supposed to interact. So roles create regular patterns of predictable behaviour that regulate individual and societal action. In contrast, an interactionist approach, which concentrates on the interactive negotiation of the social (see **symbolic interactionism**) attempts to account for differences in the way individuals play their roles. Interactionists argue that roles are not fixed, but are fluid and actively negotiated through interaction. While we do adopt or are assigned certain roles, we have the ability to adapt these roles creatively or even ignore their associated rules of behaviour.

Debates and controversies

Whether roles are fixed or negotiated, they're often not that easy to manage. Roles can have incompatible demands (role strain) (i.e. trying to be the boss who is both motivator and task master), or they can be at odds with other roles we play (role conflict) (i.e. when an executive is also a mother). Individuals can also have difficulty choosing between various roles (role confusion). This often happens when worlds collide (i.e. when you're both coach and father to a team member). All of these situations demand that individuals become active in defining the boundaries of the roles they adopt.

Practical application

We live in a world of rapid *social change,* and roles that were once clear and unambiguous are now in constant flux. The rules of established roles seem to be ever shifting. We're juggling a greater number of roles, many of which are incompatible, and we're sometimes forced to abandon roles that have been central to our sense of *self* (i.e. getting divorced or being made redundant). For functionalists, the question is whether this has ramifications for our social order. Interactionists, however, would be interested in how this affects the negotiation of both roles themselves and our personal *identity*.

Key figures

Anthropologist Ralph Linton and sociologist Talcott Parsons were instrumental in developing a functionalist account of roles/role theory. Key interactionists who explored role negotiation include social psychologist George Herbert Mead and sociologist Erving Goffman.

> *There comes a point in many people's lives when they can no longer play the role they have chosen for themselves. When that happens, we are like actors finding that someone has changed the play.*
>
> **Brian Moore** (1921–1999)
> Irish novelist – quoted in
> *Sunday Times*, London, 15 April 1990

Recommended readings

While most sociology texts introduce roles and role theory, for more depth it's really worth going to the source. For a functionalist account, turn to Linton's *The Study of Man: An introduction* (1937) or Parsons' *The Social System* (*1951* 1991). For the interactionist approach, turn to Mead's *Mind, Self, and Society* (*1934* 1967) or Goffman's *The Presentation of Self in Everyday Life* (1959).

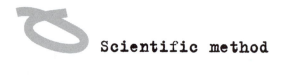

Scientific method

Longer explanation

We want to know things, we want to uncover, discover, and understand. And we want this done in ways that produce credible, authentic **knowledge**. Our goal is to come up with 'truth'. But does truth need a gatekeeper? Well, most think it does. And in our modern world we tend to give this job to science, in particular, scientific method, which provides us with step-by-step procedures for the production of legitimate knowledge. This procedure goes something like this: (1) come up with a **theory**; (2) use that theory to deduce (see **deduction**) more specific propositions or **hypotheses**; (3) gather data – often through experimental design; (4) analyse the data; and (5) draw conclusions that may or may not support hypothesis. It's our modern-day control mechanism that not only allows us to screen those who might say 'trust me, I just know', 'it came to me in a dream', or 'it was revealed to me by an angel', but also offers us protection from those who accept the premise of scientific method, but might practise shoddy science tainted with personal biases, political agendas, sloppy procedures, and/or flawed logic.

Debates and controversies

There are three major concerns here. The first concerns the dominance of scientific knowing over any other type (e.g. intuition, mysticism, or revelation). While our belief in science may run deep, science is still a product of a particular historical period – one that may eventually move on. The second concern is about the discrepancy between the rules of scientific method and its actual practice. Some theorists argue that accounts of research simply retrofit scientific method on top of much more haphazard procedures. The final concern is about the appropriateness of scientific method to social science inquiry. While many social scientists accept the premises of scientific method, others argue that it constrains social research and restricts broader exploration and theory building.

Practical application

If you accept that scientific method is appropriate for the natural sciences, the question is whether its rules should be applied to **social science research** where it is difficult, if not impossible, for researchers to detach themselves from the object of their inquiry. How social scientists answer this question is fundamental to their orientation to knowledge production and their conduct of social science research.

Key figures

Key figures here go as far back as Aristotle, who subdivided knowledge into different areas, René Descartes, who established principles for scientific method, Charles Sanders Peirce, who articulated rules for hypothesis testing, and Karl Popper, who further argued all hypotheses must be falsifiable.

> There are two objectionable types
> of believer: those who believe
> the incredible and those who
> believe that 'belief' must be
> discarded and replaced
> by 'the scientific method'.
>
> **Max Born** (1882–1970) Nobel Prize
> winning physicist – in *Natural
> Philosophy of Cause and Chance* (1949)

Recommended readings

For a good introduction to the application of scientific method, try *A Beginner's Guide to Scientific Method* (Carey 2003) or *Scientific Method in Practice* (Gauch 2002). To delve more deeply into theory and history, turn to *Scientific Method* (Gower 1996) or *Science Rules: A Historical Introduction to Scientific Methods* (Achinstein 2004).

Secularization

> ## Core definition
> The process by which religious institutions, creeds, beliefs, and practices lose their social significance.

Longer explanation

So what's happened to religion? Not that long ago we in the West were surrounded by all things religious, and in particular, all things Christian. At home we put up pictures of God, Christ and the Virgin Mary and we prayed to them before going to sleep. At school (even the public ones) Christian beliefs were reinforced in both formal and informal ways. Religion was also part of the greater *community*, for example, through the YMCA, which actually stands for the Young Men's Christian Association. We attended church every Sunday and it was central to our sense of community. And while separation of church and state may have been the rhetoric, references to God by our leaders, public Christian holidays, and slogans like 'in God we trust' saw religion become part of both personal and national identity. So has this changed? Has *society* become increasingly secular? Well, many social theorists think it has, and argue that as societies become more rational, as we embrace scientific rather than religious explanations, and as we become exposed to a broad array of beliefs systems, it's difficult for any religion to maintain a stronghold on personal and social consciousness. As evidence, they cite political policies of separation of church and state, the decline of religious public *authority* and social activities, a shift in religion as personal choice rather than social obligation, and broad patterns of religious disaffiliation.

Debates and controversies

There's definitely weight in the secularization argument, but there's also evidence that individuals, communities, and nations are not quite ready to abandon religion. This is particularly true in times of instability. In fact, God has actually regained quite a stronghold in personal, social and national consciousness since '9/11', with several religious denominations experiencing recent periods of growth.

Practical application

The secularization thesis has generally been explored in relation to Western Christianity, and debates here are certainly worth engagement. But there's also the opportunity to explore secularization in relation to both **developing countries** and alternative religions. In a world where religion and religious beliefs account for a tremendous amount of political unrest, understanding trends related to individual, social and political religiosity is quite critical.

Key figures

Many key figures in the social sciences, for example Marx, Weber and Durkheim, argued that secularization would be a consequence of **modernity**. Forces, including the development of modern science, the growth of rationalization, shifts in community **solidarity**, and **alienation** caused by **capitalist** modes of production, would be religion's demise. Theorists such as Peter Berger, Rodney Stark, and N. J. Demerath continue the study of secularization in the contemporary world.

> As for science versus religion,
> I am issuing a restraining order.
> Science must remain 500 yards
> away from religion at all times.
>
> **Judge Schneider** (The Simpsons)

Recommended readings

Western secularization is a topic that generates tremendous debate and a number of authors have attempted to capture the complexity of this social phenomenon. Have a look at God is Dead: Secularization in the West (Bruce 2002), Secularization and Cultural Criticism: Religion, Nation, and Modernity (Pecora 2006), Secularization and Its Discontents (Bates 2006) or The Secularization Debate (Olson and Swatos 2000).

 Self

Core definition
An individual's awareness of being a distinct social identity.

Longer explanation
Did you know that when a baby is born it doesn't even know that the thing over there called 'foot' is his or hers? A baby has no sense of self, not even a physical one. But by the time we are adults, we're suppose to know who we are at much more sophisticated levels than this. We should have an inner or psychological sense of self that is responsible for our feelings. This is the sense of self that makes us run, hide, laugh and cry. We should also have an outer or sociological presentation of self – the self (or *identities*) we present to the world, which of course can shift depending on who we are interacting with. Then there's the philosophical sense of self – self as *subject* with a consciousness that allows us to travel through the world knowing that 'I' exist. Finally, for many, there's a spiritual sense of self that underpins the relationship between self and a higher power and provides a position on the self in an afterlife.

Debates and controversies
Figuring out who we are and how we relate to the world has been the goal of biologists, philosophers, psychologists, sociologists and theologians alike. But each approaches the self with a distinct focus. There is little consensus, and controversies rage within and between disciplines. As psychologist and philosopher Erich Fromm once said, 'Man is the only animal for whom his own existence is a problem which he has to solve' (*1947* 1990). Who would have thought 'who am I?' would be such a tricky question.

Practical application
We live in a world where the only thing that seems constant is change. And this isn't easy on our sense of self. Whether it's instability in self image, difficulty in negotiating varied *roles*, battered self-esteem, shaken self-confidence, incongruent self-awareness, loss of spiritual self, or a confused sense of identity, exploring the negotiation of self is central in understanding the social world and our place within it.

Key figures

Key figures cut across various disciplines and include Descartes and Kant, philosophers who explored consciousness and being, psychologist Sigmund Freud, who explored the unconscious, psychologist Erik Erikson, who identified eight developmental stages of 'man', social theorists Marx and Althusser, who looked at the self as a product of material conditions/ideology, social psychologist George Mead, who articulated the distinction between I and me, ethnomethodologist Erving Goffman, who explored the presentation of self, and postmodern theorists Lacan and Foucault, who emphasized the role of language and discourse in creating the self.

> And remember, no matter where
> you go, there you are.
>
> *Confucius* (551–479 BC) Chinese
> philosopher – attributed

Recommended readings

A number of works will introduce you to the 'self', including *The Handbook of Self and Identity* (MacDonald et al. 2005), *Individual Self, Relational Self, Collective Self* (Sedikides 2002), and *Self in Social Psychology: Essential Readings* (Baumeister 1999). Also of interest here are the Recommended readings under **identity**, **personality** and **subject**.

 Semiotics

Longer explanation

What do the letters p-i-g stand for? A pig, of course. But for those into semiotics, there's no 'of course' about it. A semiotician would go beyond the surface and point out a number of things we generally take for granted, like why the letters p-i-g are the designated 'signifier' of that fat, four-legged, pink animal (the signified), rather than any other string of arbitrary letters. They'd also point to the variability of the signified. For example, the word 'pig' could conjure up an image of a dangerous wild boar, but it might also trigger an image of fat dirty farmyard beast or a famous cartoon pig like Porky, Wilbur or Babe. Semioticians would also suggest that the letters p-i-g can stand for more than just an animal; it can also stand for deeper and more abstract concepts like gluttony or boorishness. Semiotics therefore looks at the whole concept of signs and sign systems (which includes symbols and icons as well as words) and how they allow human communication and meaning-making.

Debates and controversies

While semiotics has definitely established itself as a major strand of inquiry in both linguistic and humanities, there are theorists who question its value in the social sciences. The most common critiques are that semiotics (1) only describes human communication and does not offer social explanations or predictions of the future; (2) is of little practical utility; (3) relies on analysis that is *subjective* with no clear criteria for assessing validity of interpretations; (4) ignores the complexities of human language acquisition which make decoding linguistic signs extraordinarily difficult.

Practical application

Signs are powerful things (just think of the power that a glimpse of the Golden Arches can have on a hungry child). Now there are some things we recognize as overt signs and symbols, for example a flag or logo. But semiotics reminds us that almost everything around us is part of a sign system. How our signs are created and used by various institutions, such as governments, the media, and marketing sectors, to manipulate our social consciousness is highly applicable in the social sciences.

Key figures

In the early twentieth century, semiotics was developed by US pragmatist Charles Peirce, who identified three types of sign: icons, which resemble what they signify; indexes, which are indicative of something (e.g. spots signifying measles); and symbols, which are arbitrary. In Europe, Swiss linguist Ferdinand de Saussure argued that signs are composed of signifiers (representations like words or symbols) and signified (mental concepts). Another key figure here is Roland Barthes, who developed social semiotics (the study of social and cultural signs) in the mid-twentieth century.

> In the rough, a symbol is a sign
> that stands for something. ...
> Before a noise, etc., may become
> a symbol, something must exist
> for the symbol to symbolize.
>
> **Alfred Korzybski** (1879–1950)
> Father of general semantics –
> in *Science and Sanity* (1933)

Recommended readings

For a clear introduction to general semiotics, I'd turn to either *Semiotics: The Basics* (Chandler 2004) or *Introducing Semiotics* (Cobley 2005). For an introduction to social semiotics, try *Introducing Social Semiotics* (van Leeuwen 2004). If you'd like to delve into seminal writings, turn to *Classic Readings in Semiotics* (Perron and Danesi 2003).

 **Sexuality**

Core definition

Sexual interests and behaviours that includes physiological, psychological, social, cultural, emotional and spiritual dimensions.

Longer explanation

In 2000, the Bloodhound Gang reminded us that, 'You and me baby ain't nothin' but mammals, so let's do it like they do on the Discovery Channel'. If only it were that simple. But for us humans, who tend to be social, religious, political, power hungry, *prejudiced*, judgemental, manipulative, emotional, guilt-ridden, confused, and self-reflective, it was never going to be without complication. Yes, human sexuality involves the relatively straightforward physiological dimensions of the sex act, but it also includes the interplay of all the social and psychological dimensions unique to humans. So for us, sexuality encompasses: sexual orientations and *identity* driven by both biological and social forces; the scope of acceptable and unacceptable sexual behaviours which are often tied to morality, *cultural* and religious *norms*, and legal sanctions; as well as the more psycho-social dimensions of sex such as partner expectations and our need for things like love, fear, security, *power*, and control.

Debates and controversies

As 'mammals', our sexuality is indeed based on primal instinct and is something we think of as personal rather than cultural or political. But as intellectual, social, political, and religious mammals, our sexuality is much more. In fact, in our *socially constructed* world, many argue that sexuality is not just a product of cultural forces, but that it's actually used by governments, religious institutions, communities and even families to both define us (e.g. as normal or deviant) as well as control us.

Practical application

The range of social science applications here is virtually endless and as a start includes things like sexual development, identity, orientations and lifestyles; the relationship between sexuality and social institutions (such as the family, the church, and the law); social and cultural norms, traditions and rituals; biological vs. socially constructed sexual stereotypes and sexual deviance; pornography; prostitution; homophobia; gay rights; sexual harassment and abuse; **patriarchy**; queer theory; the role of the media and advertising; the **body**; sexism; **feminism**; and cross-cultural practices. The list goes on and on.

Key figures

Any number of theorists have engaged in wide-ranging debates on sexuality. For example, Freud argued that sexual drives are innate in infants, while Alfred Kinsey was the first to survey Americans about their sexual desire and activities. Foucault explored discourses of sexuality and how they regulate populations, while any number of feminists have explored sexuality and gender in a patriarchal world (see Key figures under **feminism** and patriarchy).

> Understand that sexuality is
> as wide as the sea.
>
> **Derek Jarman** (1942–1994)
> British filmmaker, artist, author –
> in '1940s', At Your Own Risk:
> A Saint's Testament (1992)

Recommended readings

For contemporary texts that cover a range of issues, I'd turn to *Human Sexuality in a World of Diversity* (Rathus et al. 2004) or *Understanding Human Sexuality* (Hyde and Delamater 2006). If you're after a bit more theoretical depth, turn to *Sexualities: Identities, Behaviours, and Society* (Kimmel and Plante 2004), *Sex Matters: The Sexuality and Society Reader* (Stombler et al. 2006), or *Culture, Society and Sexuality: A Reader* (Aggleton 2006).

 Social change

Core definition

The alteration, adaptation, modification or transformation of social structures, social institutions, socio-cultural characteristics, social relations or socio-political ideology.

Longer explanation

Change: some fear and loathe it and actively fight against it, others welcome it and attempt to advocate and fight for it. Either way, nothing ever stays the same. Social change in unavoidable and much of the social sciences is dedicated to understanding its causes, nature, rate, direction, and implications. Now, social change is just about as broad as social science itself, so it's quite useful to explore change across a number of dimensions. Social change can be understood according to scale – from micro (family/**community**) to macro (nation/global) levels. It also ranges in scope – from particular actions and behaviours to **radical** (see **critical**/**radical**) paradigm shifts. It has a pace – from sudden and radical to gradual and incremental – and a duration – from short- to long-term. There are causes – changes to modes of production, political upheaval, public/legal policy, environmental change, natural evolution, population shifts, cultural diffusion, **class** conflict, **technological** change, mass media, **social movements**, and **ideological** shifts – and of course various drivers of the process (e.g. social groups, the **power** elite, intellectuals, governments, religious institution, and community).

Debates and controversies

One of the legacies of **modern** thinking (see **modernity**) is that change equals progress, and that social change evolves towards a utopian end. But change is never one-sided and for all the supposed progress and good, there are always costs. So while some social theorists still look at social change as an overall progression, others argue that it can be regressive (particularly for some sectors of **society**), while still others argue that it's cyclical and has little impact on development in any linear direction.

Practical application

Social scientists are in the business of understanding change, and in fact disciplines like sociology were founded on the exploration of great waves of modern change (i.e. *industrialization*, *capitalism*, *democracy*, *technology*, and mass migration). But these waves do not stand still. *Capitalism* and *industrialization* are still moving throughout the 'third world', *developed nations* are moving into a *post-industrial* phase, governments are in a constant state of flux, technology continues to move at the rate of knots, and we are becoming ever more *globalized*. Without a doubt, social change will stay on the social scientist's agenda.

Key figures

In one way or another, all sociology's founding fathers were in the business of understanding social change. And while theorists like August Comte, Herbert Spencer and Emile Durkheim argued that society would progress through evolutionary stages, it was Karl Marx who argued that change is brought about by *class* conflict and can be both radical and *revolutionary*.

> Once social change begins, it cannot be reversed. ... We have seen the future, and the future is ours.
>
> *Cesar Chavez* (1927-1993)
> Labour organizer,
> social activist – attributed

Recommended readings

For a solid introduction to a broad range of social change theories, I'd have a look at *Social Change* (Vago 2003), *Social Theory and Social Change* (Noble 2000), *Paradigms of Social Change: Modernization, Development, Transformation, Evolution* (Schelke et al. 2001), or *Revolutions: A Worldwide Introduction to Political and Social Change* (Sanderson 2005).

Social constructionism

Longer explanation

Real, true, and solid things like money, race, gender and religion exist out there in the world, don't they? Well, no one would argue that these things don't exist. In fact, such things make up a large part of our lived reality. But it's the nature of their existence that's debated. Many theorists argue that events and social phenomena have an independent and objective existence, but social constructivists argue that we actually create social phenomena. Only then do they become embedded into our world as 'real'. Money is certainly real, but it would only be paper and bits of metal if we didn't socially construct its meaning. And when it comes to things like race and gender, social constructivists argue that rather than essential biological truths, these constructs are better understood as categories defined by shared socio-cultural beliefs and practices. The same can be said of religion. Rather than an objective reality, social constructivists argue that religion is a dynamic construct that reflects the needs of various social groups. In this way, social constructivism reminds us that things that we assume are 'natural' are actually cultural artifacts created through social interactions.

Debates and controversies

Does it matter if constructs like race and gender are social rather than biological? Many think it does. If we see such constructs as biological realities, then we'll believe they're stable and immutable. But if we accept them as social constructs, they become dynamic and can and will change to reflect current social realities. This acceptance of dynamism takes the steam out of arguments related to the inherent supremacy of one race or gender over another.

Practical application

The more phenomena we accept as constructed, the more we are able to *deconstruct* and reconstruct. So in a socially constructed world, the possibilities are endless. How those with **power**, as well as those simply going through the motions of their daily lives, act to create the social is fascinating. On a different note, social constructionism is also of interest to researchers who all need to consider whether knowledge is simply a social product or whether it's based on objective truths not affected by the social world.

Key figures
While theorists as diverse as Karl Marx, Karl Manheim, Alfred Schütz, William Thomas and Talcott Parsons have argued that our world is constructed through social processes, the concept is most closely associated with Peter Berger and Thomas Luckmann whose 1967 work, *The Social Construction of Reality,* generated tremendous debate on the topic.

> *Things are not what they seem. ...*
> *Social reality turns out to have*
> *many layers of meaning.*
>
> **Peter Berger** (1929-) US sociologist –
> in *Invitation to Sociology* (1963)

Recommended readings
I'd start with Berger and Luckmann's seminal work, *The Social Construction of Reality* (1967). But if you'd rather go with a more contemporary introduction, try *Social Constructionism* (Burr 2003), *An Invitation to Social Construction* (Gergen 1999) or *The Social Construction of What?* (Hacking 2000). To delve into the work of a number of authors, try *Social Construction: A Reader* (Gergen and Gergen 2003).

 Social control

Longer explanation

In the words of Austin Powers, 'Oh Behave!' And this is exactly what 'society' needs us to do, so it works at controlling our behaviours in order to avoid chaos and maintain social order. Now, getting us to 'behave' is actually a complex process that involves a number of tactics and several key players. As for tactics, they can be divided into two main categories. This first involves socializing appropriate beliefs into an individual's consciousness. When this happens a society's values, norms, morals and *ideologies* abide deeply within an individual – this is a very effective means of social control. The second is through more coercive methods where there's a threat of sanction. Our laws, for example, are coercive in that breaking them will incur a loss of money and/or freedom. But even at an informal level, breaching social norms can lead to criticism, ostracism, shaming as well as internal guilt. Okay, so who are the key players in maintaining social control? Well, at the level of ideology, the family, the church, schools, the media, the government, and even the workplace all socialize and indoctrinate in ways that establish and maintain social control. And these same social institutions have systems of punishment (and reward) that attempt to control those who may want to breach norms and rules in spite of socializing practices.

Debates and controversies

There's no doubt that we need mechanisms of social control. Imagine driving a car without them. But the question is whether they're always designed for the public good, as the political rhetoric would have us believe. Social control in all its subtle and overt forms can also be explored as a means for maintaining the inequity that exist in all societies.

Practical application

In a **globalizing** world, it's becoming harder and harder to establish a common worldview. Within any one society, individuals answer to a number of religious, familial, and cultural codes. So relying on **socialization,** or even sanctions for social control, is becoming more and more problematic. How **communities** come to reach mutual understanding and equitable systems of control in a **multicultural** world will be a crucial question in the social sciences for some time to come.

Key figures

A number of key figures, including **functionalists** such as Emile Durkheim and Talcott Parsons and **Marxist** such as Karl Marx and Louis Althusser, have explored the role of socialization and ideology in maintaining social order. Also interesting here is Michel Foucault, who argues that **modern** (see **modernity**) society is one of surveillance and control that reaches into all aspects of our lives and our psyches.

> That a society controls the behavior
> of its members is a universal;
> but the methods, the particulars
> of that control, vary from
> one culture to another.
>
> **Kenneth L. Pike** (1912–2000) US linguist
> and anthropologist – in 'Mixtec
> Social Credit Rating', *Proceedings
> of the National Academy of Sciences* (1986)

Recommended readings

For an introduction to deviance and social control, try *Understanding Social Control* (Innes 2003), *Deviance and Social Control: A Reader* (Weitzer 2001) or *Punishment and Social Control* (Blomberg and Cohen 2003). Also interesting is *Mass Media, Social Control, and Social Change: A Macrosocial Perspective* (Demers and Viswanath 1998) and Foucault's seminal work *Discipline and Punish (1977* 1995), which explores social control in **modernity**.

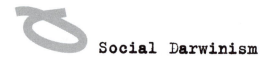

Social Darwinism

Core definition
The application of Darwinian evolutionary theory to social phenomena.

Longer explanation
You know the show *Survivor*, where the goal is to 'outwit, outplay, outlast', well this show was clearly conceived by a social Darwinist. In the mid-nineteenth century, Charles Darwin argued that species evolve through natural selection where the fittest survive to pass on their traits. Social Darwinism is the broad application of these ideas to the social realm. So for social Darwinists, survival of the fittest is the natural rule by which various **communities**, races, tribes, and even individuals thrive or die off. In other words 'outwit, outlast, outplay … survive'. Not only does this mean that the strongest races, tribes, and individuals will reign supreme, it also suggests that the weakest will die off, and in fact need to, if society is to 'evolve'.

Debates and controversies
There's some controversy over whether social Darwinism is an accurate description of social processes, but the main controversy lies in how it has been used politically, often to justify non-interventionist policies. To that end, social Darwinism has been used to argue against regulating **capitalist** markets – let those who are able, survive. It's also been used to justify social inequities and to argue against providing support to disadvantaged individuals or social groups. In fact, extreme social Darwinists argue against any altruism because it interferes with evolutionary principles and obstructs social progress. The strong have a right, and in fact a social obligation, to become increasingly dominant. Social Darwinism has thus been called on to justify the right to **colonize** 'weaker' or more 'primitive' nations as well as to justify eugenics (strengthening hereditary traits through various interventions (e.g. selective breeding, genetic engineering)). Hitler even used social Darwinism as a justification for Nazism.

Practical application
Most social scientists recognize that the complexity of socio-cultural contexts makes it impossible to equate social and biological phenomena. Nonetheless,

belief in the 'survival of the fittest' still runs deep within the modern psyche (think of reality TV shows such as *Survivor*, *The Apprentice*, *The Biggest Loser*, where the weakest get voted off). How this manifests in attitudes towards things like gender, race, **class**, and educational level as well as the policies of multi-national corporations in an ever-globalizing world gives social Darwinism tremendous currency.

Key figures

Social Darwinism actually predates Darwin's theories. In fact, in the late eighteenth century, Thomas Malthus argued that population growth would cause inadequate food supply leading the weakest to starve. Not only did this influence Darwin, it also influenced Herbert Spencer, the philosopher most closely associated with social Darwinism who actually coined the phrase 'survival of the fittest'. Francis Galton, the founder of eugenics (and also Darwin's half-cousin) is also influential here. Interestingly, Darwin himself was sceptical of the ability to apply his evolutionary theory to the social.

> We have unmistakable proof that
> throughout all past time, there has
> been a ceaseless devouring
> of the weak by the strong.
>
> **Herbert Spencer** (1820–1903)
> British philosopher –
> in *First Principles* (1862)

Recommended readings

A good place to start is with *Social Darwinism* (Dickens 2000) or *Darwinism in Philosophy, Social Science and Policy* (Rosenberg 2000). For a historical overview, turn to *In Search of Human Nature: The Decline and Revival of Darwinism in American Social Thought* (Degler 1992) or *Social Darwinism in European and American Thought, 1860–1945* (Hawkins 1997).

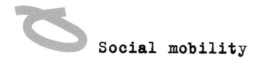

Social mobility

Core definition

The extent to which an individual's social status can change over a life course or between generations.

Longer explanation

How hard is it for the farmer's daughter to become a lawyer? Is a child born into a family from the lowest echelons of **society** tied to that fate? Can the factory-floor labourer make it to manager? Well, not only are such life opportunities dependent on ambition and effort, they're also dependent on a society's social mobility. Across the globe there are societies where it's almost impossible, despite merit or even wealth, to leave the social strata to which you're born. But in **democratic** societies, the rhetoric is that regardless of gender, race, religion, or your family's social standing, with hard work you can become anything you want. The reality, however, can be quite different. Democratic societies may not have a legally defined class or caste system, and no official moratorium on social mobility, but it's still not easy for the disadvantaged to get ahead. Inequities in school funding, overt and subtle **discrimination** (see **predjudice/ discrimination**), labelling, class-consciousness, as well as the opportunities money can buy and the hardship poverty creates, means that achieving upward mobility when you are underprivileged is an exception rather than a rule.

Debates and controversies

One issue here is whether social mobility is a zero-sum game. In other words, for every person who moves upwards, does someone else need to move downwards, or can societies support an overall upward trend? A decrease in blue-collar labour in some **developed countries** suggests that overall upward mobility may be possible. But a boom is often followed by a bust, and moving industries to **developing countries** has its own social and economic implications for workers in those countries.

Practical application

We live in a world that has a growing divide between the rich and the poor, increased rates of migration, **industrial** growth in developing nations, and shifts towards **post-industrialism** in developed nations. And all of this affects patterns of social mobility, making the construct highly relevant in contemporary society.

Key figures

Social mobility became a distinct object of sociological investigation with the publication of Pitirim Sorokin's *Social and Cultural Mobility* in 1927. Since that time, any number of researchers, for example Wilbert Moore, David Glass, Seymour Lipset, Peter Blau and Otis Duncan, have engaged in debates on the social mobility and its appropriate measurement (see **socioeconomic status**).

> Individuals have always, as individuals, shown themselves stronger than the prevailing system, and have broken through it. ... But these exceptions have been negligible in comparison with the millions who have conformed to it.
>
> **C. C. North** Early social researcher – in *Social Differentiation* (1926)

Recommended readings

A classic here is Strauss's *Contexts of Social Mobility: Ideology and Theory* (*1971* 2006). For a more contemporary overview, try *Analyzing Inequality: Life Chances and Social Mobility in Comparative Perspective* (Svallfors 2005), *Mobility and Inequality: Frontiers of Research in Sociology and Economics* (Morgan et al. 2006), *Research in Social Stratification and Mobility* (Leicht 2005) or *Social Mobility and Modernization* (Rotberg 2000). Also worth a look is *The Social Mobility of Women* (Payne 1990).

 Social movements

> ## Core definition
> Individuals united by a common purpose who act *collectively* to promote or resist political or *social change*.

Longer explanation

For many of us, social movements, whether they target specific issues (legalizing marijuana) or reflect major social divisions (civil rights), whether they're conservative (criminalizing abortion) or liberal (anti-capital punishment), reformative (advocating environmental protection laws) or *radical* (stopping capitalist exploitation) (see **critical/radical**), peaceful (Gandhi's fight for Indian independence) or violent (armed resistance), global (anti-*globalization*) or regional/local (fighting for farm subsidies), have always been part of our reality. We tend to accept such movements as part of our *democratic* framework. In fact, they are seen as central to tackling social issues not adequately addressed by institutionalized political processes. Social movements, however, are actually quite a new phenomenon, which only emerged with large population centres, the right to free speech, and the ability to communicate with the masses. And social movement theories, which attempt to understand causes, initiation/origin, *leadership*, organization, participants (who and why), resources, networks, structures, life-cycle, dynamics, effects, events, and environments, continue to evolve.

Debates and controversies

While social movements may be a key social change process, they're not all successful. Some never get off the ground; the organization is poor, causes are questionable, and mobilizing the masses just doesn't happen. Other times the system being fought is too entrenched or too powerful to overcome (think anti-*globalization*) or there may be alternative social movements working in opposition (pro-life vs. pro-choice). And of course in some nations, social movements are extraordinarily risky (e.g. the Tiananmen Square massacre of student protestors in China in 1989).

Practical application

Most realize that government policy sometimes reflects only a segment of the population or lags behind shifts in public opinion. And social movements (which have been around since the eighteenth century but really proliferated in the 1960s) have been a common, and often successful, means of rallying public support and pressuring governments to adopt (or sometimes resist) change. Social movements are thus a fascinating topic for anyone interested in social reform or social transformation.

Key figures

Theorists who have contributed to our understanding of social movements include Henri de Saint-Simon, who first used the term to characterize French social protests in the early eighteenth century, and Karl Marx, who in the nineteenth century explored *class* conflict and *revolution*. More recent theorists working in this area include Herbert Blumer, Neil Smesler, Ernesto Laclau, Chantal Mouffe, Doug McAdams, Charles Tilly, Mancur Olson, Alain Touraine, and Craig Calhoun.

> Sixties movements were grounded in a democratic vision: a belief that all people should be included as full members of society, that individuals become empowered through meaningful social participation.
>
> Edward P. Morgan (1910–1993) US journalist, author – in The 60s Experience (1991)

Recommended readings

I'd start with *Social Movements: An Introduction* (Porta and Diani 2006) or *The Social Movements Reader: Cases and Concepts* (Goodwin and Jasper 2003). Other interesting choices include *Social Movements, 1768–2004* (Tilly 2004), *Social Movements: An Anthropological Reader* (Nash 2004) and *Self, Identity, and Social Movements* (Stryker et al. 2000).

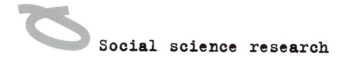

Social science research

Core definition

Systematic investigation of the social world that makes a contribution to *knowledge*.

Longer explanation

While the definition above may seem clear and concise, it doesn't clarify (1) what constitutes a systematic investigation and (2) what qualifies as a contribution to knowledge. Now as far as systematic investigation goes, research approaches in the social sciences are extremely broad and can range from highly 'scientific' approaches that follow **positivist** rules of **scientific method** reliant on **hypothesis** testing to more **post-positivist** approaches that can be participative, collaborative, **inductive** (see **deductive/inductive reasoning**), idiographic and exploratory. As far as what qualifies as a contribution to knowledge, the range is similarly broad. Social science research can have any number of goals, ranging from basic or pure research that attempts to produce and expand theoretical knowledge to much more applied research that addresses real-world issues related to the nature of problems, their potential solutions, and the evaluation of various change initiatives.

Debates and controversies

A major debate here is whether social science research can ever stand up to the exacting standards of natural science research. Some say yes, and rigorously apply the rules of scientific method to the social. Others suggest that the social needs to be researched in alternative ways that can still produce authentic understandings. Still others suggest that the social world is constantly being constructed and is therefore impossible to capture through any research process. This has led to a great internal debate over the most appropriate ways to capture the social world and what research goals are most appropriate. For example, if social truth is, in fact, elusive and ever-shifting, then applied approaches that actually make a contribution to situation improvement, may be seen as having greater value than research that is purely theoretical.

Practical application

The conduct of research is a central activity across all the social sciences and is likely to be part of any degree you attempt. Several entries in this book can help you work through the basics. From the most theoretical to the most applied, these include *epistemology* (*knowledge*, *theory/social theory*, *positivism*, *post-positivism*, *empiricism*, *social interactionism*); logic (*causation*, *deductive/inductive reasoning*, *grounded theory*); *methodology* (*scientific method*, *hypothesis/hypothetico-deductive method*, *action research*, *ethnography*, *ethnomethodology*, *phenomenology*); *methods*; data (*qualitative/quantitative*); and *research credibility* (*positivist* and *post-positivist*).

Key figures

This is such a broad topic that the list of key figures is unending. I'd be more specific and look at the topics highlighted above and explore the key figures listed in those entries.

> Research is formalized curiosity.
> It is poking and prying
> with a purpose.
>
> *Zora Neale Hurston* (1891–1960)
> African-American novelist,
> anthropologist – in *Dust
> Tracks on a Road* (1942).

Recommended readings

There are about a billion social science research methods books on the market including my own, *The Essential Guide to Doing Research* (O'Leary 2004) and *Researching Real-World Problems* (O'Leary 2005). Other good choices are *Introduction to Social Research: Quantitative and Qualitative Approaches* (Punch 2005) and *The Basics of Social Research* (Babbie 2004). But if you want to narrow in, I'd run through the Recommended readings for the various entries listed under Practical application.

Social stratification

Longer explanation
You know there's a good chance you've already been subjected to a stratified classification system over which you had little control. Schools, for example, often stratify kids according to perceived ability which sets them down a particular educational path. As adults we are again classified and stratified, but this time according to things like *socioeconomic status.* And while we have little power over the process, the classifications we are assigned can have a major impact on life opportunities.

Debates and controversies
When it comes to education there are those who see stratification as *functional*. You need to challenge those at the top so they can get as far as they can go and you need to help those who are struggling so that they too can reach their potential. But the 'against' side screams inequity. They claim that stratification leads to *labelling* and *discrimination*, and creates a self-fulfilling prophecy where those relegated to the bottom have no expectations to live up to. These are some of the same arguments that surround stratification based on socioeconomic status. *Functionalists* claim that societal stratification is necessary since those at the top need to be rewarded if they're to take on more crucial societal roles. *Critical theorists*, however, claim that stratification perpetuates inequity and exploitation, and keeps those at the bottom of the hierarchy in their place. In the West we may not have a caste system where social stratification is non-negotiable and without opportunity for *social mobility*, but there's plenty of evidence to suggest that Western systems of social stratification are far from open and meritorious. Critical theorists argue that they positively reek of racial, ethnic, and gender-based discrimination that only serves the wealthy.

Practical application

Whether the perspective is sociological, philosophical, economic, social-psychological or political, inequity, such as that captured in social stratification systems, is a key theme. How such inequities are measured, understood, created, used, manipulated, maintained, perpetuated, and overcome is of critical importance across the social sciences.

Key figures

Theorists who have argued the necessity of social stratification include functionalists Emile Durkheim and Talcott Parsons. More critical theorists who have contributed to this area include Marx, who was instrumental in the exploration of **class** division, class conflict, and class-based exploitation, and Max Weber, who explored stratification along social, economic and political lines.

> I am worried that we will become
> a stratified economy ... where
> the prosperous and the advantaged stay
> prosperous, and the poor and
> disadvantaged stay poor.
>
> **Lawrence Summers** (1954–)
> US economist, politician, academic –
> quoted in *Seattle Post Intelligencer*,
> 27 September 2005

Recommended readings

Worth a look here are *Social Stratification and Inequality* (Kerbo 2002) and *Social Stratification: Class, Race, and Gender in Sociological Perspective* (Grusky 2000). I also like *Social Class and Stratification: Classic Statements and Theoretical Debates* (Levine 2006) and *Research in Social Stratification and Mobility* (Leicht 2005).

 Socialism

Core definition

An economic system in which the means of production and distribution are collectively owned and controlled, usually by government.

Longer explanation

In *Measure for Measure*, Shakespeare wrote, 'What's mine is yours, and what is yours is mine'. Well, this sense of **collectivity** is the premise of socialism: an economic system that attempts to overcome the inequities associated with **capitalism**. In fact, socialism arose from critiques of the inequities associated with the privately owned means of production of the industrial revolution (see **industrialization**). Socialism is premised on a belief in shared ownership and production, which avoids exploitation; state regulation of economic activities, which leads to high levels of efficiency; government allocation of resources, which leads to equity; dissolution of private property, which eradicates social **class** and class conflict; and decisions based on common good, which leads to a form of **democracy**.

Debates and controversies

An old Polish proverb goes, 'Under capitalism man exploits man; under socialism the reverse is true'. In other words, the goals of socialism are stronger in theory than in practice. Under most socialist states exploitation was not eradiated, efficiency was lacking, inequity in the distribution of resources was pronounced, social classes remained, and the 'party' made many decisions without democratic processes.

Practical application

I think Winston Churchill was right when he said: 'The inherent vice of capitalism is the unequal sharing of blessings; the inherent virtue of socialism is the equal sharing of miseries.' When it comes to finding the economic system and form of society that brings the greatest level of overall prosperity in the most equitable fashion, we truly struggle. How, in an ever-**globalizing** world, we work towards **capital** growth while balancing issues related to social **justice** and increasing environmental threats is a timely economic and socio-political issue that often brings socialist doctrine to the fore.

Key figures

While eighteenth-century theorists such as François Noël Babeuf, Robert Owen, Charles Fourier, and Henri de Saint-Simon were some of the first to propose socialist doctrine in response to inequity, the figures most closely associated with socialism are Marx and Engels, who in the nineteenth century saw socialism as a transitionary stage between the private ownership of capitalism and state free *communism*. Contemporary Emile Durkheim saw socialism as a response to the *anomie* associated with capitalism, while Weber warned that putting the economy fully in the hands of the state could lead to huge restrictions of freedom.

> I am for socialism. ... I seek the social ownership of property, the abolition of the propertied class, and the sole control of those who produce wealth.
>
> *Roger Baldwin* (1884–1981), Civil libertarian – quoted in the *Harvard Class Book of 1935*, 'Thirty Years Later' (1935)

Recommended readings

For unbeatable historical context, I'd have a look at Marx and Engel's *The Communist Manifesto* (*1848* 2004). For a more contemporary introduction, try *Socialism: A Very Short Introduction* (Newman 2005), *Understanding Socialism: An Introduction to Ideas and Issues* (Williams and Mcmullen 2007), or *Socialism* (Howard 2001). Other good choices include *Heaven on Earth: The Rise and Fall of Socialism* (Muravchik 2003) and *The Case for Socialism* (Maass 2005).

Socialization

Longer explanation
We come into the world a screaming heap with no sense of **self**, others, or the 'rules' of the society into which we're born. We don't know what the world expects of us, and we don't know what's acceptable. But it doesn't take long before we're functioning members of society who not only know the rules, but who've actually adopted and internalized them. Socialization begins at birth (primary socialization) with the family taking on the major socializing role, but it continues throughout childhood and adolescence with school, peers groups, and the media influencing a secondary stage of socialization. An ongoing third stage occurs throughout adulthood as individuals fill social roles that have more specific expectations (e.g. employee, soldier, partner, parent, retiree). While processes of socialization are often explicit and overt (e.g. being told what do to or being punished for breaches), they can also be much more implicit and subtle (learning by example or being given praise for conformance).

Debates and controversies
While it's easy to articulate **theories** related to particular aspects of socialization, for example, theories on early childhood socialization, adult socialization, enculturation, or socialization into sects and cults, it's more difficult to articulate a unified theory. Socialization is extremely broad-ranging and runs throughout the life course, with a host of socializing agents and huge implications for both personal and social **identity**. This makes it difficult to capture as a singular process. Additionally, research into socialization often runs along disciplinary lines with psychologists, anthropologists, and sociologists each taking a distinct perspective.

Practical application
As the process that turns biological entities into social beings, socialization is absolutely central in the social sciences. Of particular contemporary interest

are socializing influences outside traditional **community** structures of family, school, church and peers. In a **postmodern** (see **postmodernity**) world, children are increasingly exposed to things like the internet, movies, TV, music and even video games, which many argue weakens traditional ideals and creates confusion in values and norms.

Key figures

Key figures include Freud, who considered the **superego** (see **id/ego/superego**) the 'moral' part of the mind that internalizes and embodies parental and societal values, Jean Piaget, who proposed four stages of cognitive development, George Herbert Mead, who distinguished between I (the active self) and me (the socialized self), Erik Erikson, who proposed eight stages of human development, and Talcott Parsons, who saw socialization as learning to fill roles prescribed by the social system.

> *Socialization gives us the tools to fill our ... roles. They are our building blocks.*
>
> **Warren Farrell** (1943–)
> US writer and 'masculinist' –
> Interview with attorney/author
> J. Steven Svoboda, 22 September 1996

Recommended readings

Socialization experiences are extremely diverse and broad-ranging. Works that can help open the door to this area include *Early Socialization* (Schaffer 1995), *New Frontiers in Socialization* (Settersten and Owens 2002) and *Parent – Child Socialization in Diverse Cultures* (Roopnarine and Carter 1992).

 Society

Core definition

At a socio-political level, a society is an extended group of individuals residing within a bounded geographic area, subject to common political *authority* and law, has mutual institutions, and shares a distinctive *culture*. At a broader level, a society is any social grouping that comes together, or is lumped together, on the basis of some shared characteristic or interest.

Longer explanation

This won't be a new term to you, so I'm going to focus here on socio-political understandings of society and unpack the two very distinct connotations of the term. The first is when societies are contrasted, often negatively, with *communities*. Under this line of thought, communities are seen as cohesive groups of people who share a sense of belonging, while societies are larger social groupings that are a part of loose and impersonal *bureaucratic/* economic systems. The second connotation is much more positive (and is almost at odds with the first) and occurs when societies are contrasted with the *state*. Here the state is understood as socio-political institutions that govern a population, while societies are the people of a nation that need to fight from over-control by the state.

Debates and controversies

There are two key controversies here. The first is that there isn't a term more fundamental to the social sciences, yet it's one of the hardest terms to capture. In addition to the connotations mentioned above, society is used in numerous ways, for example *capitalist* society, high society, the Society for the Protection of Ancient Buildings, or British society. The usage is, in fact, so broad that some theorists question its power as a social construct. The second controversy is whether societies actually exist as defined entities, or whether, as Oscar Wilde once stated, 'society exists only as a mental concept; in the real world there are only individuals'.

Practical application

Society is the framework, context and underpinning of all the social sciences. In fact, it's what defines social. It is therefore important for social science students to engage critically with this construct and question our casual everyday use of the term.

Key figures

Key figures here include Ferdinand Tönnies, who distinguished cohesive communities from larger bureaucratic societies, and Emile Durkheim, who saw societies are real, ever-evolving entities. Louis Althusser viewed societies as economic, *ideological* and political relationships, while Anthony Giddens argued that societies should be understood as social systems not limited by national boundaries.

> Society is held together by our need;
> we bind it together with legend, myth,
> coercion...
>
> *James Baldwin* (1924-1987) US author –
> in 'Everybody's Protest Novel',
> *Partisan Review* (1949)

Recommended readings

A good place to start is with introductory works such as *Power and Society: An Introduction to the Social Sciences* (Dye 2004) or *Society: The Basics* (Macionis 2005). To delve more deeply into the topic, try *Civil Society* (Edwards 2004) or *The Civil Society Reader* (Hodgkinson and Foley 2003). If you'd prefer to delve into a classic, try Tönnies' *Tönnies: Community and Civil Society* (*1887* 2001).

Sociobiology

Longer explanation

We know that genetics determines things like physical characteristics, certain diseases, and even aspects of *personality*. But what about social behaviours? Do genes play a role here? Well, sociobiologists argue that in the animal kingdom, social behaviours are genetically determined. In fact, they argue that through natural selection, behaviours leading to survival of the genetic line become predominant in the species. So just as evolution might see camouflaging white fur growing on animals living in the snow, social behaviours that allow genetic survival also become part of our evolutionary heritage. In the animal kingdom, this manifests in mama bears being willing to die to protect their young, lionesses who'll care for nieces and nephews but not those unrelated, and apes who engage in cooperative or altruistic behaviours that benefit the community. But what about us humans? Does this apply to us? Are our behaviours learned, socialized, cultural, and environmental? Or, as sociobiologists would argue, are they a natural part of our animalistic evolutionary makeup?

Debates and controversies

Most social scientists would argue that sociobiology is overly *reductionist* and does not acknowledge the complexity of human interactions or the significance of environmental factors in human development. As highly *socialized* animals, the importance of instinct is often questioned. Nonetheless, this is pretty interesting stuff – particularly when applied to things like human mating. For example, take the stereotype of a young man who just wants to get laid and a young woman more interested in finding a life-long partner. Most sociologists would look at this scenario via the cultural expectations related to sexual behaviours, such as the vilification of 'easy' women and the prowess associated with male sexual exploits. But a sociobiological explanation might be that survival of the genetic line is best served by men spreading their sperm as far and wide as possible, and women attempting to find a mate willing to help raise the offspring she bears.

Practical application

Cultural influences are undeniably central in the development of the human self. But so too are the influences of our genetic makeup. Social scientists who are willing to overcome our tendency to **dichotomize** (nature vs. nurture) and explore the complex interactions at work between the two factors will add much to our understanding.

Key figures

In the mid-1970s, Richard Dawkins argued that genetic survival is the key to species survival, and that behaviours evolve in order to protect genes. Around the same time E. O. Wilson argued that natural selection influences not only the social behaviours of 'lower' animals, but of humans as well.

> The difference in mind between man
> and the higher animals, great as
> it is, is certainly one of
> degree and not of kind.
>
> **Charles Darwin** (1809–1882)
> British naturalist – in *The
> Descent of Man* (1871)

Recommended readings

A good place to start is with *Defenders of the Truth: The Sociobiology Debate* (Segerstrale 2001), *Why Men Won't Ask for Directions: The Seductions of Sociobiology* (Francis 2005) and *The Triumph of Sociobiology* (Alcock 2003). Also worth a look are the instrumental works of Wilson, *Sociobiology: The New Synthesis* (*1975* 2000) and Dawkins, *The Selfish Gene* (*1976* 2006).

 Socioeconomic status

Longer explanation

Researchers have long known that where we fall in the social hierarchy has innumerable consequences on life opportunities (see *social stratification*). But hierarchies aren't all about money or occupational status. Researchers have found that a composite of factors are important in determining life prospects. Socioeconomic status (SES) is an attempt to combine the most relevant variables in a single measure. It allows researchers to understand relative hierarchical standing while avoiding artificial *class* divisions that many argue are less relevant in supposedly classless societies like the USA.

Debates and controversies

Socioeconomic status is a construct that appears throughout social science literature. But while definitions are quite standard, there's no clear standard for the construct's measurement. Researchers often combine variables they feel are most important (and there is a lot of debate here, for example occupation vs. income, income vs. educational attainment) or they turn to variables readily available in existing databases. So when researchers present findings related to SES, they aren't always talking about the same thing.

Practical application

Socioeconomic status has in wide application to the social sciences and has been correlated with a huge range of variables. Lower SES, for example, has been associated with physical health concerns such as obesity, diabetes, heart disease, asthma, and occupational health and safety threats; mental health concerns such as depression, anxiety, suicide and low self-esteem; crime and deviance, including involvement in prostitution, gangs and drugs; negative attitudes towards *authority*; lower levels of motivation to succeed in school/work; social isolation; and lower expectations for children – not to mention how others perceive and interact with individuals of various backgrounds. This was well explored by British director Paul Almond in his *Seven Up!* series. The series, which began in 1964 and has been followed up every seven years since, interviews 14 British children from diverse socioeconomic backgrounds about their lives and hopes for the future. The most recent installment shows the 'children', now aged 49, reflecting on a lifetime of challenges and opportunities – much of which is, if not determined by, then certainly influenced by, their socioeconomic/class background.

> *I completely disagree with the notion that race is a factor or that their socioeconomic status is at all a factor.*
>
> **Russ Knocke** Spokesman for the Department of Homeland Security responding to criticisms of racism and classism over what many considered a highly inadequate response to the devastation caused by Hurricane Katrina in New Orleans, quoted in *Newsday*, 3 September 2005

Recommended readings

For a well-rounded introduction, turn to *Social Stratification: Class, Race, and Gender in Sociological Perspective* (Grusky 2000) and *Renewing Class Analysis* (Crompton et al. 2001). I also like *Socioeconomic Status, Parenting, and Child Development* (Bornstein and Bradley 2002) and *Political and Economic Determinants of Population Health and Well-Being: Controversies and Developments* (Navarro and Muntaner 2004). And if you get a chance, I'd certainly check out Paul Almond's *Seven Up!* series.

Sociolinguistics

Core definition

A branch of linguistics that studies how language affects and is affected by social relations.

Longer explanation

Traditional linguistic studies often disregard the social and focus on internal aspects of language, such as sounds and sounds patterns, word structures, sentence formation, and meanings. But sociolinguistics reminds us that language has a close relationship with the social world. The way we verbally express ourselves can influence our social opportunities and our social opportunities influence the way we express ourselves. In fact, if you shut your eyes and listen to a person speak, their accent, diction, words, expressions, and grammar are likely to clue you into a number of social distinctions that might include things like region, *socioeconomic status*, ethnicity, religion and, even without voice, gender. Language can thus act as a source of *self* and group *identity*. I'm going old school now, but the 1980 film *Airplane* provides a great insight into the cultural *solidarity* offered by language. In the film, a stewardess is having a hard time understanding an African-American who's speaking 'jive'. An older woman played by Barbara Billingsley (the mother in the 1950s sitcom *Leave it to Beaver*) pipes up, 'Oh Stewardess, I speak Jive', and in a hilarious scene not only translates the 'language' of a particular subculture, but invades a *cultural* space that older white women simply don't enter.

Debates and controversies

Unfortunately, it's not all about benefits such as solidarity. Sociolinguistic distinctions also aid our ability to stereotype and act with *prejudice* and *discrimination*. So while they may offer a strong sense of belonging, they can also act to pigeonhole individuals and limit social opportunities. Particular linguistic patterns, however, can be learnt (have you ever noticed how all newsreaders, including those speaking languages other than English, use the same cadence and rhythm?). This allows those who wish to be identified in mainstream (or alternative) ways to adopt linguistic patterns that can alter social perceptions.

Practical application

In a world where communication, not just within subcultures but across them, is central to our social relationships, sociolinguistics, with its focus on the social power of the spoken word, should be of particular interest. Sociolinguistics can also be instrumental in the exploration of constructs like self-identity, social identity and group solidarity.

Key figures

William Labov, who argued that variations in linguistics patterns are correlated with levels of *social stratification*, is considered the founding father of sociolinguistics. Other theorists who have explored the relationship between language and various social factors include Robin Lakoff, Basil Bernstein, Norman Fairclough, and Dell Hymes.

> Language is power, life and the instrument of culture, the instrument of domination and liberation.
>
> *Angela Carter* (1940-1992) British postmodern novelist – interview, 1 August 1985

Recommended readings

Good introductory works here include *Sociolinguistics: An Introduction to Language and Society* (Trudgill 2001) and *An Introduction to Sociolinguistics* (Wardhaugh 2005). To delve a bit deeper, I'd recommend *Sociolinguistics: A Reader* (Coupland and Jaworski 1997) and *Sociolinguistics: The Essential Readings* (Paulston and Tucker 2003).

 **Solidarity**

Longer explanation

How important are our *community* ties? Do we need to belong to something? Is there power in being united? Well, as former German Chancellor Gerhard Schröder once said, it'd be a 'cold and inhumane society without solidarity'. We simply don't do well on our own. We need each other, we need to belong, and we need to feel we're part of something greater than ourselves. If not, isolation and *alienation* can cause depression, anxiety and even lead to suicide. Now, not that long ago, solidarity was something we found close to home. We were part of a community where those around us had shared beliefs, values, *ethics*, religion, lifestyles, and even extended family – something Durkheim called mechanical solidarity. But in a modern world, we're often removed from these traditional sources of belonging and find that solidarity relies on the dependence that comes with having specialized roles in a world with complex divisions of labour – this is know as organic solidarity.

Debates and controversies

While the pressures of *modernity* may have removed us from traditional notions of community, I'd argue that mechanical solidarity has not fully given way to organic solidarity. In fact, in a world that's quite quickly gone from 'traditional' to 'modern' to '*postmodern*' (see *postmodernity*), we've actually been able to re-imagine community. So while our physical neighbourhoods may not be a source of common ground, like-minded (and sometimes geographically dispersed) individuals have found ways of gathering on the internet, through special interest groups and clubs, and through various *social movements* (it's difficult to rally for *social change* if you don't have solidarity).

Practical application

It's fascinating to explore shifts in sources of solidarity found in a postmodern world. And while many struggle to find a sense of place in an impersonal, often urban, jungle (see **urbanization**), others successfully search for belonging through things such as Eastern spirituality, new age philosophies, born-again Christian groups, cults, sects, and gangs, as well as an amazing range of virtual groups that abound on the internet.

Key figures

It was Durkheim who argued that industrial **capitalism** would cause a shift from mechanical to organic solidarity. But other thinkers also saw industrial capitalism as a threat to traditional sources of community. Weber, for example, argued that ever-growing **bureaucracies** would dehumanize and **alienate** workers, while Marx argued that the exploitative nature of capitalist production would see workers lose touch with others and even themselves (see **anomie**). Marx further argued that worker solidarity would be needed to force **social change**.

> *People were looking for opportunities to act in solidarity, not only with the community, but across the state.*
>
> **Rachel Lazar** Director of El Centro migrant support agency – quoted in *Tribune,* 7 April 2006

Recommended readings

Of interest here are *Problem of Solidarity: Theories and Models* (Doreian and Fararo 1998), *Social Solidarities: Theories, Identities and Social Change* (Crow 2001) and *Group Cohesion, Trust and Solidarity* (Thye and Lawler 2002). If you're interested in the relationship between solidarity and modernity, Durkheim's *The Division of Labor in Society* (*1893* 1997) is worth a look. I'd start with Book I, Chapters 2–7.

 **(The) State**

Core definition

A set of socio-political institutions that has the *authority* to govern the population of a geographically bounded territory.

Longer explanation

This is actually quite a tricky word that overlaps, and is sometimes used synonymously with, nation/country (a geographical region) and government (individuals in a position of power who run a nation). But the state (which generally outlives a government) is actually a set of institutions, such as the army, police, legal system, regulatory bodies, and administrative divisions, that have the authority to control a population through social integration (creating a sense of nationhood) (see *nationalism*) and legitimate force (making and enforcing laws). There are three theories of state – pluralist, elitist and *Marxist*. Pluralists argue that power is dispersed across a number of competing interest groups who each attempt to influence public policy. The elitist view, however, is that not all interest groups are equal. Political processes ensure that a nexus of elites retain *power* across state institutions. Marxists would generally agree with the elitist premise, but see this nexus of influence more directly tied to *capitalist* interests.

Debates and controversies

So where does the state start and finish? Well, the institutions that make up a state are in constant flux. For example, regulatory bodies can be created or disbanded and government institutions can become privatized. It's also difficult to draw a line between the state and civil society. For example, the phrase 'separation of church and state' actually points to the close relationship of the two, with Marxists arguing that institutions like the church, schools, and even the family have a role in transferring state *ideology*.

Practical application

There was a time when nomadic people wandered across lands that were not 'claimed' and not controlled by socio-political institutions. But those days are long gone. The entirety of the world's inhabitable land is now divided into states, generally nation-states, which have become a central political unit. But development of a global economy and the growth of international institutions are threatening the autonomy and control of nation-states and is beginning to change how we understand and engage with this construct.

Key figures

Niccolò Machiavelli introduced the concept of the state in the mid-sixteenth century, but it wasn't until the mid-seventeenth century that a more rigorous account was offered by Thomas Hobbes and John Locke. In the early twentieth century, Max Weber offered an influential definition that stressed the role of legitimate violence in state rule, while Louis Althusser in the mid-twentieth century identified both repressive state apparatus, such as the army and police, which controlled populations by force, and ideological state apparatus, such as the church, school and family, which controlled populations by influencing beliefs.

> For centuries we have been living in the society where not laws but people ruled, where there was no legal state.
>
> **Nursultan Nazarbayev** (1940-) President of Kazakhstan, speech to the Eighth Session of the Assembly of the People of Kazakhstan, 24 October 2001

Recommended readings

Works I'd recommend here include *Social Theory, the State and Modern Society* (Marinetto 2007), *Governance, Politics and the State* (Pierre 2000), *The State: Its History and Development Viewed Sociologically* (Oppenheimer 1999) and *Globalization and State Power: A Reader* (Kreiger 2005).

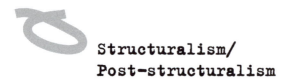

Structuralism/
Post-structuralism

Core definition

Structuralism is a theoretical positioning that observable social phenomena are the products of unobservable social structures, and that these hidden structures underlie the apparent randomness of things like *cultures*, languages, and texts. Post-structuralism emerged as a critique of structuralism's search for underlying structures and emphasizes the importance of both the individual and historical/cultural contexts in creating reality.

Longer explanation

So what should have priority? Is it what manifests itself, such as a particular language, a cultural practice, a text? Or do we need to look deeper? Should we be looking for underlying universal rules and overarching patterns that give shape and structure to languages, cultural practices or texts? Well, structuralism, which became prominent in the later half of the twentieth century, is an approach to *critical* analysis that looks for deep hidden structures and relationships rather than studying isolated, material things. So rather than look at the subtleties within a language, the exploitative practices in a particular office, or merits of a certain movie, structuralists would be interested in the universal rules of language learnt by children across the globe, the modes of production that determine patterns of exploitation, and the plot devices and universal storylines that manifest in popular movies.

But wait. Don't we lose an awful lot if we only focus on deeper structures? What about the legitimacy of the local, or the *power* and *agency* of the individual, or the intention of the author, or the importance of historical context? Don't we need to take this into account? Well, this is the thinking that gave rise to post-structuralism. Post-structuralism reasserts the importance of the subject, the local, and the historical, and questions the whole notion of *metanarratives* and universals.

Debates and controversies

So who has the answer – structuralists, post-structuralists, or the theorists that will come next? We're a unique species, able to theorize about the world that creates us and create the world we theorize about. With so much complexity, it's important to remember that one valid point of view does not invalidate the rest. There's bound to be room for interplay between various schools of thought.

Practical application

As *globalization* sees the world become ever smaller, there's a growing need to understand the structures underlying various cultures – as well as a need to understand the local, the contextual, and the particular. Structuralism and post-structuralism, particularly explored in concert, can add much to our cultural knowledge.

Key figures

Key structuralists include Ferdinand de Saussure in linguistics, Claude Lévi-Strauss in anthropology, Roland Barthes in literary and cultural studies, Jacques Lacan in psycho-analysis and Louis Althusser in *Marxist* theory. Figures associated with post-structuralism include Barthes (his later work), Jacques Derrida, who introduced *deconstruction*, and Michel Foucault (although he did not identify himself in this way).

> Structuralism claims to discover permanent structures behind or beneath things ... it's most extreme practitioners [in direct contrast to post-strucutralists] deny the significance of history.
>
> **Donald D. Palmer** US author – in *Structuralism and Poststructuralism for Beginners* (1997)

Recommended readings

If this is a new area for you, I'd start with *Structuralism and Poststructuralism for Beginners* (Palmer 1997). To delve into the structuralist arena, try *Structuralism* (Sturrock 2003). For more on post-structuralism, try *Understanding Poststructuralism* (Williams 2005).

 Subject

Core definition

In philosophy, subjects are thinking individuals who are 'actors' in society. While the nature of subjects is increasingly called into question, it has long been synonymous with 'I' or '*self*' and the autonomy implied by these words.

Longer explanation

I know who I am. I am me. I make my own decisions. I write my own script. I have *agency*. I act in self-determining ways. As a subject, I reside in my body and I am self-knowing. At least this is the myth. But do I really know myself? After all, I have an unconscious and subconscious that I can't really fathom. And what if the autonomy I think I have is just an illusion? What if I'm not a self-determining subject, but rather a cultural product? A product who is 'subjected' to things like material conditions, *ideology*, language, *discourse*? What if, in reality, I have very little empowerment? This is the debate that leaves the term 'subject' without firm ground. The stable coherent self that was once taken for granted is now a highly unstable construct. 'Subjects' are open to interpretation.

Debates and controversies

The struggle to define the contemporary subject highlights a number of key tensions in *social theory*. For example, are we a stable coherent self from birth (nature) or are we the products of *socialization* (nurture)? Do we control our destiny (agency) or are our paths predetermined (*determinism*)? Does language reflect our reality or is reality created through language (see *discourse*)? As long as these debates exist, 'subject' will remain a contested term.

Practical application

At one level, the concept of subject is of interest to anyone trying to understand what creates, and what is, the self. But because this concept highlights a number of theoretical tensions (as mentioned above) the 'subject' is a fantastic window for exploring these *dichotomies*.

Key figures

The subject as a coherent and stable self can be traced back to the theorists of *humanism*, such as Protagoras, Cicero, Voltaire, John Stuart Mill, and Bertrand Russell. Several theorists, however, have presented the subject as fragmented and constructed, causing us to reconsider this portrayal. Freud's work on the unconscious questioned whether subjects should be seen as coherent and self-aware. Marx argued that material conditions play a role in the development of the subject and that *capitalism* causes workers to be *alienated*. Althusser also believed subjects are products of societal forces, particularly ideology, while Lacan explored the subject as a construct of language. Finally, Foucault emphasized the role of discourse and *power* in subject development.

> *Who am I? How did I come to be here? How did I come into the world? Why was I not consulted? And if I am compelled to take part in it, where is the director? I want to see him.*
>
> **Søren Kierkegaard** (1813–1855) Danish philosopher – attributed

Recommended readings

For a good introduction to the coherent subject as conceptualized in humanism, try *Humanism: An Introduction* (Herrick 2005). For both psycho-analytic and philosophical reflections on the creation of subjects, I like *Becoming a Subject: Reflections in Philosophy and Psychoanalysis* (Cavell 2006) and *The Ticklish Subject: The Absent Centre of Political Ontology* (Žižek 2000). Also worth a look is *The Well-Tempered Self: Citizenship, Culture, and the Postmodern Subject* (Miller 1993).

Subjectivism

Longer explanation

So what is truth? Is truth something that's sitting out there waiting for us to discover it? Are there objective certainties that sit outside personal experience? Or are we part of the truth and is the truth a part of us? Well, subjectivists would say that the only truth is that of the individual–his or her perspective or point of view. For example, say you wanted to know what going to high school is really like – the best time of your life, torturous, fun, humiliating? Subjectivists would say it's impossible to find an objective answer here. The only truth resides in the person being asked. Or consider what your father was like when you were growing up. Just because your brother or sister may see it very, very differently, it doesn't make your reality any less real.

Debates and controversies

We might not have a problem agreeing that snakes slither. Most accept this as objective fact. But are snakes disgusting? Even though many would agree, we know there are people who love slithery creatures. So we accept 'snakes are disgusting' as a subjective claim. But it gets a lot trickier and more controversial when you ask about things like the reality of God, whether homosexuality is wrong, or if modern art is over-valued. The line between fact and opinion, between objective truth and subject claim, can become quite blurred. In fact in a *postmodern* world (see *postmodernity*) highly sceptical of answers that don't recognize the political and complex nature of knowledge, what scientists once accepted as discoverable truths are increasingly called into question.

Practical application

A key application here is in the conduct of research. When I started my PhD, I remember being told two things that were supposedly critical to my success. The first was to choose a topic I was passionate about (after all my research could take more than a couple years). Second, I must approach my study with complete objectivity. Hmmm... passionate objectivity – that was going to be tricky! Nowadays the hard-and-fast rules of research objectivity that reigned under a **positivist** framework have shifted with more recent **post-positivist** perspectives acknowledging the subjectivity of both researchers and the researched.

Key figures

A number of important theorists have argued that subjectivities must be acknowledged in the quest for, and production of, knowledge. Such theorists include Søren Kierkegaard, who argues that objectivity is highly limited, and phenomenologists such as Edmund Husserl, Jean-Paul Sartre, and Maurice Merleau-Ponty, who argue that phenomena can only be understood as they present themselves in direct experience.

> *Objectivity requires taking subjectivity into account.*
>
> **Lorraine Code** (1937–) Canadian philosopher – in *What Can She Know? Feminist Theory and the Construction of Knowledge* (1991)

Recommended readings

For an interesting introduction, try *Subjectivity and Selfhood: Investigating the First-Person Perspective* (Zahavi 2006). To get a handle on a range of subjectivity theories, I'd turn to *Self and Subjectivity* (Atkins 2005) or *Subjectivity: Theories of the Self from Freud to Haraway* (Mansfield 2001). For budding researchers, I'd also recommend *The I in Science: Training to Utilize Subjectivity in Research* (Brown 1996).

Symbolic interactionism

Core definition

Sociological perspective that focuses on the way individuals interpret social symbols (gestures, signs, and language) and subsequently interact with each other to create social realities.

Longer explanation

What would happen if you were pinched? Well, if a pinch is simply a stimulus, then the reaction might be 'ouch!' But a symbolic interactionist would say that this type of straightforward behavioural explanation is too simple for intellectually and socially complex humans. What we tend to do is read and interpret the symbolic cues within the social situation before engaging in purposive and creative interaction. So let's go back to the pinch. A symbolic interactionist would say that a pinch is not just a pinch and our reaction to it will depend on the meaning we assign to it. So, say you were pinched by a snot-nosed four year-old. In this case you might be annoyed and hiss, 'what do you think your doing!' But if you were a child and a babysitter pinched you with malice, your reaction might be extremely fearful tears. Then again, if we are snuck up on by a close friend, you might take it in fun and try your best to give one back. So your response isn't just based on the physical pinch stimulus, but the symbolic meaning attached to it.

Debates and controversies

This highly interactive approach is not without criticism. It's argued that symbolic interactionism is too micro in focus and ignores fundamental macro sociological issues such as the role of *culture* and social structures. It's also criticized for its emphasis on the *self* as dynamic, emergent and reactionary, which downplays the importance of inherent genetic traits or stable *personality* characteristics.

Practical application

Symbolic interactionists argue that humans communicate through a world of complex symbols and engage in intricate interpretative work that actually creates the social world. It recognizes that individuals are not passive in making meaning and establishing social order and therefore offers a non-traditional angle on social reality. Social scientists can therefore use symbolic interactionism to not only explore how we go about creating our selves, but also how we go about shaping **society**.

Key figures

Herbert Blumer coined the term in 1937 and argued that the way people act/react in any situation depends on how they interpret that situation's symbolic cues. His theories are based on the work of George Herbert Mead, who argued that individuals are social actors who take on purposive and creative **roles** that construct the self as well as social realities. Other theorists who have explored the relationship between the self and the construction of the social include Harold Garfinkel and Erving Goffman (see Recommended readings below).

> *(In) symbolic interaction ...
> human beings interpret or 'define'
> each other's actions instead of
> merely reacting to each
> other's actions.*
>
> **Herbert Blumer** (1900–1987) US
> sociologist – in 'Society as Symbolic
> Interaction', Rose, A. *Human Behavior
> and Social Process* (1962)

Recommended readings

If you're after a good contemporary overview, I'd suggest *Symbolic Interactionism: An Introduction, An Interpretation* (Charon 2006) or *Handbook of Symbolic Interactionism* (Reynolds 2004). Seminal readings worth a look include Mead's *Mind, Self, and Society* (*1934* 1967), Blumer's *Symbolic Interactionism: Perspective and Method* (*1969* 1986), Goffman's *The Presentation of Self in Everyday Life* (1959), Garfinkel's *Studies in Ethnomethodology* (1967) and Berger and Luckmann's *The Social Construction of Reality* (1967).

Systems theory

Core definition

A *theory* that stresses the importance of exploring the world at the level of systems made up of interdependent and interacting parts.

Longer explanation

Systems theory is all about trying to recognize and understand the complexity of the relationships that make up all systems. For example, at a biophysical level, understanding the human body not only requires an understanding of various parts (i.e. the heart, lungs, veins, muscles and skin), but also requires holistic consideration of how they are dependent on each other and how they work together to make the system function. The same argument applies to social systems. A systemic approach to understanding families, for example, not only requires an understanding of the various *roles* within a family (i.e. father, mother and child), but also an understanding of the relationships between those roles and how those relationships affect the family itself. Put simply, systems theory focuses on relationships among elements of a system and not just the elements as isolated parts.

Debates and controversies

Within the social sciences, the exploration of various components of systems, as well as the exploration of systems as unified wholes, tends to override the exploration of the complex and interwoven relationships within systems. In part, this is because it can be extremely difficult to capture the complex web of interrelations that might be occurring with any system, let alone understand the significance of those relationships on the shape and form of the system itself. Additionally, systems theory is critiqued for its overemphasis on understanding how balance and equilibrium are maintained within social systems, thereby limiting its ability to explain social conflict and *social change*.

Practical application

Systems thinking has been quite influential in the study of social systems where boundaries are seen as fairly well defined (e.g. organizations, management systems, political systems and economic systems). Systems theory, however, can add a valuable window into the exploration of almost all social phenomena since most can be understood as a rich nexus of interrelating parts.

Key figures

Systems theory has developed through a number of disciplines so there are quite a few key players. In the social sciences, theorists who have contributed to systems thinking include Herbert Spencer, Vilfredo Pareto, Lawrence Henderson, Margaret Mead and, most notably, Talcott Parsons. Parsons, who is most closely associated with social systems theory, argued that the equilibrium of social systems depends on the balance of exchange between subsystems related to money, *power*, influence and commitments.

> *The whole is more than*
> *the sum of its parts.*
>
> *Aristotle* (384–322 BC)
> Greek philosopher –
> in *Metaphysics* (336–323 BC)

Recommended readings

General Systems Theory (Skyttner 2006), *The Systems View of the World: A Holistic Vision for Our Time* (Lazlo 1996) and *General Systems Theory – Beginning with Wholes* (Hanson 1995) all provide a good introduction to systems theory and systems thinking. To delve more deeply into social systems theory, have a look at *The Emerging Consensus in Social Systems Theory* (Bausch 2001) or Parsons and Smelser's seminal work, *Economy and Society* (1956).

 **Technology**

Core definition

The application of science to material and social resources in order to create instruments and processes that satisfy human desires and extend human capability.

Longer explanation

Technology has been around as long as humankind. And while the 50GB MP4 player that you can wear like a charm on a necklace might seem a bit more advanced than the first stone tool, technological innovations have always been linked to fundamental changes in our political, social, economic, and personal worlds. I mean, just imagine what the world was like before and after the control of fire or the development of agriculture. And what kind of world would it be without music, paper, thread, education, or, heaven forbid, television and beer? And what about electricity and how it allowed us to control day and night, or waste disposal and it's impact on human health. Then again, you can also try to imagine a world without machine guns, missiles, nuclear bombs, or *bureaucracy*. Good, bad or ugly, technology is not just something we humans create, it's also something that transforms our world (and us) in profound ways.

Debates and controversies

We definitely have the intelligence and motivation to create technology, but do we have the common sense to use it in appropriate, just, and fair ways? Does technology really satisfy human desires and extend human capability? Well, not always, and certainly not for everyone. We sometimes push forward with technology without pausing to ask whether advances are making us any happier (there are plenty of times I'd like to throw my mobile phone out the window). Also, technology represents *power*, and power has always been wielded in inequitable ways. For example, we talk about the world being connected by the internet; too bad about a third of the world's population is without electricity, let alone a computer and modem. And of course, when we do 'help' the developing world, we sometimes apply Western technology without considering its appropriateness and sustainability for local contexts.

Practical application

Technology is advancing across all areas at astounding rates. And we're not just talking about things like weapons or computers, we're also talking about processes as diverse as creating genetically modified foods or delivering distance education. How an unending array of technological advances impacts all sectors of society in both positive and negative ways makes technology an incredibly important social science construct.

Key figures

Given that technology is the application of science, any scientist (including social scientists) whose work is applied can be considered a contributor here. With the rapid pace of technological change, however, social theorists such as Radovan Richta and Steve Woolgar have begun to open up a defined area called technological theory.

If we continue to develop our technology
without wisdom or prudence, our servant
may prove to be our executioner.

Omar Bradley (1893-1981)
US general - attributed

Recommended readings

There are several interesting works. I like *Science and Technology in World History: An Introduction* (McClellan and Dorn 2006), *Culture and Technology* (Murphie and Potts 2003), *Culture + Technology: A Primer* (Slack and Wise 2005), *The Social Shaping of Technology* (MacKenzie and Wajcman 1999) and *Transforming Technology: A Critical Theory Revisited* (Feenberg 2002).

 Teleology

Core definition

An approach to understanding the world which premises final causes, ends and purposes.

Longer explanation

This term generally describes belief systems in which end purposes are the only way to understand phenomena. Now, this can manifest in how decisions and behaviours are judged. The argument here is that the ends justifies the means, and that acts are not intrinsically right or wrong; they can only be judged by their consequences. Good decisions are those that meet their objectives. Teleology also manifests in arguments of function over form. For example, rather than being able to walk simply because we have legs, the teleological argument is that we have legs because we need to walk, ears because we need to hear, a brain because we need to think. Such function over form arguments actually imply a designer. Cars have headlights so we can see in the dark. It's not a coincidence that they allow us to do it, they are purposely designed that way. So the question is if the natural world is purposefully designed (i.e. we have legs so we can walk), then who's the designer? Well, many would say, 'God of course!' And this is the teleological argument for intelligent design and evidence of God.

Debates and controversies

In the 1980s my mother had a t-shirt that said 'Shit Happens' – and believe it or not, that pretty much sums up arguments against teleology. There's no plan, no greater purpose, no design, and no designer. History and life might just be a series of random happenings. 'Shit Happens' even covers human existence. Another ice age, a meteor strike, or a mutating virus may have seen evolution take a turn where humans may not have made it into existence.

Practical application

You may not be familiar with the word 'teleology', but you're probably familiar with teleological arguments, like when people say, 'it must be God's will' or 'it may look like a mess, but at least it works'. Oprah Winfrey often calls on teleology when she talks about the need to find out why you were put on the planet. This points to deep-seeded teleological beliefs that permeate human thinking and make the term highly relevant in understanding the construction of knowledge in biological, sociological, psychological, philosophical, and theological realms.

Key figures

Teleological arguments have existed since Greek antiquity, with Plato and Aristotle both arguing that understandings must take into account final causes. The eighteenth-century philosopher Kant used teleology to argue for God's existence, while the nineteenth-century theorists William James and Charles Peirce projected human purpose on to nature. Georg Hegel is also important here since he called on teleological arguments to understand the whole of history.

> Strange is our situation here upon
> earth. Each of us comes for a short
> visit, not knowing why, yet sometimes
> seeming to a divine purpose.
>
> **Albert Einstein** (1879–1955)
> German-born US theoretical physicist –
> in *Mein Weltbild* (1931)

Recommended readings

Realism Regained: An Exact Theory of Causation, Teleology, and the Mind (Koons 2000) and *Teleological Realism: Mind, Agency, and Explanation* (Sehon 2005) offer introductions to philosophical teleological arguments. Also worth a look are *Teleology and the Norms of Nature* (Fitzpatrick 2000), *Social Action: A Teleological Account* (Miller 2001) and *Aristotle on Teleology* (Johnson 2006).

Theory/social theory

Longer explanation

It's not easy to capture how the world works. Nonetheless we observe, contemplate and do our best to put forth well-founded theories that explain and predict the world around us. But **knowledge** continually advances and even when we think we have the answer, we're often proven wrong. Phoebe from *Friends* captures this when she asks 'science guy' Ross:

> Wasn't there a time when the brightest minds in the world believed that the world was flat? And, up until like what, 50 years ago, you all thought the atom was the smallest thing, until you split it open, and this like, whole mess of crap came out.

But we don't give up. We continually attempt to prove (and disprove) our theories (often by following **scientific method** or more specifically, **hypothetico-deductive methods**) and end up accepting, correcting, modifying, and rejecting these theories.

Now it's certainly tough to come up with accurate theories that explain the natural world, but in the social world, where it's accepted that socio-historic context creates social realities, it's even more difficult. Universal truth is hard to find, and theories vary according to the **paradigms** operating within particular socio-historic periods (although many **postmodern** (see **postmodernity**) theorists say this is the case for the natural sciences as well). Key social theories include **conflict theory**, **functionalism**, **symbolic interactionism**, and **structuralism**.

Debates and controversies

A contentious point of debate here is whether social theories stand up to the exacting standards of 'scientific' theories. Many researchers in the biophysical sciences suggest that they don't. But even within the social sciences you'll find that some researchers adopt a highly scientific approach to theory via *hypothesis* testing, while others point to the flaws of this approach and opt to develop more abstract or philosophical theories that may not be 'testable' (see *social science research*).

Practical application

We like to think of theories in terms of truth. But in both the natural and social sciences we find that truth, especially everlasting truth, is awfully hard to come by. An approach here is to think of theories, particularly social theories, in terms of their utility, that is how useful they might be in helping us to understand and improve the human condition.

Key figures

In terms of general theory building/testing, key figures include René Descartes, Charles Sanders Peirce, and Karl Popper. The list of key social theorists is unending and includes major thinkers such as Auguste Comte, Emile Durkheim, Max Weber, Karl Marx, John Stuart Mill, George Herbert Mead, and Michel Foucault. The Recommended readings below will give you a taste of the breadth here.

> Without theory, there
> are no questions.
>
> **William Edwards Deming** (1900-1993)
> US, professor, author,
> consultant – in *Review of*
> *The Prophet of Quality* (1992)

Recommended readings

For readings on general theory building and testing turn to the entries for *scientific method* and *hypothesis/hypothetico-deductive method*. For an introduction to social theory, try *Making Sense of Social Theory: A Practical Introduction* (Powers 2004), *Contemporary Sociological Theory: Expanding the Classical Tradition* (Wallace and Wolf 2005), *Social Theory: The Multicultural and Classic Readings* (Lemert and Catalano 2004) and *Readings in Social Theory* (Farganis 2003). To engage with particular social theories turn to Recommended readings for *conflict theory*, *functionalism*, *structuralism* and *symbolic interactionism*.

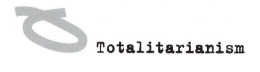 Totalitarianism

Core definition

Omnipotent political systems that through *ideological* and repressive means attempt to regulate all spheres of human life in order to attain a utopian vision.

Longer explanation

There have been many leaders and governments that have attempted to achieve a utopian vision, for example, *societies* based on liberty and freedom (see *liberalism*) or non-exploitative classless societies (see *socialism* and *communism*). And while some visions themselves can be problematic (Hitler's dream of an all-powerful Aryan race), it's the extent to which a *state* will go to achieve its vision that's the real issue. Totalitarian states, which are often led by dictators who have full control over the police, military, media, economy, education system, and even religious institutions, use ideological means such as intensive state propaganda to control their citizens' attitudes, beliefs and values (see *hegemony*). Dissent is not tolerated and is quashed by coercive means such as mass surveillance, restriction of free speech and even terror tactics. Examples of totalitarian states include Mussolini's Italy, Hitler's Germany, Stalin's Soviet Union, Mao's China, and Pinochet's Chile.

Debates and controversies

Totalitarianism is a loaded term and is probably best understood as a characterization or ideal type. Very few 'totalitarian' states are as singular in power as the term suggests. They're often plural in that several interest groups, for example the military, political officials, and industrialists, vie for power and influence. Also, states described as totalitarian are not the only ones guilty of using ideological and repressive means to manipulate and control citizens. '*Democratic*' states often impose *patriarchal* and *capitalist norms* that systemically silence large segments of the population. In times of political turmoil, democratic states have also been known to suppress dissent through various means, some of which have been considered repressive.

Practical application

While many totalitarian states were a product of the chaotic aftermath of the First World War, the term has not been relegated to the history books. At one extreme, it's being used to describe states under **fundamentalist** Islamic law. At the other, it's used to characterize the exercise of global power by the US Bush administration. The political, social and economic implications of such **discursive** processes are rich ground for contemporary social scientists.

Key figures

In the early twentieth century, the Italian philosopher Giovanni Gentile used the term 'totalitarian' to describe Mussolini's rule of Italy, while French anarchist Victor Serge used it to describe Stalin's Soviet Union. More contemporary theorists of totalitarianism include theorists as diverse as Karl Popper, Hannah Arendt, Carl Friedrich, and Zbigniew Brzezinski.

> Everything in the State, nothing outside the State, nothing against the State.
>
> **Benito Mussolini** (1883–1945) Italian dictator – attributed

Recommended readings

Some good choices here include *Totalitarianism and the Modern Conception of Politics* (Halberstam 2000), *Totalitarianism: The Inner History of the Cold War* (Gleason 1997), *Fascism, Totalitarianism, and Political Religion* (Griffin 2005) and Arendt's seminal work, *The Origins of Totalitarianism* (*1951* 2004). I also like *Did Somebody Say Totalitarianism?: Five Interventions in the (Mis)Use of a Notion* (Žižek 2002).

Urbanization

Core definition

The migration of people from overseas or from rural areas to urban areas, which increases both an urban area's density and extent.

Longer explanation

Did you know that in 1800 only 3% of the world's population lived in urban areas? That figure is now about 50% with more than 450 cities with a million people plus. That's a lot of urban growth in what is, historically, an incredibly short period of time. So why has there been such mass urbanization and what are its implications? Well, urban growth is a by-product of shifts from agricultural to industrial economies. As industry developed, there was a need for a centralized pool of workers and a corresponding opportunity for the rural poor to migrate to cities in search of a better life. This has left **developed countries** with massive urban centres, while **developing countries** continue to experience unprecedented urban growth. On the upside, such urban centres can provide a huge range of goods and services, including education, medical services, transport, and recreation. All urban areas, however, have enormous economic disparity. In fact, many of the poor that are needed to support an urban centre's infrastructure are unable to live comfortably within city limits.

Debates and controversies

Poverty, inequity, isolation, **alienation**, lack of community, poor planning, poor infrastructure, inadequate transportation, inadequate waste disposal, high rates of depression and suicide, increased obesity and diabetes, environmental degradation... Yes, urban areas can offer a host of economic and social advantages, but they also offer complicated challenges of the greatest significance.

Practical application

No use lamenting the past, we live in a highly urbanized world. The question is how we can best manage our cities in ways that maximize their economic and social benefits. I'd argue that social scientists need to work hand in hand with government officials, city planners, and environmental managers if we are to meet the challenges posed by continued urbanization.

Key figures

While several contemporary researchers work in this field, it was Georg Simmel who opened up this area of investigation in the early twentieth century by exploring the links between the physical characteristics of cities and the social characteristics of its residents. Louis Wirth also attempted to understand patterns of urban social life and classified urban areas according to their size, density and social heterogeneity. In the 1970s, Marxist Manuel Castell explored cities as sites for the mass consumption necessary for *capitalist* systems to reproduce themselves.

> We want to live in a small
> community ... and yet we want all
> the facilities of the city. ...
> We want to have very intense
> urban experiences and yet we want the
> open space right next to us.
>
> *Moshe Safdie* (1938–)
> Israeli-born Canadian architect and
> urban designer – attributed

Recommended readings

Urbanization is part and parcel of the modern world and there are a number of readings that can help you explore its various dimensions. Have a look at *Urban Life and Society* (Gold 2001), *Postmetropolis: Studies of Cities and Regions* (Soja 2000), *Urban Sprawl and Public Health: Designing, Planning, and Building for Healthy Communities* (Frumkin et al. 2004), *The Landscape Urbanism Reader* (Walsheim 2006), and *Managing Urban Futures: Sustainability and Urban Growth in Developing Countries* (Keiner et al. 2005).

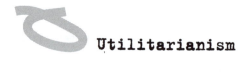
Utilitarianism

Core definition

The belief that morally right actions are those that produce the greatest good or greatest happiness for the greatest number of people.

Longer explanation

In the 1996 movie *Extreme Measures*, Gene Hackman plays Dr Lawrence Myrick, a neurosurgeon desperate to generate spinal growth in order to cure paralysis. To do this he needs to experiment on a few homeless men, isn't that a fair price to pay for a cure? Dr Myrick thinks so and, relying on a classic utilitarian argument, is willing to sacrifice a few men at the bottom of the social hierarchy if it will bring about greater societal benefits. Basically, in utilitarianism, what's right is what produces the greatest good/happiness for the greatest number. Now one major branch of utilitarianism concentrates on acts and argues that actions must be judged on the basis of likely consequences. The other concentrates on rules and bases decisions on the importance of a rule to society. For example, imagine a police officer has conducted an illegal search of a suspected drug dealer. An 'act' utilitarian might argue that this search is morally right because it's likely to get a dealer off the streets. A 'rule' utilitarian, however, would argue that if we don't uphold constitutional rights, the detriment to society will be much greater than that caused by a few more dealers.

Debates and controversies

Let's go back to *Extreme Measures* for a moment. I didn't tell you about Hugh Grant's character, Dr Guy Luthan, who's morally offended by utilitarian Myrick at two levels. First, he's offended that it's the weak of **society** that get exploited. Second, he believes it's impossible to quantify the value of any human life. Well, these are actually two of the main arguments against utilitarianism. Okay, you may be thinking, hold on, it's just a movie. But although utilitarianism aims for the greatest good/happiness, it's been used throughout history to rationalize horrendous human rights violations, including slavery, the death penalty, and torture.

Practical application

Very few decisions please everyone. There's always perceived inequity. And whether it's a genuine ethical stance or political rhetoric, 'the greatest good for the greatest number' has been called on as a justification for everything from individual actions to social/public policy, laws, economic reforms, political action, and war. This makes utilitarianism not only a key ethical construct, but a powerful sociological one as well.

Key figures

Key figures here include several nineteenth-century British philosophers, such as Jeremy Bentham, who proposed the greatest happiness principle, John Stuart Mill, who argued that intellectual and cultural pleasures are more valuable than physical pleasures, and Henry Sidgwick, who argued that no one should act in ways that risk their own happiness.

> The said truth is that it is
> the greatest happiness of
> the greatest number that is
> the measure of right and wrong.
>
> Jeremy Bentham (1748–1832) British
> philosopher, political theorist –
> in Fragment of Government (1776).

Recommended readings

Good choices here include *Contemporary Ethics: Taking Account of Utilitarianism* (Shaw 1998) and *Utilitarianism as a Public Philosophy* (Goodin 1995). If you'd prefer to delve into the work of classic theorists, try *Political Thought in England: The Utilitarians from Bentham to J. S. Mill* (Davidson 2006) or seminal works by Bentham, *Selected Writings on Utilitarianism* (*1789* 2000) and Mill, *Utilitarianism* (*1863* 2005).

Bibliography/reading list

Achinstein, P. (2004) *Science Rules: A Historical Introduction to Scientific Methods.* Baltimore, MD: The Johns Hopkins University Press.

Adam, B., Beck, U. and Van Loon, J. (2000) *The Risk Society and Beyond: Critical Issues for Social Theory.* London: Sage.

Adler, F. and Laufer, W. S. (eds) (1999) *The Legacy of Anomie Theory.* Somerset, NJ: Transaction.

Aggleton, P. (2006) *Culture, Society and Sexuality: A Reader.* London: Routledge.

Agnew, J. A. (2005) *Hegemony: The New Shape of Global Power.* Philadelphia: Temple University Press.

Albert, M. (2004) *Thought Dreams: Radical Theory for the 21st Century.* Winnipeg: Arbeiter Ring.

Alchin, N. (2006) *Theory of Knowledge.* London: Hodder Murray.

Alcock, J. (2003) *The Triumph of Sociobiology.* New York: Oxford University Press.

Ali, T. (2003) *The Clash of Fundamentalisms: Crusades, Jihads and Modernity.* London: Verso.

Alinsky, S. (*1971* 1989) *Rules for Radicals.* New York: Vintage Books.

Alperson, P. (ed.) (2002) *Diversity and Community: An Interdisciplinary Reader.* London: Blackwell.

American Psychological Society (2004) *Current Directions in Personality Psychology Reader.* Englewood Cliffs, NJ: Prentice-Hall.

Ameriks, K. (ed.) (2000) *The Cambridge Companion to German Idealism.* Cambridge: Cambridge University Press.

Anderson, B. (2006) *Imagined Communities: Reflections on the Origin and Spread of Nationalism.* London: Verso.

Anderson, B. J. (2000) *Doing the Dirty Work?: The Global Politics of Domestic Labour.* London: Zed Books.

Appiah, K. A. (2004) *The Ethics of Identity.* Princeton, NJ: Princeton University Press.

Archer, M. S. (2003) *Structure, Agency and the Internal Conversation.* Cambridge: Cambridge University Press.

Arendt, H. (*1951* 2004) *The Origins of Totalitarianism.* New York: Schocken Books.

Atkins, K. (2005) *Self and Subjectivity.* London: Blackwell.

Atkinson, P., Coffey, A., Delamont, S., Lofland, J. and Lofland, L. (eds) (2001) *Handbook of Ethnography.* London: Sage.

Atmanspacher, H. and Bishop, R. (2002) *Between Chance and Choice: Interdisciplinary Perspectives on Determinism.* Exeter, UK: Imprint Academic.

Avineri, S. and de-Shalit, A. (1992) *Communitarianism and Individualism.* Oxford: Oxford University Press.

Axtmann, R. (ed.) (2003) *Understanding Democratic Politics: An Introduction*. Thousand Oaks, CA: Sage.

Azzouni, J. (2006) *Deflating Existential Consequence: A Case for Nominalism*. Oxford: Oxford University Press.

Babbie, E. (2004) *The Basics of Social Research*. Belmont, CA: Wadsworth.

Baghramian, M. (2004) *Relativism*. London: Routledge.

Ball, T. and Dagger, R. (2003) *Ideals and Ideologies: A Reader*. White Plains, NY: Longman.

Bardhan, P., Bowles, S. and Wallerstein, M. (eds) (2006) *Globalization and Egalitarian Redistribution*. Princeton, NJ: Princeton University Press.

Barker, C. and Galasinski, D. (2001) *Cultural Studies and Discourse Analysis: A Dialogue on Language and Identity*. London: Sage.

Barrentine, L. B. (1999) *An Introduction to Design of Experiments: A Simplified Approach*. Milwaukee, WI: ASQ Quality Press.

Barry, B. M. (2005) *Why Social Justice Matters*. Cambridge: Polity Press.

Bartos, O. J. and Wehr, P. (2002) *Using Conflict Theory*. Cambridge: Cambridge University Press.

Bates, S. (2006) *Secularization and Its Discontents*. New Haven, CT: Yale University Press.

Baum, W. (2004) *Understanding Behaviorism: Behavior, Culture, and Evolution*. Malden, MA: Blackwell.

Baumeister, R. (ed.) (1999) *Self in Social Psychology: Essential Readings*. New York: Psychology Press.

Bausch, K. (2001) *The Emerging Consensus in Social Systems Theory*. New York: Springer.

Baylis, J., Smith, S. and Owens, P. (2004) *The Globalization of World Politics: An Introduction to International Relations*. Oxford: Oxford University Press.

Beatley, T. (2004) *Native to Nowhere: Sustaining Home and Community in a Global Age*. Washington, DC: Island Press.

Beauchamp, T. L. (2001) *Philosophical Ethics: An Introduction to Moral Philosophy*. Columbus, OH: McGraw-Hill.

Beck, U. (1992) *Risk Society: Towards a New Modernity*. London: Sage.

Beck, U. and Beck-Gernsheim, E. (2002) *Individualization: Institutionalized Individualism and Its Social and Political Consequences*. London: Sage.

Becker, H. (*1963* 1997) *Outsiders*. New York: Free Press.

Bell, D. (*1976* 2001) *The Coming of Post-Industrial Society: A Venture in Social Forecasting*. New York: Basic Books.

Bennett, A. (2005) *Culture and Everyday Life*. London: Sage.

Bennett, J. M. (2006) *History Matters: Patriarchy and the Challenge of Feminism*. Philadelphia: University of Pennsylvania Press.

Benson, P. (2001) *Ethnocentrism and the English Dictionary*. London: Routledge.

Bentham, J. (*1789* 2000) *Selected Writings on Utilitarianism*. Ware, Hertfordshire, UK: Wordsworth.

Bentz, V. M. and Shapiro, J. J. (1998) *Mindful Inquiry in Social Research*. London: Sage.

Berger, P. L. and Luckmann, T. (1967) *The Social Construction of Reality*. New York: Doubleday.

303

Bernstein, R. J. (1999) *The Praxis and Action: Contemporary Philosophies of Human Activity*. Philadelphia. University of Pennsylvania Press.

Berreby, D. (2005) *Us and Them: Understanding Your Tribal Mind*. New York: Little, Brown and Company.

Bertuglia, C. S. and Vaio, F. (2005) *Nonlinearity, Chaos, and Complexity: The Dynamics of Natural and Social Systems*. Oxford: Oxford University Press.

Best, S. and Kellner, D. (1991) *Postmodern Theory*. New York: The Guilford Press.

Bewes, T. (2002) *Reification: Or the Anxiety of Late Capitalism*. London: Verso.

Bhabha, H. (2004) *The Location of Culture*. London: Routledge.

Biaggi, C. (2006) *The Rule of Mars: Readings on the Origins, History and Impact of Patriarchy*. Manchester, CT: Knowledge, Ideas & Trends, Inc.

Bicchieri, C. (2005) *The Grammar of Society: The Nature and Dynamics of Social Norms*. Cambridge: Cambridge University Press.

Blanck, G. and Blanck, R. (1992) *Ego Psychology*. New York: Columbia University Press.

Blauner, R. (1964) *Alienation and Freedom: The Factory Worker and His Industry*. Chicago: University of Chicago Press.

Blomberg, T. and Cohen, S. (2003) *Punishment and Social Control*. Chicago: Aldine Transaction.

Blommaert, J. (2005) *Discourse: A Critical Introduction*. Cambridge: Cambridge University Press.

Blumer, H. (*1969* 1986) *Symbolic Interactionism: Perspective and Method*. Berkeley: University of California Press.

Boghossian, P. A. (2006) *Fear of Knowledge: Against Relativism and Constructivism*. Oxford: Oxford University Press.

BonJour, L. (1997) *In Defence of Pure Reason: A Rationalist Account of A Priori Justification*. Cambridge: Cambridge University Press.

BonJour, L. (2005) *The Structure of Empirical Knowledge*. Cambridge, MA: Harvard University Press.

Bornstein, M. H. and Bradley, R. H. (eds) (2002) *Socioeconomic Status, Parenting, and Child Development*. Hillsdale, NJ: LEA, Inc.

Bourdieu, P. (1986) 'The Forms of Capital', in J. G. Richardson (ed.), *Handbook for Theory and Research for the Sociology of Education*. Westport, CT: Greenwood Press. pp. 241–58.

Bourdieu, P. and Wacquant, L. (1992) *An Invitation to Reflexive Sociology*. Chicago: University of Chicago Press.

Bowles, S. and Gintis, H. (eds) (1999) *Recasting Egalitarianism: New Rules for Communities, States and Markets*. London: Verso.

Branzei, R., Dimitrov, D. and Tijs, S. (2005) *Models in Cooperative Game Theory*. New York: Springer.

Brown, J. R. (1996) *The I in Science: Training to Utilize Subjectivity in Research*. Oslo: Scandinavian University Press.

Brown, T. and Smith, L. (eds) (2002) *Reductionism and the Development of Knowledge*. Hillsdale, NJ: LEA, Inc.

Browning, G. K. (2000) *Lyotard and the End of Grand Narratives*. Cardiff: University of Wales Press.

Bruce, S. (2002) *God is Dead: Secularization in the West*. London: Blackwell.

Bubner, R. (2003) *The Innovations of Idealism*. Cambridge: Cambridge University Press.

Burr, V. (2003) *Social Constructionism*. New York: Psychology Press.

Butler, C. (2003) *Postmodernism: A Very Short Introduction*. Oxford: Oxford University Press.

Callinicos, A. (2004) *Making History: Agency, Structure, and Change in Social Theory*. Leiden, Netherlands: Brill Academic Publishers.

Campbell, J. K., O'Rourke, M., and Shier, D. (eds) (2004) *Freedom and Determinism*. Cambridge, MA: The MIT Press.

Carey, S. S. (2003) *A Beginner's Guide to Scientific Method*. Belmont, CA: Wadsworth.

Carlisle, R. and Lide, J. (2002) *The Complete Idiot's Guide to Communism*. New York: Alpha Books.

Carrier, M., Roggenhofer, J., Kupper, G. and Blanchard, P. (eds) (2004) *Knowledge and the World: Challenges Beyond the Science Wars*. New York: Springer.

Casullo, A. (2003) *A Priori Justification*. Oxford: Oxford University Press.

Cavell, M. (2006) *Becoming a Subject: Reflections in Philosophy and Psychoanalysis*. Oxford: Oxford University Press.

Chandler, D. (2004) *Semiotics: The Basics*. London: Routledge.

Charmaz, K. C. (2006) *Constructing Grounded Theory: A Practical Guide through Qualitative Analysis*. London: Sage.

Charon, J. M. (2006) *Symbolic Interactionism: An Introduction, An Interpretation*. Englewood Cliffs, NJ: Prentice-Hall.

Childs, P. (2000) *Modernism*. London: Routledge.

Chomsky, N. (2003) *Hegemony or Survival: America's Quest for Global Dominance*. New York: Metropolitan Books.

Christensen, L. B. (2000) *Experimental Methodology*. Boston: Allyn & Bacon.

Clarke, A. E. (2005) *Situational Analysis: Grounded Theory after the Postmodern Turn*. London: Sage.

Clifford, M. (2001) *Political Genealogy after Foucault: Savage Identities*. London: Routledge.

Cobley, P. (2005) *Introducing Semiotics*. New York: Totem Books.

Coghlan, D. and Brannick, T. (2004) *Doing Action Research in Your Own Organization*. London: Sage.

Colding, J. and Berkes, F. (2000) *Linking Social and Ecological Systems: Management Practices and Social Mechanisms for Building Resilience*. Cambridge: Cambridge University Press.

Collier, M. J. (2000) *Constituting Cultural Difference through Discourse*. London: Sage.

Comte, A. (*1855* 2003) *Positive Philosophy of Auguste Comte, Part 1/Part 2*. Whitefish, MT: Kessinger.

Conee, E. and Sider, T. (2005) *Riddles of Existence: A Guided Tour of Metaphysics*. Oxford: Oxford University Press.

Connolly, W. E. (2005) *Pluralism*. Durham, NC: Duke University Press.

Cooper, F. (2005) *Colonialism in Question: Theory, Knowledge, History*. Berkeley: University of California Press.

Coser, L. A. (*1956* 1999) *Functions of Social Conflict*. London: Routledge.

Cottingham, J. (1988) *The Rationalists*. Oxford: Oxford University Press.

Coughlin, L., Wingard, E. and Hollihan, K. (eds) (2005) *Enlightened Power: How Women are Transforming the Practice of Leadership*. Hoboken, NJ: Jossey-Bass.

Coulon, A. (1995) *Ethnomethodology*. London: Sage.

Coupland, N. and Jaworski, A. (eds) (1997) *Sociolinguistics: A Reader*. New York: Palgrave Macmillan.

Creswell, J. W. (2002) *Research Design: Qualitative, Quantitative, and Mixed Methods Approaches*. Thousand Oaks, CA: Sage.

Creswell, J. W. and Plano Clark, V. L. (2006) *Designing and Conducting Mixed Methods Research*. Thousand Oaks, CA: Sage.

Croce, B. (2004) *Historical Materialism and the Economics of Karl Marx*. Whitefish, MT: Kessinger.

Crompton, R., Scott, J., Devine, F. and Savage, M. (eds) (2001) *Renewing Class Analysis*. London: Blackwell.

Crow, G. (2001) *Social Solidarities: Theories, Identities and Social Change*. Buckingham: Open University Press.

D'Amato, P. (2006) *The Meaning of Marxism*. Chicago: Haymarket Books.

Dahl, R. A. (2000) *On Democracy*. New Haven, CT: Yale University Press.

Dahrendorf, R. (1959) *Class and Class Conflict in Industrial Society*. Stanford, CA: Stanford University Press.

Darder, A., Torres, R. D. and Baltodano, M. (eds) (2002) *The Critical Pedagogy Reader*. London: Falmer Press.

Davidson, W. J. (2006) *Political Thought in England: The Utilitarians from Bentham to J. S. Mill*. Whitefish, MT: Kessinger.

Davies, T. (1996) *Humanism*. London: Routledge.

Davis, M. G. (1997) *Game Theory: A Nontechnical Introduction*. New York: Dover Publications.

Dawkins, R. (*1976* 2006) *The Selfish Gene*. Oxford and New York: Oxford University Press.

de Beauvoir, S. (*1949* 1989) *The Second Sex*. New York: Vintage Books.

Dean, K., Joseph, J., Roberts, J. and Wight, C. (2006) *Realism, Philosophy and Social Science*. New York: Palgrave Macmillan.

Degler, C. N. (1992) *In Search of Human Nature: The Decline and Revival of Darwinism in American Social Thought*. Oxford: Oxford University Press.

Delanty, G. and Strydom, P. (2003) *Philosophies of Social Science*. Maidenhead: Open University Press.

Demers, D. and Viswanath, K. (eds) (1998) *Mass Media, Social Control, and Social Change: A Macrosocial Perspective*. Ames, IA: Iowa State Press.

Denise, T. C., White, N. and Peterfreund, S. P. (eds) (2004) *Great Traditions in Ethics*. Belmont, CA: Wadsworth.

Denny, D. (2005) *Risk and Society*. London: Sage.

Denzin, N. and Lincoln, Y. (eds) (2003) *The Landscape of Qualitative Research: Theories and Issues*. Thousand Oaks, CA: Sage.

Denzin, N. and Lincoln, Y. (2005) *The Sage Handbook of Qualitative Research*. Thousand Oaks, CA: Sage.

Depken, C. (2005) *Microeconomics Demystified*. Columbus, OH: McGraw-Hill.

Derrida, J. (*1976* 1998) *Of Grammatology*. Baltimore, MD: Johns Hopkins University Press.

Descartes, R. (*1641* 1993) *Discourse on Method and Meditations on First Philosophy*. Indianapolis: Hackett.

Dickens, P. (2000) *Social Darwinism: Linking Evolutionary Thought to Social Theory*. Buckingham: Open University Press.

Diehl, P. F. (2005) *The Politics of Global Governance: International Organizations in an Interdependent World*. Boulder, CO: Lynne Rienner.

Doreian, P. and Fararo, T. (1998) *Problem of Solidarity: Theories and Models*. London: Routledge.

Dotter, D. L. (2004) *Creating Deviance: An Interactionist Approach*. Lanham, MD: AltaMira Press.

Dovido, J. F., Glick, P. and Rudman, L. A. (eds) (2005) *On the Nature of Prejudice: Fifty Years after Allport*. London: Blackwell.

Doyle, D. H. and Pamplona, M. A. V. (eds) (2006) *Nationalism in the New World*. Athens, GA: University of Georgia Press.

Draper, H. and Haberkem, E. (2005) *Karl Marx's Theory of Revolution: War and Revolution*. Alameda, CA: Center for Socialist History.

Dresser, N. (2005) *Multicultural Manners: Essential Rules of Etiquette for the 21st Century*. New York: John Wiley & Sons.

du Gay, P. (2000) *In Praise of Bureaucracy: Weber–Organization–Ethics*. London: Sage.

Dunn, J. (2006) *Democracy: A History*. New York: Atlantic Monthly Press.

Durant, R. F., Fiorino, D. J. and O'Leary, R. (2004) *Environmental Governance Reconsidered: Challenges, Choices, and Opportunities*. Cambridge, MA: The MIT Press.

During, S. (2005) *Cultural Studies*. Abingdon, UK: Taylor & Francis.

During, S. (2007) *The Cultural Studies Reader*. Abingdon, UK: Taylor & Francis.

Durkheim, E. (*1893* 1997) *The Division of Labor in Society*. New York: Free Press.

Durkheim, E. (*1895* 1982) *The Rules of Sociological Method*. New York: Free Press.

Durkheim, E. (*1897* 1997) *Suicide*. New York: Free Press.

Durkheim, E. (*1906* 1974) *Sociology and Philosophy*. New York: Free Press.

Dye, T. R. (2004) *Power and Society: An Introduction to the Social Sciences*. Belmont, CA: Wadsworth.

Edwards, M. (2004) *Civil Society*. Cambridge: Polity Press.

Eldridge, M. (1998) *Transforming Experience: John Dewey's Cultural Instrumentalism*. Nashville, TN: Vanderbilt University Press.

Ellis, B. D. (2002) *The Philosophy of Nature: A Guide to the New Essentialism*. Montreal: McGill-Queen's University Press.

Erikson, E. (*1959* 1994) *Identity and the Life Cycle*. New York: W. W. Norton & Co.

Ertman, M. and Williams, J. (eds) (2005) *Rethinking Commodification: Cases and Readings in Law and Culture*. New York: New York University Press.

Evans, M. and Lee, E. (eds) (2002) *Real Bodies: A Sociological Introduction*. New York: Palgrave Macmillan.

Eve, R. A. and Horsfall, S. (eds) (1997) *Chaos, Complexity, and Sociology: Myths, Models, and Theories*. London: Sage.

Ewen, R. B. (2003) *An Introduction to Theories of Personality*. Hillsdale, NJ: LEA, Inc.

Fairbrother, P. and Rainnie, A. (2006) *Globalisation, State and Labour*. London: Routledge.

Faja, M. A. (2006) *Dynamic Functionalism*. Cambridge: Cambridge University Press.

Farganis, J. (ed.) (2003) *Readings in Social Theory*. Columbus, OH: McGraw-Hill.

Feagin, S. and Maynard, P. (eds) (1998) *Aesthetics*. Oxford: Oxford University Press.

Feenberg, A. (2002) *Transforming Technology: A Critical Theory Revisited*. New York: Oxford University Press.

Ferguson, R., Gever, M., Minh-Ha, T. and West, C. (eds) (1992) *Out There: Marginalization and Contemporary Culture*. Cambridge, MA: The MIT Press.

Festinger, L. (1957) *Theory of Cognitive Dissonance*. Stanford, CA: Stanford University Press.

Finlay, L. and Gough, B. (2003) *Reflexivity: A Practical Guide for Researchers in Health and Social Sciences*. London: Blackwell.

Fisher, A. (2001) *Critical Thinking*. Cambridge: Cambridge University Press.

Fisher, A. T., Sonn, C. C. and Bishop, B. J. (eds) (2002) *Psychological Sense of Community: Research, Applications, and Implications*. New York: Springer.

Fitzpatrick, W. (2000) *Teleology and the Norms of Nature*. London: Garland.

Fleischacker, S. (2005) *A Short History of Distributive Justice*. Cambridge, MA: Harvard University Press.

Flynn, S. M. (2005) *Economics for Dummies*. New York: IDG Books Worldwide.

Fogelin, R. (2001) *Routledge Philosophy Guidebook to Berkeley and the Principles of Human Knowledge*. London: Routledge.

Foley, D. (1986) *Understanding Capital: Marx's Economic Theory*. Cambridge, MA: Harvard University Press.

Foran, J. (ed.) (2003) *The Future of Revolutions: Rethinking Radical Change in the Age of Globalization*. London: Zed Books.

Foucault, M. (*1969* 2002) *Archeology of Knowledge*. London: Routledge.

Foucault, M. (*1977* 1995) *Discipline and Punish*. London: Vintage.

Foucault, M. (1980) *Power/Knowledge: Selected Interviews and Other Writings, 1972–1977*. New York: Pantheon.

Foucault, M. (1984) *The Foucault Reader*. New York: Pantheon.

Fowler, F. J. Jr. (2001) *Survey Research Methods*. Thousand Oaks, CA: Sage.

Francis, R. C. (2005) *Why Men Won't Ask for Directions: The Seductions of Sociobiology*. Princeton, NJ: Princeton University Press.

Francis, D. and Hester, S. (2004) *An Invitation to Ethnomethodology*. London: Sage.

Fraser, N. (1997) *Justice Interruptus*. London: Routledge.

Freeden, M. (2003) *Ideology: A Very Short Introduction*. Oxford: Oxford University Press.

Freedman, E. (2003) *No Turning Back: The History of Feminism and the Future of Women*. New York: Ballantine Books.

Freud, S. (*1923* 1962) *The Ego and the Id*. New York: W. W. Norton & Co.

Friedan, B. (*1963* 2001) *The Feminine Mystique*. New York: W. W. Norton & Co.

Friedman, G. (1997) *Agency, Structure and International Politics*. London: Routledge.

Friere, P. (*1970* 2000) *Pedagogy of the Oppressed*. London: Continuum.

Fromm, E. (*1947* 1990) *Man for Himself*. New York: Owl Books.

Frosh, S. (1999) *The Politics of Psychoanalysis: An Introduction to Freudian and Post-Freudian Theory*. New York: New York University Press.

Frumkin, H., Frank, L. and Jackson, R. J. (2004) *Urban Sprawl and Public Health: Designing, Planning, and Building for Healthy Communities*. Washington, DC: Island Press.

Fuchs, D. (2005) *Against Essentialism: A Theory of Culture and Society*. Cambridge, MA: Harvard University Press.

Fulcher, J. (2004) *Capitalism: A Very Short Introduction*. Oxford: Oxford University Press.

Gadamer, H. (*1960* 2005) *Truth and Method*. London: Continuum.

Gallagher, C. and Greenblatt, S. (2001) *Practicing New Historicism*. Chicago: University of Chicago Press.

Garfinkel, H. (1967) *Studies in Ethnomethodology*. Englewood Cliffs, NJ: Prentice-Hall.

Gauch, H. G. Jr. (2002) *Scientific Method in Practice*. Cambridge: Cambridge University Press.

Gaus, G. F. (2003) *Contemporary Theories of Liberalism: Public Reason as a Post-Enlightenment Project*. London: Sage.

Geertz, C. (1973) *The Interpretation of Cultures*. New York: Basic Books.

Gelman, S. A. (2005) *The Essential Child: Origins of Essentialism in Everyday Thought*. Oxford: Oxford University Press.

Gergen, K. J. (1999) *An Invitation to Social Construction*. London: Sage.

Gergen, M. M., and Gergen, K. J. (eds) (2003) *Social Construction: A Reader*. London: Sage.

Gerth, H. and Mills, C. W. (1958) *From Max Weber: Essays in Sociology*. New York: Oxford University Press.

Giddens, A. (1986) *The Constitution of Society: Outline of the Theory of Structuration*. Berkeley, CA: University of California Press.

Giddens, A. (1991) *Modernity and Self-Identity: Self and Society in the Late Modern Age*. Stanford, CA: Stanford University Press.

Giddens, A. (1991) *The Consequences of Modernity*. Stanford, CA: Stanford University Press.

Giddens, A. and Diamond, P. (eds) (2005) *The New Egalitarianism*. Cambridge: Polity Press.

Gill, R. (2006) *Theory and Practice of Leadership*. London: Sage.

Glaser, B. and Strauss, A. (1967) *The Discovery of Grounded Theory*. Chicago: Aldine Transaction.

Gleason, A. (1997) *Totalitarianism: The Inner History of the Cold War*. New York: Oxford University Press.

Goffman, E. (1959) *The Presentation of Self in Everyday Life*. New York: Anchor Books.

Gold, H. (2001) *Urban Life and Society*. Englewood Cliffs, NJ: Prentice-Hall.

Goldblatt, D. and Brown, L. B. (2004) *Aesthetics: A Reader in Philosophy of the Arts*. Englewood Cliffs, NJ: Prentice-Hall.

Goldstone, J. A. (2002) *Revolutions: Theoretical, Comparative, and Historical Studies*. Belmont, CA: Wadsworth.

Goodin, R. E. (1995) *Utilitarianism as a Public Philosophy*. Cambridge: Cambridge University Press.

Goodsell, C. T. (2003) *The Case for Bureaucracy: A Public Administration Polemic*. Washington, DC: CQ Press.

Goodwin, J. and Jasper, J. M. (eds) (2003) *The Social Movements Reader: Cases and Concepts*. London: Blackwell.

Gorard, S. (2003) *Quantitative Methods in Social Science*. London: Continuum.

Gower, B. (1996) *Scientific Method*. London: Routledge.

Gray, J. (1995) *Liberalism*. Minneapolis, MN: University of Minnesota Press.

Gray, J. (2004) *Men are from Mars, Women are from Venus*. New York: Harper Paperbacks.

Grayling, A. C. (2003) *Meditations for the Humanist: Ethics for a Secular Age*. Oxford: Oxford University Press.

Greer, G. (*1970* 2002) *The Female Eunuch*: New York: Farrar, Straus and Giroux.

Griffin, R. (ed.) (1995) *Fascism*. Oxford: Oxford University Press.

Griffin, R. (2005) *Fascism, Totalitarianism, and Political Religion*. London: Routledge.

Griswold, W. (2003) *Cultures and Societies in a Changing World*. Thousand Oaks, CA: Pine Forge Press.

Grondin, J. and Weinsheimer, J. (1997) *Introduction to Philosophical Hermeneutics*. New Haven, CT: Yale University Press.

Groves, R. M., Fowler, F. J., Couper, M. J., Lepkowski, J. M., Singer, E. and Tourangeau, R. (2004) *Survey Methodology*. New York: John Wiley & Sons.

Grusky, D. (ed.) (2000) *Social Stratification: Class, Race, and Gender in Sociological Perspective*. Boulder, CO: Westview Press.

Guba, E. (ed.) (1990) *The Paradigm Dialog*. Thousand Oaks, CA: Sage.

Gubrium, J. F. and Holstein, J. A. (2001) *Handbook of Interview Research: Context and Method*. Thousand Oaks, CA: Sage.

Haack, S. (ed.) (2006) *Pragmatism, Old and New: Selected Writings*. Loughton, Essex: Prometheus Books.

Hacking, I. (2000) *The Social Construction of What?* Cambridge, MA: Harvard University Press.

Halberstam, M. (2000) *Totalitarianism and the Modern Conception of Politics*. New Haven, CT: Yale University Press.

Hall, S. and du Gay, P. (eds) (1996) *Questions of Cultural Identity*. London: Sage.

Hall, S., Held, D., Hubert, D. and Thompson, K. (eds) (1996) *Modernity: An Introduction to Modern Societies*. London: Blackwell.

Hamilton, P. (1996) *Historicism*. London: Routledge.

Handelman, H. (2002) *The Challenge of Third World Development*. Englewood Cliffs, NJ: Prentice-Hall.

Hanson, B. (1995) *General Systems Theory – Beginning with Wholes*. Abingdon, UK: Taylor & Francis.

Harmon-Jones, E. and Mills, J. (eds) (1999) *Cognitive Dissonance: Progress on a Pivotal Theory in Social Psychology*. Washington, DC: American Psychological Association.

Harvey, D. (2005) *The New Imperialism*. Oxford: Oxford University Press.

Haugaard, M. (2002) *Power: A Reader*. Manchester: Manchester University Press.

Hawkes, D. (2003) *Ideology*. London: Routledge.

Hawkins, M. (1997) *Social Darwinism in European and American Thought, 1860–1945: Nature as Model and Nature as Threat*. New York: Cambridge University Press.

Hazelrigg, L. E. (1989) *Social Science and the Challenge of Relativism: A Wilderness of Mirrors: On Practices of Theory in a Gray Age*. Gainesville, FL: University Press of Florida.

Hearn, J. (2006) *Rethinking Nationalism: A Critical Introduction*. New York: Palgrave Macmillan.

Hechter, M. and Opp, K. (2001) *Social Norms*. London: Sage.

Heinberg, R. (2005) *The Party's Over: Oil, War and the Fate of Industrial Societies*. Gabriola Island, BC: New Society Publishers.

Held, D. (1997) *Models of Democracy*. Stanford, CA: Stanford University Press.

Held, D. and McGrew, A. G. (eds) (2002) *Governing Globalization: Power, Authority and Global Governance*. Cambridge: Polity Press.

Hendry, J. and Wong, H. W. (eds) (2006) *Dismantling the East–West Dichotomy*. London: Routledge.

Herda, E. A. (1999) *Research Conversations and Narrative: A Critical Hermeneutic Orientation in Participatory Inquiry*. New York: Praeger.

Hergenhahn, B. R. and Olson, M. (2006) *An Introduction to Theories of Personality*. Englewood Cliffs, NJ: Prentice-Hall.

Herrick, J. (2005) *Humanism: An Introduction*. Loughton, Essex: Prometheus Books.

Hobsbawn, E. J. (1999) *Industry and Empire: The Birth of the Industrial Revolution*. New York: New Press.

Hobson, J. (*1902* 1965) *Imperialism*. Ann Arbor, MI: University of Michigan Press.

Hodgkinson, V. and Foley, M. W. (eds) (2003) *The Civil Society Reader*. Medford, MA: Tufts University Press.

Honderich, T. (2002) *How Free Are You?: The Determinism Problem*. Oxford: Oxford University Press.

Howard, M. W. (ed.) (2001) *Socialism*. Loughton, Essex: Humanity Books.

Huemer, M. (ed.) (2002) *Epistemology: Contemporary Readings*. London: Routledge.

Humphrey, J. A. (2005) *Deviant Behavior*. Englewood Cliffs, NJ: Prentice-Hall.

Husserl, E. (2003) *The Phenomenology of Husserl: Selected Critical Readings*. Madison, WI: University of Wisconsin Press.

Hyde, J. S. and Delamater, J. (2006) *Understanding Human Sexuality*. Columbus, OH: McGraw-Hill.

Innes, M. (2003) *Understanding Social Control*. Buckingham: Open University Press.

Isajiw, W. (*1968* 2003) *Causation and Functionalism in Sociology*. London: Routledge.

Ives, P. (2004) *Language and Hegemony in Gramsci*. London: Pluto Press.

Jablon, J. R., Dombro, A. L. and Dichtelmiller, M. L. (1999) *The Power of Observation*. Florence, KY: Thomson Delmar Learning.

Jacquette, D. (2002) *Ontology*. Montreal: McGill-Queen's University Press.

Jain, J. (ed.) (2005) *Women in Patriarchy: Cross-Cultural Readings*. Jaipur: Rawat Publications.

James, C. L. R. (2005) *Notes on Dialectics: Hegel, Marx, Lenin*. London: Pluto Press.

James, W. (*1931* 2005) *Pragmatism*. McLean, VA: IndyPublish.com.

Jameson, F. (1992) *Postmodernism, or The Cultural Logic of Late Capitalism*. Durham, NC: Duke University Press.

Jameson, F. (2002) *A Singular Modernity: Essay on the Ontology of the Present*. London: Verso.

Javier, A. (2006) *Liberalism Against Liberalism*. London: Routledge.

Johnson, A. G. (1997) *The Gender Knot: Unravelling Our Patriarchal Legacy*. Philadelphia: Temple University Press.

Johnson, R. (2006) *Aristotle on Teleology*. Oxford: Oxford University Press.

Jones, A. L. (*1909* 2004) *Logic, Inductive and Deductive: An Introduction to Scientific Method*. Whitefish, MT: Kessinger.

Jones, R. H. (2000) *Reductionism: Analysis and the Fullness of Reality*. Lewisburg, PA: Bucknell University Press.

Joule, R. V. (1996) *A Radical Dissonance Theory*. Abingdon, UK: Taylor & Francis.

Jung, C. (*1934* 1991) *The Archetypes and the Collective Unconscious*. London: Routledge.

Kain, P. J. (2005) *Hegel and the Other: A Study of the Phenomenology of Spirit*. Albany, NY: State University of New York Press.

Kallis, A. (ed.) (2002) *Fascism Reader*. London: Routledge.

Kant, I. (*1783* 2004) *Prolegomena to Any Future Metaphysics*. Cambridge: Cambridge University Press.

Kapferer, B. (ed.) (2005) *The Retreat of the Social: The Rise and Rise of Reductionism*. Oxford: Berghahn Books.

Katz, H. and Kochan, T. (2003) *An Introduction to Collective Bargaining and Industrial Relations*. Columbus, OH: McGraw-Hill.

Katz, J. J. (1997) *Realistic Rationalism*. Cambridge, MA: The MIT Press.

Keil, L. D. and Elliott, E. W. (eds) (1997) *Chaos Theory in the Social Sciences: Foundations and Applications*. Ann Arbor, MI: University of Michigan Press.

Keiner, M., Koll-Schretzenmayr, M. and Schmid, W. A. (eds) (2005) *Managing Urban Futures: Sustainability and Urban Growth in Developing Countries*. Williston, VT: Ashgate.

Kekes, J. (2003) *The Illusions of Egalitarianism*. Ithaca, NY: Cornell University Press.

Kelly, D. H. and Clarke, E. J. (2003) *Deviant Behavior: A Text-Reader in the Sociology of Deviance*. New York: Worth Publishers.

Kenworthy, L. (2004) *Egalitarian Capitalism: Jobs, Incomes, and Growth in Affluent Countries*. New York: Russell Sage Foundation Publications.

Kerbo, H. (2002) *Social Stratification and Inequality*. Columbus, OH: McGraw-Hill.

Kim, J. and Sosa, E. (eds) (1999) *Metaphysics: An Anthology*. London: Blackwell.

Kimmel, M. S. and Plante, R. F. (2004) *Sexualities: Identities, Behaviours, and Society*. Oxford: Oxford University Press.

Kingsland, W. (2005) *Materialism vs. Idealism*. Whitefish, MT: Kessinger.

Knight, M. (1995) *Humanist Anthology: From Confucius to Attenborough*. Loughton, Essex: Prometheus Books.

Kolakowski, L. (*1978* 2005) *Main Currents of Marxism: The Founders, the Golden Age, the Breakdown*. New York: W. W. Norton & Co.

Kolmar, W. and Bartowski, F. (2003) *Feminist Theory: A Reader*. Columbus, OH: McGraw-Hill.

Kolocotroni, V., Goldman, J. and Taxidou, O. (1999) *Modernism: An Anthology of Sources and Documents*. Chicago: University of Chicago Press.

Koons, R. C. (2000) *Realism Regained: An Exact Theory of Causation, Teleology, and the Mind*. Oxford: Oxford University Press.

Kraidy, M. M. (2005) *Hybridity, or The Cultural Logic of Globalization*. Philadelphia: Temple University Press.

Kreiger, J. (ed.) (2005) *Globalization and State Power: A Reader*. White Plains, NY: Longman.

Kuhn, H. W. (ed.) (1997) *Classics in Game Theory*. Princeton, NJ: Princeton University Press.

Kuhn, T. (*1962* 1996) *The Structure of Scientific Revolutions*. Chicago: University of Chicago Press.

Kukathas, C. and Schott, G. (2006) *Multiculturalism*. London: Blackwell.

Kumar, K. (2005) *From Post-Industrial to Post-Modern Society: New Theories of the Contemporary World*. London: Blackwell.

Lazlo, E. (1996) *The Systems View of the World: A Holistic Vision for Our Time*. Cresskill, NJ: Hampton Press.

Le Sueur, J. (2003) *The Decolonization Reader*. London: Routledge.

Lechte, J. (2006) *Fifty Key Contemporary Thinkers*. London: Routledge.

Lee, R. M. (2000) *Unobtrusive Methods in Social Research*. Buckingham: Open University Press.

Lehman, H. and Roth, G. (eds) (1995) *Weber's Protestant Ethic: Origins, Evidence, Contexts*. Cambridge: Cambridge University Press.

Lehmann, E. L. and Romano, J. P. (2005) *Testing Statistical Hypotheses*. New York: Springer.

Leicht, K. T. (ed.) (2005) *Research in Social Stratification and Mobility*. St Louis, MO: JAI Press.

Lemert, C. and Catalano, S. (eds) (2004) *Social Theory: The Multicultural and Classic Readings*. New York: HarperCollins.

Lenin, V. (*1916* 1969) *Imperialism the Highest Stage of Capitalism*. New York: International Publishers.

Levin, M. D. (1993) *Modernity and the Hegemony of Vision*. Berkeley: University of California Press.

Levine, R. (2006) *Social Class and Stratification: Classic Statements and Theoretical Debates*. Lanham, MD: Rowman & Littlefield.

Lincoln, B. (1995) *Authority: Construction and Corrosion*. Chicago: University of Chicago Press.

Lincoln, Y. S. and Guba, E. G. (1985) *Naturalistic Inquiry*. Thousand Oaks, CA: Sage.

Linton, R. (1937) *The Study of Man: An introduction*. New York: Appleton-Century.

Lofland, J. and Lofland, L. H. (2003) *Analyzing Social Settings: A Guide to Qualitative Observation and Analysis*. Belmont, CA: Wadsworth.

Longhurst, B., McCracken, S., Ogborn, M., Smith, G. and Baldwin, E. (eds) (2000) *Introducing Cultural Studies*. Athens, GA: University of Georgia Press.

Lopes, D. M. and Gaut, B. (eds) (2002) *The Routledge Companion to Aesthetics*. London: Routledge.

Lukács, G. (1972) *History and Class Consciousness*. Cambridge, MA: The MIT Press.

Lynch, M. P. (1998) *Truth in Context: An Essay on Pluralism and Objectivity*. Cambridge, MA: The MIT Press.

Lyon, D. (1999) *Postmodernity*. Minneapolis, MN: University of Minnesota Press.

Lyotard, J. (1984) *The Postmodern Condition: A Report on Knowledge*. Minneapolis, MN: University of Minnesota Press.

Lyotard, J. (1999) *Postmodern Fables*. Minneapolis, MN: University of Minnesota Press.

Maass, A. (2005) *The Case for Socialism*. Chicago: Haymarket Books.

MacDonald, G., Leary, M. R., Tangney, J. P. (eds) (2005) *The Handbook of Self and Identity*. New York: The Guilford Press.

Machan, T. (2002) *Capitalism and Individualism*. Christchurch, NZ: Cybereditions.

Macionis, J. J. (2005) *Society: The Basics*. Englewood Cliffs, NJ: Prentice-Hall.

MacKenzie, D. and Wajcman, J. (eds) (1999) *The Social Shaping of Technology*. Columbus, OH: McGraw-Hill.

MacKinnon, B. (2003) *Ethics: Theory and Contemporary Issues*. Belmont, CA: Wadsworth.

Malinowski, B. (*1944* 2001) *Scientific Theory of Culture and Other Essays*. London: Routledge.

Mansfield, N. (2001) *Subjectivity: Theories of the Self from Freud to Haraway*. New York: New York University Press.

Marinetto, M. (2007) *Social Theory, the State and Modern Society*. Buckingham: Open University Press.

Marino, G. (2004) *Basic Writings of Existentialism*. New York: Modern Library.

Marra, M. A. (ed.) (2001) *A History of Modern Japanese Aesthetics*. Honolulu: University of Hawaii Press.

Marsden, G. M. (2006) *Fundamentalism and American Culture: The Shaping of Twentieth-century Evangelicalism, 1870–1925*. Oxford: Oxford University Press.

Marshall, C. and Rossman, G. B. (2006) *Designing Qualitative Research*. Thousand Oaks, CA: Sage.

Marshall, G. (1997) *Repositioning Class: Social Inequality in Industrial Societies*. London: Sage.

Marx, K. and Engels, F. (*1845* 1998) *The German Ideology: Including Thesis on Feuerbach*. Loughton, Essex: Prometheus Books.

Marx, K. and Engels, F. (*1848* 2004) *The Communist Manifesto*. Plymouth: Broadview Press.

Marx, K. (*1844* 1988) *The Economic and Philosophic Manuscripts of 1844*. Loughton, Essex: Prometheus Books.

Marx, K. (1845) *Thesis of Freurbach*. Available at: http://www.marxists.org/archive/marx/works/1845/theses/theses.htm

Marx, K. (*1859* 1979) *Contribution to the Critique of Political Economy*. New York: International Publishers.

Marx, K. (*1867* 1999) *Das Kapital*. S. Levitsky (trans). Washington, DC: Galeway Editions.

Marx, K. (*1891* 2004) *Wage Labor and Capital*. Boston: Digireads.com.

Maxim, P. S. (1999) *Quantitative Research Methods in the Social Sciences*. Oxford: Oxford University Press.

May, T. (2006) *Reflexivity*. London: Sage.

Mayo, P. (2004) *Liberating Praxis: Paulo Freire's Legacy for Radical Education and Politics*. New York: Praeger.

McClellan III, J. E. and Dorn, H. (2006) *Science and Technology in World History: An Introduction*. Baltimore, MD: Johns Hopkins University Press.

McLaren, P. (2006) *Life in Schools: An Introduction to Critical Pedagogy in the Foundations of Education*. Boston: Allyn & Bacon.

McNiff, J. and Whitehead, J. (2002) *Action Research: Principles and Practice*. London: Routledge.

McRobbie, A. (2005) *The Uses of Cultural Studies: A Textbook*. London: Sage.

Mead, G. H. (*1934* 1967) *Mind, Self, and Society: From the Standpoint of a Social Behaviorist*. Chicago: University of Chicago Press.

Menand, L. (ed.) (1997) *Pragmatism: A Reader*. New York: Vintage Books.

Merton, R. (*1949* 1968) *Social Theory and Social Structure*. New York: Free Press.

Messer, D. and Dockrell, J. (1998) *Developmental Psychology: A Reader*. New York: Hodder Arnold.

Mill, J. S. (*1859* 2006) *On Liberty*. Lanham, MD: Rowman & Littlefield.

Mill, J. S. (*1863* 2005) *Utilitarianism*. McLean, VA: IndyPublish.com.

Miller, D. L. (2000) *Introduction to Collective Behavior and Collective Action*. Long Grove, IL: Waveland Press.

Miller, S. (2001) *Social Action: A Teleological Account*. Cambridge: Cambridge University Press.

Miller, T. (1993) *The Well-Tempered Self: Citizenship, Culture, and the Postmodern Subject*. Baltimore, MD: Johns Hopkins University Press.

Mills, C. W. (*1956* 2000) *The Power Elite*. Oxford: Oxford University Press.

Monks, R. A. G and Minow, N. (2003) *Corporate Governance*. London: Blackwell.

Moore, B. N. and Parker, R. (2005) *Critical Thinking*. Columbus, OH: McGraw-Hill.

Moran, D. (2000) *Introduction to Phenomenology*. London: Routledge.

Moran, D. and Mooney, T. (2002) *The Phenomenology Reader*. London: Routledge.

Morgan, S. L., Grusky, D. B. and Fields, G. S. (eds) (2006) *Mobility and Inequality: Frontiers of Research in Sociology and Economics*. Stanford, CA: Stanford University Press.

Moser, P. K. and Carson, T. L. (eds) (2000) *Moral Relativism: A Reader*. Oxford: Oxford University Press.

Moskowitz, G. B. (2004) *Social Cognition: Understanding Self and Others*. New York: The Guilford Press.

Moya, P. and Hames-Garcia, M. (eds) (2000) *Reclaiming Identity: Realist Theory and the Predicament of Postmodernism*. Berkeley: University of California Press.

Muller, J. Z. (1997) *Conservatism*. Princeton, NJ: Princeton University Press.

Muravchik, J. (2003) *Heaven on Earth: The Rise and Fall of Socialism*. New York: Encounter Books.

Murolo, P. and Chitty, A. (2003) *From the Folks Who Brought You the Weekend: A Short, Illustrated History of Labor in the United States*. New York: New Press.

Murphie, A. and Potts, J. (2003) *Culture and Technology*. New York: Palgrave Macmillan.

Murphy, C. (ed.) (2004) *Global Institutions, Marginalization and Development*. London: Routledge.

Myerson, G. (2001) *Teach Yourself 101 Key Ideas: Existentialism*. Columbus, OH: McGraw-Hill.

Mythen, G. and Walklate, S. (2006) *Beyond the Risk Society*. Maidenhead: Open University Press.

Nash, J. (2004) *Social Movements: An Anthropological Reader*. London: Blackwell.

Navarro, V. and Muntaner, C. (eds) (2004) *Political and Economic Determinants of Population Health and Well-Being: Controversies and Developments*. Amityville, NY: Baywood.

Nelson, A. (2005) *Companion to Rationalism*. London: Blackwell.

Newman, M. (2005) *Socialism: A Very Short Introduction*. Oxford: Oxford University Press.

Nietzsche, F. (*1887* 2003) *The Genealogy of Morals*. New York: Dover Publications.

Niezen, R. (2005) *A World Beyond Difference: Cultural Identity in the Age of Globalization*. London: Blackwell.

Noble, T. (2000) *Social Theory and Social Change*. New York: Palgrave Macmillan.

Norman, R. (1998) *The Moral Philosophers: An Introduction to Ethics*. Oxford: Oxford University Press.

Norman, R. (2004) *On Humanism*. London: Routledge.

Nozick, R. (1977) *Anarchy, State and Utopia*. New York: Basic Books.

O'Brien, D. (2006) *An Introduction to the Theory of Knowledge*. Cambridge: Polity Press.

O'Leary, Z. (2004) *The Essential Guide to Doing Research*. London: Sage.

O'Leary, Z. (2005) *Researching Real-World Problems: A Guide to Methods of Inquiry*. London: Sage.

Oderberg, D. S. (2006) *Real Essentialism*. London: Routledge.

Ollman, B. (1977) *Alienation: Marx's Conception of Man in a Capitalist Society*. Cambridge: Cambridge University Press.

Ollman, B. (2003) *Dance of the Dialectic: Steps in Marx's Method*. Champaign, IL: University of Illinois Press.

Olson, W. H. Jr. and Swatos, D. V. A. (2000) *The Secularization Debate*. Lanham, MD: Rowman & Littlefield.

Oppenheimer, F. (1999) *The State: Its History and Development Viewed Sociologically*. Chicago: Aldine Transaction.

Ore, T. E. (ed.) (2005) *The Social Construction of Difference and Inequality: Race, Class, Gender and Sexuality*. Columbus, OH: McGraw-Hill.

Osborne, M. J. (2003) *An Introduction to Game Theory*. Oxford: Oxford University Press.

Osterhammel, J. (2005) *Colonialism: A Theoretical Overview*. Princeton, NJ: Markus Wiener.

Page, M. E. and Sonnenburg, P. M. (eds) (2003) *Colonialism: An International Social Cultural and Political Encyclopedia*. Santa Barbara, CA: ABC-Clio.

Palmer, D. D. (1997) *Structuralism and Poststructuralism for Beginners*. London: Writers & Readers Publishing.

Palmer, M. (1998) *Yin and Yang: Understanding the Chinese Philosophy of Opposites and How To Apply It To Your Everyday Life*. London: Piatkus Books.

Papa, M. J., Singhal, A. and Papa, W. (2005) *Organizing for Social Change: A Dialectic Journey of Theory and Praxis*. London: Sage.

Parker, N. and Sim, S. (1998) *A–Z Guide to Modern Social and Political Theorists*. Englewood Cliffs, NJ: Prentice-Hall.

Parson, K. (2003) *The Science Wars: Debating Scientific Knowledge and Technology*. Loughton, Essex: Prometheus Books.

Parsons, T. (*1951* 1991) *The Social System*. London: Routledge.

Parsons, T. and Smelser, N. J. (1956) *Economy and Society*. London: Routledge.

Passas, N. and Agnew, R. (eds) (1997) *The Future of Anomie Theory*. Boston: Northeastern University Press.

Passmore, K. (2002) *Fascism: A Very Short Introduction*. Oxford: Oxford University Press.

Paulston, C. B. and Tucker, R. G. (eds) (2003) *Sociolinguistics: The Essential Readings*. London: Blackwell.

Paxton, R. O. (2005) *The Anatomy of Fascism*. New York: Vintage Books.

Payne, G. (1990) *The Social Mobility of Women*. London: Falmer Press.

Payne, R. J. and Nassar, J. R. (2002) *Politics and Culture in the Developing World: The Impact of Globalization*. White Plains, NY: Longman.

Pearl, J. (2000) *Causality: Models, Reasoning, and Inference*. Cambridge: Cambridge University Press.

Pecora, V. P. (2006) *Secularization and Cultural Criticism: Religion, Nation, and Modernity*. Chicago: University of Chicago Press.

Perkinson, H. J. (2005) *The Inevitability of Conservatism*. Frederick, MD: PublishAmerica.

Perron, P. and Danesi, M. (eds) (2003) *Classic Readings in Semiotics*. Ottawa, ON: Legas Publishing.

Phemsiter, P. (2006) *Rationalists: Descartes, Spinoza and Leibniz*. Cambridge: Polity Press.

Pierre, J. (2000) *Governance, Politics and the State*. New York: Palgrave Macmillan.

Pieterse, J. N. (2003) *Globalization and Culture*. Lanham, MD: Rowman & Littlefield.

Pinchot, G. and Pinchot, E. (1994) *The End of Bureaucracy and the Rise of the Intelligent Organization*. San Francisco: Berrett-Koehler.

Pipes, R. (2003) *Communism: A History*. New York: Modern Library.

Pitcher, P. (1997) *The Drama of Leadership*. New York: John Wiley and Sons.

Plous, S. (ed.) (2002) *Understanding Prejudice and Discrimination*. Columbus, OH: McGraw-Hill.

Poletiek, F. (2001) *Hypothesis Testing Behaviour*. New York: Psychology Press.

Pontell, H. N. (2004) *Social Deviance: Readings in Theory and Research*. Englewood Cliffs, NJ: Prentice Hall.

Popper, K. (*1959* 2002) *The Logic of Scientific Discovery*. London: Routledge.

Popper, K. (*1961* 2002) *The Poverty of Historicism*. London: Routledge.

Porta, D. D. and Diani, M. (2006) *Social Movements: An Introduction*. London: Blackwell.

Powell, J. N. (1998) *Postmodernism for Beginners*. London: Writers & Readers Publishing.

Powell, J. N. (2005) *Deconstruction for Beginners*. London: Writers & Readers Publishing.

Powers, C. H. (2004) *Making Sense of Social Theory: A Practical Introduction*. Lanham, MD: Rowman & Littlefield.

Prior, L. (2003) *Using Documents in Social Research*. London: Sage.

Pritchard, S. (2006) *An Introduction to Multiculturalism*. London: Sage.

Punch, K. (2005) *Introduction to Social Research: Quantitative and Qualitative Approaches*. London: Sage.

Rathus, S. A., Nevid, J. S. and Fichner-Rathus, L. (2004) *Human Sexuality in a World of Diversity*. Boston: Allyn & Bacon.

Rawls, J. (*1971* 1999) *A Theory of Justice*. Cambridge, MA: Belknap Press.

Reason, P. and Bradbury, H. (2001) *Handbook of Action Research: Participative Inquiry and Practice*. London: Sage.

Reichenbach, H. (2006) *Experience and Prediction: An Analysis of the Foundations and the Structure of Knowledge*. Notre Dame, IN: University of Notre Dame Press.

Rella, F. (1994) *The Myth of the Other: Lacan, Foucault, Deleuze, Bataille*. University Park, MD: Maisonneuve Press.

Rescher, N. (2005) *Reason and Reality: Realism and Idealism in Pragmatic Perspective*. Lanham, MD: Rowman & Littlefield.

Reynolds, L. T. (2004) *Handbook of Symbolic Interactionism*. Lanham, MD: AltaMira Press.

Rheingold, H. (2000) *The Virtual Community: Homesteading on the Electronic Frontier*. Cambridge, MA: The MIT Press.

Ricœur, P. (1981) *Hermeneutics and the Human Sciences: Essays on Language, Action and Interpretation*. Cambridge: Cambridge University Press.

Riley, J. (2006) *Mill's Radical Liberalism: An Essay in Retrieval*. London: Routledge.

Ritzer, G. (*1995* 2004) *The McDonaldization of Society*. Thousand Oaks, CA: Pine Forge Press.

Ritzer, G. (1998) *The McDonaldization Thesis: Explorations and Extensions*. Thousand Oaks, CA: Sage.

Ritzer, G. (2002) *McDonaldization: The Reader*. Thousand Oaks, CA: Pine Forge Press.

Roberts, R. (1995) *Religion and the Transformations of Capitalism*. London: Routledge.

Robinson, D. (2004) *Introducing Empiricism*. New York: Totem Books.

Rodriguez-Pereyra, G. (2002) *Resemblance Nominalism: A Solution to the Problem of Universals*. Oxford: Oxford University Press.

Roncaglia, A. (2005) *The Wealth of Ideas: A History of Economic Thought*. Cambridge: Cambridge University Press.

Roopnarine, J. L. and Carter, D. B. (eds) (1992) *Parent–Child Socialization in Diverse Cultures*. St Louis, MO: Ablex.

Rose, L. and Denters, B. (eds) (2005) *Comparing Local Governance: Trends and Developments*. Basingstoke: Palgrave Macmillan.

Rosenbach, W. E. and Taylor, R. L. (eds) (2006) *Contemporary Issues in Leadership*. Boulder, CO: Westview Press.

Rosenberg, A. (2000) *Darwinism in Philosophy, Social Science and Policy*. Cambridge: Cambridge University Press.

Rosenstand, N. (2002) *The Moral of the Story: An Introduction to Ethics*. Columbus, OH: McGraw-Hill.

Rotberg, R. I. (ed.) (2000) *Social Mobility and Modernization: A Journal of Interdisciplinary History Reader*. Cambridge, MA: The MIT Press.

Roush, S. (2006) *Tracking Truth: Knowledge, Evidence, and Science*. Oxford: Oxford University Press.

Royle, N. (ed.) (2000) *Deconstructions: A User's Guide*. New York: Palgrave Macmillan.

Rubin, H. J. and Rubin, I. S. (2004) *Qualitative Interviewing: The Art of Hearing Data*. Thousand Oaks, CA: Sage.

Russell, B. (*1949* 1995) *Authority and the Individual*. London: Routledge.

Rutherford, J. (2003) *Identity: Community, Culture and Difference*. London: Lawrence and Wishart.

Ruthven, M. (2004) *Fundamentalism: The Search for Meaning*. Oxford: Oxford University Press.

Said, E. W. (1994) *Culture and Imperialism*. New York: Vintage Books.

Salmon, W. C. (ed.) (1997) *Causality and Explanation*. Oxford: Oxford University Press.

Sanderson, S. K. (2005) *Revolutions: A Worldwide Introduction to Political and Social Change*. Boulder, CO: Paradigm.

Sardar, Z. (2005) *Introducing Cultural Studies*. New York: Totem Books.

Sartre, J. P. (1993) *Essays in Existentialism*. Bristol: Carol Publishing Corporation.

Schacht, R. (1994) *The Future of Alienation*. Champaign, IL: University of Illinois Press.

Schaffer, R. (ed.) (1995) *Early Socialization*. Leicester: British Psychological Society.

Schelkle, W., Krauth, W., Kohli, M. and Elwert, G. (eds) (2001) *Paradigms of Social Change: Modernization, Development, Transformation, Evolution*. New York: Palgrave Macmillan.

Scheurich, J. (1997) *Research Method in the Postmodern*. London: Falmer Press.

Schick, T. (ed.) (1999) *Readings in the Philosophy of Science: From Positivism to Postmodern.* Columbus, OH: McGraw-Hill.

Schmitt, R. (2002) *Alienation and Freedom.* Boulder, CO: Westview Press.

Schneir, M. (1994) *Feminism: The Essential Historical Writings.* New York: Vintage Books.

Schor, J. B. (2004) *Born to Buy: The Commercialized Child and the New Consumer Culture.* New York: Scribner.

Scott, J. (2001) *Power.* Cambridge: Polity Press.

Scruton, R. (2002) *The Meaning of Conservatism.* Chicago: St Augustine's Press.

Sedikides, C. (ed.) (2002) *Individual Self, Relational Self, Collective Self.* New York: Psychology Press.

Segerstrale, U. (2001) *Defenders of the Truth: The Sociobiology Debate.* New York: Oxford University Press.

Sehon, S. (2005) *Teleological Realism: Mind, Agency, and Explanation.* Cambridge, MA: The MIT Press.

Settersten, R. A. Jr. and Owens, T. J. (eds) (2002) *New Frontiers in Socialization.* St Louis, MO: JAI Press.

Shachar, A. (2006) *Multiculturalism: A Critical Introduction.* London: Routledge.

Shapiro, I. (2003) *The State of Democratic Theory.* Princeton, NJ: Princeton University Press.

Shaw, W. H. (1998) *Contemporary Ethics: Taking Account of Utilitarianism.* London: Blackwell.

Sherman, F. T. and Torbert, W. R. (2000) *Transforming Social Inquiry, Transforming Social Action.* New York: Springer.

Shilling, C. (2003) *The Body and Social Theory.* London: Sage.

Shook, J. (2003) *The Chicago School of Pragmatism* (4 vols). Bristol: Thömmes Continuum.

Shook, J. and Margolis, J. (eds) (2006) *A Companion to Pragmatism.* London: Blackwell.

Sider, T. (2003) *Four-Dimensionalism: An Ontology of Persistence and Time.* Oxford: Oxford University Press.

Simmel, G. (*1908* 1964) *Conflict and the Web of Group Affiliations.* New York: Free Press.

Singer, J. (2000) *Blake, Jung, and the Collective Unconscious: The Conflict between Reason and Imagination.* Berwick, ME: Nicolas-Hays.

Skinner, B. F. (*1971* 2002) *Beyond Dignity and Freedom.* Indianapolis, IN: Hackett.

Skocpol, T. (1994) *Social Revolutions in the Modern World.* Cambridge: Cambridge University Press.

Skyttner, L. (2006) *General Systems Theory.* Hackensack, NJ: World Scientific.

Slack, J. D. and Wise, J. M. (2005) *Culture + Technology: A Primer.* New York: Peter Lang.

Smart, B. (1999) *Resisting McDonaldization.* London: Sage.

Smith, A. D. (2001) *Nationalism: Theory, Ideology, History.* Cambridge: Polity Press.

Snow, C. P. (*1959* 1993) *The Two Cultures.* Cambridge: Cambridge University Press.

Soja, E. W. (2000) *Postmetropolis: Studies of Cities and Regions.* London: Blackwell.

Sokolowski, R. (2000) *Introduction to Phenomenology.* New York: Cambridge University Press.

Solomon, R. C. (ed.) (2004) *Existentialism.* Oxford: Oxford University Press.

Sorokin, P. (1927) *Social and Cultural Mobility.* New York: Free Press.

Speth, J. G. (2003) *Worlds Apart: Globalization and the Environment.* Washington, DC: Island Press.

Stangor, C. (ed.) (2000) *Stereotypes and Prejudice: Essential Readings.* New York: Psychology Press.

Steiner, F. (2002) *Human Ecology: Following Nature's Lead.* Washington, DC: Island Press.

Steinmetz, G. (ed.) (2005) *The Politics of Method in the Human Sciences: Positivism and Its Epistemological Others.* Durham, NC: Duke University Press.

Sterns, P. (1998) *The Industrial Revolution in World History.* Boulder, CO: Westview Press.

Steup, M. and Sosa, E. (eds) (2005) *Contemporary Debates in Epistemology.* London: Blackwell.

Stiglitz, J. E. (2003) *Globalization and Its Discontents.* New York: W. W. Norton & Co.

Stombler, M., Baunauch, D. M., Burgess, E. O., Donnelly, D. and Simonds, W. (2006) *Sex Matters: The Sexuality and Society Reader.* Boston: Allyn & Bacon.

Storey, J. (ed.) (1996) *What is Cultural Studies?: A Reader.* New York: Hodder Arnold.

Strasser, S. (2003) *Commodifying Everything: Relationships of the Market.* London: Routledge.

Strauss, A. (*1971* 2006) *The Contexts of Social Mobility: Ideology and Theory.* Chicago: Aldine Transaction.

Strauss, A. and Corbin, J. M. (1998) *Basics of Qualitative Research: Techniques and Procedures for Developing Grounded Theory.* Thousand Oaks, CA: Sage.

Stringer, E. (1999) *Action Research.* Thousand Oaks, CA: Sage.

Stryker, S., Owens, T. J. and White, R. W. (eds) (2000) *Self, Identity, and Social Movements.* Minneapolis, MN: University of Minnesota Press.

Sturrock, J. (2003) *Structuralism.* London: Blackwell.

Surowiecki, J. (2004) *The Wisdom of Crowds.* New York: Random House.

Sutton, M. (2004) *An Introduction to Cultural Ecology.* Lanham, MD: AltaMira Press.

Svallfors, S. (ed.) (2005) *Analyzing Inequality: Life Chances and Social Mobility in Comparative Perspective.* Stanford, CA: Stanford University Press.

Swanenberg, A. (2005) *Macroeconomics Demystified.* Columbus, OH: McGraw-Hill.

Swatos, W. H. Jr. and Kaelber, L. (eds) (2005) *The Protestant Ethic Turns 100: Essays on the Centenary of the Weber Thesis.* Boulder, CO: Paradigm.

Tannen, D. (1999) *The Argument Culture: Stopping America's War of Words.* New York: Ballantine Books.

Tawney, R. H. (*1926* 1998) *Religion and the Rise of Capitalism.* Somerset, NJ: Transaction.

Taylor, F. (*1911* 2006) *The Principles of Scientific Management.* London: Echo Library.

Taylor, S. (ed.) (2002) *Ethnographic Research: A Reader.* London: Sage.

ten Have, P. (2004) *Understanding Qualitative Research and Ethnomethodology.* London: Sage.

Thomason, B. C. (1982) *Making Sense of Reification.* New York: Palgrave Macmillan.

Thrift, N. (2005) *Knowing Capitalism.* London: Sage.

Thye, S. R. and Lawler, E. J. (2002) *Group Cohesion, Trust and Solidarity.* St Louis, MO: JAI Press.

Thyer, B. A. (ed.) (2006) *The Philosophical Legacy of Behaviorism.* New York: Springer.

Tilly, C. (2004) *Social Movements, 1768–2004.* Boulder, CO: Paradigm.

Toffler, A. (1984) *The Third Wave.* New York: Bantam Books.

Toffolo, S. E. (ed.) (2003) *Emancipating Cultural Pluralism.* Albany, NY: State University of New York Press.

Tönnies, F. (*1887* 2001) *Tönnies: Community and Civil Society.* Cambridge: Cambridge University Press.

Tooley, M. (1999) *The Nature of Properties: Nominalism, Realism, and Trope Theory.* New York: Garland Press.

Torrey, R. A. (*1909* 2003) *The Fundamentals.* Grand Rapids, MI: Baker Books.

Troman, G., Jeffrey, B. and Walford, G. (eds) (2005) *Methodological Issues and Practices in Ethnography.* St Louis, MO: JAI Press.

Trudgill, P. (2001) *Sociolinguistics: An Introduction to Language and Society.* London: Penguin Books.

Turner, B. S. (1996) *The Body and Society: Explorations in Social Theory.* London: Sage.

Vago, S. (2003) *Social Change.* Englewood Cliffs, NJ: Prentice-Hall.

van Fraassen, B. C. (2004) *The Empirical Stance.* New Haven, CT: Yale University Press.

van Leeuwen, T. (2004) *Introducing Social Semiotics.* London: Routledge.

Vasquez, J. A. and Elman, C. (2002) *Realism and the Balancing of Power: A New Debate.* Englewood Cliffs, NJ: Prentice-Hall.

von Dietze, E. (2001) *Paradigms Explained: Rethinking Thomas Kuhn's Philosophy of Science.* New York: Praeger.

von Neumann, J. and Morgenstern, O. (*1944* 2004) *The Theory of Games and Economic Behavior.* Princeton, NJ: Princeton University Press.

Wallace, R. A. and Wolf, A. (2005) *Contemporary Sociological Theory: Expanding the Classical Tradition.* Englewood Cliffs, NJ: Prentice-Hall.

Wallerstein, I. (2001) *Unthinking Social Science: The Limits of Nineteenth-Century Paradigms.* Philadelphia: Temple University Press.

Walsheim, C. (ed.) (2006) *The Landscape Urbanism Reader.* Princeton, NJ: Princeton Architectural Press.

Wardhaugh, R. (2005) *An Introduction to Sociolinguistics.* London: Blackwell.

Watson, J. B. (*1930* 1998) *Behaviourism.* Somerset, NJ: Transaction.

Weber, M. (*1905* 2003) *The Protestant Ethic and the Spirit of Capitalism.* New York: Dover Publications.

Weber, M. (*1921–22* 1978) *Economy and Society.* Berkeley: University of California Press.

Webster, R. (1996) *Why Freud Was Wrong: Sin, Science and Psychoanalysis.* New York: Basic Books.

Wegner, D. M. (2003) *The Illusion of Conscious Will.* Cambridge, MA: The MIT Press.

Weill, P. and Ross, J. (2004) *IT Governance: How Top Performers Manage IT Decision Rights for Superior Results.* Boston: Harvard Business School Press.

Weiss, J. (2002) *Industrialisation and Globalisation: Theory and Evidence from Developing Countries.* London: Routledge.

Weitzer, R. (ed.) (2001) *Deviance and Social Control: A Reader.* Columbus, OH: McGraw-Hill.

Werbner, P. and Modood, T. (eds) (1997) *Debating Cultural Hybridity: Multi-Cultural Identities and the Politics of Anti-Racism.* London: Zed Books.

Whitley, B. E. and Kite, M. E. (2005) *The Psychology of Prejudice and Discrimination.* Belmont, CA: Wadsworth.

Williams, G. P. (1997) *Chaos Theory Tamed.* Washington, DC: National Academies Press.

Williams, J. (2005) *Understanding Poststructuralism.* Chesham: Acumen.

Williams, M. (2001) *Problems of Knowledge: A Critical Introduction to Epistemology.* Oxford: Oxford University Press.

Williams, R. and Mcmullen, A. (2007) *Understanding Socialism: An Introduction to Ideas and Issues.* Cheltenham: Edward Elgar.

Wilson, D. and Huff, J. O. (eds) (1994) *Marginalized Places and Populations: A Structurationist Agenda.* New York: Praeger.

Wilson, E. O. (*1975* 2000) *Sociobiology: The New Synthesis.* Cambridge, MA: Belknap Press.

Wink, J. (2004) *Critical Pedagogy: Notes from the Real World.* Boston: Allyn & Bacon.

Wittgenstein, L. (*1951* 1972) *On Certainty.* New York: Harper Perennial.

Wollstonecraft, M. (*1792* 2004) *A Vindication of the Rights of Women.* London: Echo Library.

Wood, E. M. (1995) *Democracy against Capitalism: Renewing Historical Materialism.* Cambridge: Cambridge University Press.

Woods, T. E. Jr. (2004) *The Politically Incorrect Guide to American History.* Washington, DC: Regnery Publishing Inc.

Woodward, J. (2005) *Making Things Happen: A Theory of Causal Explanation.* Oxford: Oxford University Press.

Zahavi, D. (2006) *Subjectivity and Selfhood: Investigating the First-Person Perspective.* Cambridge, MA: The MIT Press.

Zhang, W. B. (2005) *Economic Growth Theory: Capital, Knowledge and Economic Stuctures.* Williston, VT: Ashgate.

Žižek, S. (2000) *The Ticklish Subject: The Absent Centre of Political Ontology.* London: Verso.

Žižek, S. (2002) *Did Somebody Say Totalitarianism?: Five Interventions in the (Mis)Use of a Notion.* London: Verso.

Index

Collins, R., 45
colonization, 36–7
commodification, 38–9
commodity fetishism, 39, 225
communism, 40–1
community, 42–3
Comte, A., 137, 138, 197, 249, 295
conflict theory, 44–5
conservatism, 46–7
constant comparative method, 107
contract theory, 80
cooperative inquiry, 2, 3
Coser, L. A., 45
critical pedagogy, 188–9
critical, 48–9
cultural artifacts, 50
cultural studies, 50–1
culture, 52–3
Curie, M., 119

Dahl, R., 59
Dahrendorf, R., 45
Daly, M., 187
Darwin, C., 119, 255
Dawkins, R., 271
de Beauvoir, S., 19, 93, 119
de Saint–Simon, H., 155, 259, 265
de Saussure, F., 183, 245, 281
decolonization, 36
deconstruction, 54–5
deductive reasoning, 56–7
Demerath, N. J., 241
democracy, 58–9
deontology, 80
dependability, 230
dependency theory, 37
Derrida, J., 55, 199, 281
Descartes, R., 13, 181, 217,
    221, 239, 243, 295
determinism, 60–1
  biological, 60
  economic, 60
  environmental (anthropological), 60
  environmental
      (social–psychological), 60
  genetic 60
  theological, 60
developed countries, 62–3
developing countries, 62–3

deviant behaviour, 64–5
Dewey, J., 139, 207
dialectic materialism, 67
dialectic, 66–7
dichotomy, 68–9
Dilthey, W., 111
discourse, 70–1
discrimination, 210–1
divine command theory, 80
Dixon, A. C., 97
domestic labour, 30
Douglas, M., 235
dualism, 194
Duncan, O., 257
Durkheim, E., 7, 10–11, 25, 35,
    43, 65, 95, 105, 137, 143,
    163, 179, 241, 249, 253,
    263, 265, 269, 276–7, 295

ecology, 116
egalitarianism, 72–3
ego, 124–5
Einstein, A., 119, 220
Eisler, R., 187
Elliott, E., 29
empiricism, 74–5
Engels, F., 31, 40–1, 73, 113, 154–5,
    157, 265
epistemology, 76–7,
Erikson, E., 129, 243, 267
essentialism, 78–9
ethics, 80–1, 228, 230
ethnocentrism, 82–3
ethnography, 84–5
ethnomethodology, 86–7
eugenics, 254, 255
exchange value, 38
existentialism, 88–9
experimentation, 164

factor, 26
Fairclough, N., 275
Fanon, F., 37
fascism, 90–1
feminism, 92–3
Festinger, L., 33
Feuerbach, L., 157
Fine, M., 189
Firestone, S., 187

(the) state, 278–9
  elitist theory of, 278
  Marxist theory of 278
  pluralist theory of, 278
Steinem, G., 93, 119
Stove, D., 126, 219
Strauss, A., 107
structuralism, 280–1
subject, 282–3
subjectivism, 284–5, 230
Sumner, W., 83, 227
superego, 124–5
surveying, 164
symbolic interactionism, 286–7
synthesis, 66
systems theory, 288–9

Taylor, J. H., 97
taylorism,159
technology, 290–1
teleology, 292–3
text, 50, 54–5, 110
theory, 294–5
thesis, 66
thick description, 85
third world, 62
Thomas, W., 251
Tilley, C., 259
Toffler, A., 201
Tönnies, F., 43, 269
totalitarianism, 296–7
Touraine, A., 259
transferability, 230
Trotsky, L., 155
Turner, B., 19
Turner, F., 29
Tylor, E. B., 53

underdeveloped countries, 62–3
unobtrusive methods, 164

urbanization, 298–9
use–value, 38
utilitarianism, 300–1
  act, 300
  rule, 300
utility, 230, 295

validity, 228,
  external, 228
  internal, 228
values, 178
variable, 26, 122
Veblen, T., 157
Voltaire, 119, 283
von Neumann, J., 99

Walby, S., 187
Wallerstein, I., 185
Walras, L., 167
Watson, J. B., 17
Weber, M., 14–15, 20–1, 25,
    31, 45, 105, 111, 137,
    139, 149, 159, 163, 205,
    212–13, 241, 263, 265,
    277, 279, 295
Westermarck, E., 227
Whewell, W., 123
white collar, 30
William of Occam, 177
Williams, B., 195
Williams, R., 51
Wilson, E. O., 271
Wirth, L., 43, 299
Wittgenstein, L., 5, 13, 181, 195
Wollstonecraft, M., 93, 119
Woolgar, S., 291

yin–yang, 67,68

zero–sum game, 98